SAIL LOGOS

One Designs Small Boats *Continued*	470	G-Cat	GP-14	Geary 18
Gryphon	Herreshoff	Highlander	Hobie 14	Howmar Twelve
Interlake	Invitation	Isotope	Javelin	Jet 14
Laser	Lido 14	Lightning	MC	Mariner
Mercury	Moth	Nacra 5.2	110	Penguin
Phantom	Precision 16	Prindle 18	Puffer	Rascal
Raven	Rhodes 19	Sandpiper 100	Santana	Shields
Shrimp	Siren	Sirius	Skipjack	Skunk

A Field Guide
to Sailboats
of North America

A Field Guide to

Sailboats

of North America

Richard M. Sherwood

Houghton Mifflin Company · Boston
1984

Library of Congress Cataloging in Publication Data

Sherwood, Richard M.
    A field guide to sailboats of North America.

    Includes index.
    1. Sailboats—Handbooks, manuals, etc.   I. Title.
VM351.S483   1984   623.8′223′0202   84-545
ISBN 0-395-35401-3

Printed in the United States of America

M 10 9 8 7 6 5 4 3 2 1

Contents

Preface

Twenty years ago it was possible to identify just about every class of sailboat normally encountered. There were far fewer classes than there are today, and they were well known.

In the late 1950s the FRP (fiber-reinforced plastic) "chopper" gun was devised. This gun feeds resin, catalyst, and fiberglass strands through a mixing nozzle. If the mixture is sprayed onto a mold a duplicate is obtained. I had occasion to see such a gun at that time. The workers were bringing in wheelbarrows, boats, bird baths, and any other objects that caught their fancy, and happily making their personal copies. About the same time, FRP was used for the first production boats. The process required only a male or female mold, a limited investment in equipment, and semiskilled labor either to lay up by hand or to spray the fiberglass. The result, when capably done, was extremely resistant to corrosion and was light-weight. It could be colored. The immense market for production fiberglass boats soon followed.

Now there are literally thousands of different class or production boats. Recognition is difficult. Class identification marks are very helpful, but they are not always used. And, of course, sometimes the sails are down. There has been no single book designed to help identify these boats. This book has been written to help both new and experienced sailors identify boats by pinpointing distinguishing features.

In order to compile the information in this book, I sent hundreds of letters of inquiry to manufacturers. Almost all of the manufacturers are in the United States and Canada, but inquiries were also sent to England for certain sailboats exported to the United States. Class associations, or at least those that are members of the United States Yacht Racing Union, were also contacted. I am grateful to those who replied.

As anyone who has written away for information knows, the results obtained vary widely in both quality and quantity. I felt that certain statistical information on each boat was important, but it was not always forthcoming. In some cases, second and third letters, telephone calls, and even visits proved useless. There are some very good and well-known boats that unfortunately could not be included in this book because complete information on them could not be obtained.

My selection of boats for this guide is based on several criteria. Some classes simply have to be included; Olympic classes are a good example. Some types are historic. Some are very popular. Some are unusual. However, it was necessary to put a limit on the number of boats. Boats for which information was so scanty as to be worthless were excluded. For example, some manufacturers do not like to release underwater profiles. Also, very small boats have received little consideration; and boats longer than 45 feet overall have received none. Further restrictions have been necessary, and these I must admit were personal choices. While the primary purpose of this book is sailboat identification, a second is to present interesting designs and diversity of types.

The book is in two sections. The first section contains one-designs, small boats, and other boats (generally below 20 feet) that have no engines. Cruising boats and auxiliaries are in the second section. In both sections, boats are arranged by length overall (LOA).

In the drawing of each boat, short dotted lines are used to highlight notable identification features—which are also listed briefly at the beginning of the boat's description.

My deepest thanks go to Ron Jesiolowski, who did all but one or two of the drawings.

I hope this book is helpful. I will welcome information on any boat.

Richard M. Sherwood

Introduction

This section discusses the features of a boat that are most helpful for identification. As sailing has its own language, many other terms are defined in the glossary.

Class Identification

In most cases, the designer, manufacturer, or class association concerned with a small one-design boat has designed a class emblem, or logo. This usually appears on the mainsail. It is certainly the most simple and accurate means of identifying a boat. A number of these are reproduced on the endpapers of this book. Look through them to find the logo of an individual boat, note the name, then use the alphabetical index to find the boat.

A list of class associations belonging to the United States Yacht Racing Union (USYRU) appears in the Appendix. This list was current as of 1982.

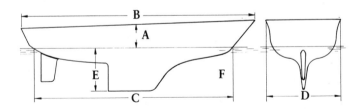

A. freeboard

B. length overall (LOA)

C. length on the waterline (LWL)

D. beam (maximum)

E. draft

F. forefoot

General Dimensions

Length overall (LOA) is the length of the boat from the farthest point forward on the bow to a similar point on the stern.

Length on the waterline (LWL) is measured with the boat upright. Freeboard is the height of the rail above water, and usually changes along the length of the boat. Draft is the maximum depth of the boat under the water. Beam is the width of the boat and may be measured on deck, at the waterline, or elsewhere. The dimension given for beam in the statistics in this book is the *maximum* beam, wherever it may occur.

Hull Sections

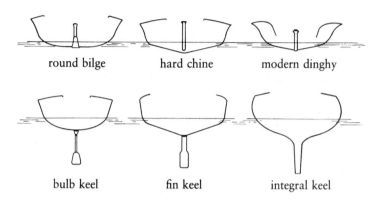

round bilge   hard chine   modern dinghy

bulb keel   fin keel   integral keel

Hulls

Most of the boats in this book are of recent design. While a few classes date to 1900 and several to 1920 and 1930, the majority were designed after World War II. Early in this century hulls tended to be quite narrow and deep, with full-length keels and rudders attached directly to the keel. (There were many deviations, however; the Star is a notable example.) Largely because of the influence of the racing rating rules, boat design has changed. The rules have changed frequently. Following each change, designs were modified to obtain the most favorable rating. Displacement, or weight, was reduced until the "ultra-light" displacement boats appeared. Displacement, however, gives a sailboat stability. Some substitute was required, and since the beam of a boat also adds stability, beam has been increased.

Except for planing hulls, the waterline of a boat has a distinct effect on speed. The longer the waterline, the faster the boat. The most recent designs have eliminated the long overhangs that were common in the early part of the century, and waterline length now approaches overall length in many classes, particularly among the smaller boats.

The friction between the boat and the water causes drag. If the area of hull in the water ("wetted surface") is small, friction is minimized. Long, deep keels with large surface areas have given way to short, narrow keels. Rudders have moved far aft, where they exert a very quick and positive control.

Most of these changes are under water and are not ordinarily seen. The aspects of modern design that are most often visible include fine bows, beam well aft, and reverse transoms, as well as the wide beam and short overhangs mentioned above.

Most boats are not designed solely for racing. In order to sell to both racing and cruising markets, production boats are a compromise. Some emphasize racing, some cruising or daysailing. But most still represent compromises, because if they were designed solely as racers or as cruisers the potential market would be limited. Some of the smaller boats are exceptions, however, as are maxi boats designed solely for racing.

Hull Cross-Sections

When a boat heels, the wind is spilled from the sails. Pressure on the sails is reduced, and often the boat sails more slowly. Too much heel may lead to a capsize. Hull shape can reduce heel by incorporating a keel or centerboard and/or by greater width.

Weight in the bottom of the boat tends to keep it upright. The lower the weight, the better. Weight is often designed into a keel, below the actual hull. In small boats it is placed in a centerboard. All boat design involves compromises, however. Heavy boats are slow in light airs and won't accelerate quickly. Deep projections limit where boats can go without running aground. The goal is to have as much weight as possible as low as possible, but not too much weight, and not too low.

(The centerboard or keel also projects below the hull for a second purpose: It plays a vital role when the boat is sailing across the wind or upwind. That component of the apparent wind which pushes the boat sideways makes it skid, which is of no use. The pressure of the water against the keel or centerboard resists that force, and the boat moves forward.)

Narrow boats are tippy, wide boats are not. A designer can add stability by making the boat wider so that as it starts to heel, buoyancy is increased. Furthermore, under the present

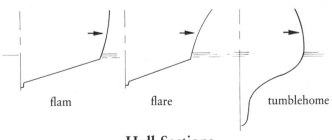

flam   flare   tumblehome

Hull Sections

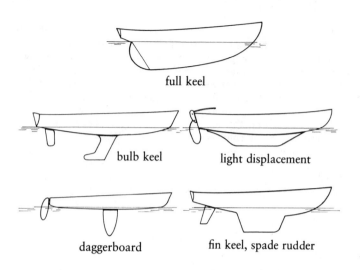

full keel

bulb keel

light displacement

daggerboard

fin keel, spade rudder

Hull Profiles

racing rules, wide beam is not penalized; that is, increasing the beam does not increase the rating as fast as increasing some other dimension, such as waterline length. But very wide-beam boats have a lot of resistance at speeds below planing speed, or in rough water. So beam is also a compromise.

Dinghys most often are round-bottom, round-bilge, or hard-chine, or have the exaggerated flare of a modern dinghy such as the International 505. An alternative to flare is flam, where the hull's sides have a convex instead of a concave curve, but where the beam at the deck is still wider than at the waterline. Another possibility is tumblehome. Here the curve is convex but the maximum beam is at the water. Flam is preferred today for most boats. Tumblehome reduces reserve buoyancy when the boat is heeled; and flare can cause tripping, turbulence, and drag. Flare, however, is frequently used at the bow, where the concave shape of the hull throws water down and out, keeping the boat drier.

Other cross-sections most commonly seen on larger boats are the bulb keel, an obvious attempt to place weight low; the fin keel, where the ballast of the keel is attached to the hull; and the integral keel.

Hull Profiles

Underwater shapes shown include a traditional hull whose full keel has an attached rudder; a bulb-keel boat; a small light-displacement keel cruiser; a dinghy with a daggerboard; and a modern high-performance racing boat with a fin keel and a spade rudder supported by a skeg.

Sheer

The line of the deck is termed sheer. While sheer may have some effect upon boat performance, it is usually chosen for appearance. Reverse sheer, for example, gives the maximum freeboard at the middle of the boat and increases stability as the boat heels; but because of its bulky appearance it is uncommon. Straight sheer is unusual. The most common is the conventional hollow sheer, where freeboard decreases from the bow going aft, and at some point begins to increase towards the stern. Variations are common. One is powderhorn or coble sheer, in which the sheer at the bow is reverse and the sheer aft is conventional.

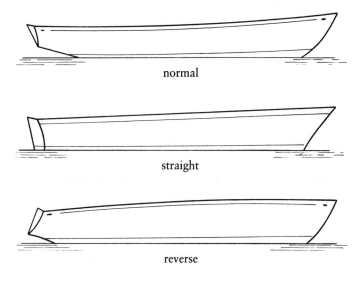

normal

straight

reverse

Sheer

Bows

The basic bow shapes are: cruiser; plumb; spoon; a longer spoon with a "chin"; and clipper. Plumb bows are often found on catboats and are frequently used for small one-design racing boats. Cruiser and spoon bows are the most common and are found on all types. Recently the spoon has evolved into a nearly straight line above the water. Clipper bows are traditional and are usually found on cruising boats. Below the bow and under water is the forefoot, which may be full or cut away. In small boats and in auxiliaries with fin keels the forefoot is almost totally cut away.

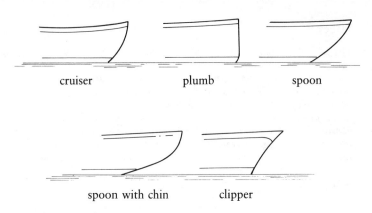

cruiser   plumb   spoon

spoon with chin   clipper

Bows

Sterns

Older and more traditional designs employ long counters which overhang the water. The transom may be vertical, angled aft, or reversed. Double-ended boats have pointed or "canoe" sterns which may or may not have the rudder mounted on the transom. Modern designs tend to have fairly wide sterns which develop from long, flat sections below the waterline leading to the stern.

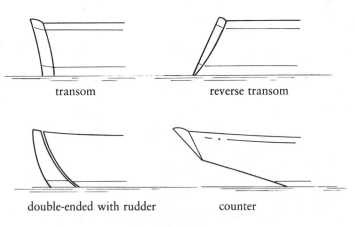

transom   reverse transom

double-ended with rudder   counter

Sterns

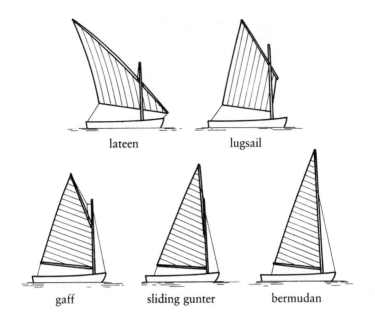

lateen   lugsail

gaff   sliding gunter   bermudan

Rigs

Although marconi or Bermuda rigs are the most common, lateen, gaff, gunter, and sliding gunter will be encountered. Ketch, yawl, and schooner rigs are most often used for cruisers.

The aspect ratio of a boat helps to describe the boat's appearance. A high aspect ratio is the equivalent of a tall rig. The aspect ratio most often used by sailors is obtained by dividing the length of the mainsail's luff by the length of its foot. (In aerodynamics a different proportion is used, where the length of the luff is divided by the area of the sail.) Tall, narrow sails have high aspect ratios, and tend to be most efficient going upwind. Low-aspect-ratio rigs are lower, broader, and more efficient off the wind.

In a masthead rig the forestay runs to the peak of the mast and the jib usually fills the entire foretriangle. In a 7/8 rig the stay runs to the point seven-eighths of the way up the mast. There are other partial rigs.

Rudders

Rudders may be keel-mounted, balanced, semibalanced, skeg-mounted, or mounted on the transom. A rudder shape typical of a catboat is also shown. Like a boat's rig, the rudder has an aspect ratio. For the rudder it is the depth of the rudder divided by the chord, or fore-and-aft dimension. A Beetle Cat's rudder has a low aspect ratio; the Soling's is high.

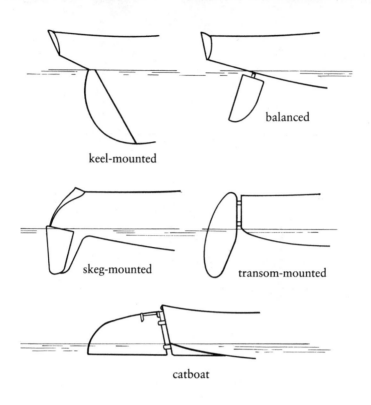

keel-mounted

balanced

skeg-mounted

transom-mounted

catboat

Rudders

Statistical Data

For the most part, the statistics given for each boat are self-explanatory. Statistics have been obtained almost entirely from manufacturers' literature. Certain notes follow which may be helpful.

Length: Overall length (LOA) is used for all small boats; for cruisers, length on the waterline (LWL) is also given. Both small and large boats appear in order of LOA, from shortest to longest.

Beam: Unless otherwise noted, beam listed is the maximum.

Draft: Where variable, as for centerboard boats, board condition is noted. Cruisers are very often available with several keel configurations, and therefore, several drafts.

Weight / Displacement: Weight is given for small one-designs, displacement for cruisers.

Sail area: If the information was available, area is given by sail; i.e., main, jib, mizzen, etc. Where no sails are specified, the boat has just one sail—the main—and its area is the one given. In some instances, the following symbols appear. They are used to obtain the rated sail areas.

I: The measured height of the foretriangle, from deck to the truck (top) of the mast.

J: The measured foretriangle base, from the forestay to the mast.

P: The measured luff of the mainsail, from head to tack.

E: The measured foot of the mainsail, from tack to clew.

Hull: If sandwich construction is noted, it is for the hull. Sandwich construction is very commonly used for decks.

Spars: Finish is not always noted. Wood and aluminum spars should always be finished. When aluminum is anodized the thin oxide film normally present, which gives aluminum its resistance to corrosion, is artificially increased in thickness. The result is an improvement in weathering characteristics and a uniform silver color. The coating may be dyed, perhaps gold, but this is unusual. Hard-coated aluminum is anodized in a modified process. The resulting oxide coating is denser and thicker than normal anodic coatings and also has a typical integral color, usually either bronze or black.

Racing Crew: Used only for small one-designs, or for boats where class rules limit crew. Comfortable capacity for daysailing is almost always higher.

First Built: "Modern" design is not always recent, and an older design may be modern indeed. Sources sometimes disagree by one or two years (and in some cases no date is available). The date used is assumed to be the most authoritative. This entry is not given for cruisers.

No. Built: Always approximate, and given for one-designs only. This information gives some idea of the boat's popularity. Frequently this figure is considered confidential by the manufacturer and is therefore not available. In some instances an estimated figure is given.

Berths: Infrequently, this figure had to be assumed.

Engine: Where possible, the type and horsepower are given.

Fuel: The type and tank capacity are given.

Head: "Standard" indicates a marine head conforming to environmental regulations.

Galley: The number of burners and the type of fuel are given.

Water: Tank capacity is given.

Rating: One-design boats may race level, or "head to head"; but when boats from different classes race against each other, more even competition is possible if a handicapping system is used. The total time for each boat is adjusted and the winner determined after the handicap is applied. In the United States, the rating and handicap are based on systems resulting in a time-on-distance correction.

IOR *(International Offshore Rule):* This rule was adopted in 1970 by the International Yacht Racing Union (IYRU) and is not a measurement, although it is given in linear feet. The IOR evolved from the rule of the American Cruising Club of America and the British Royal Ocean Racing Club. If shown, it has been provided by the manufacturer.

D–PN *(Portsmouth Number):* The Portsmouth yardstick is a widely used method of rating different classes sailing the same course. The numbers represent the length of time boats take to sail a common but unspecified distance. They are useful for comparing boats. A smaller number indicates a faster boat. Portsmouth numbers used here were taken from the 1979 compilation of Portsmouth numbers by the United States Yacht Racing Union (USYRU). Portsmouth numbers may be corrected into handicaps for different wind strengths, but here only the primary number has been given. When "suspect" is used it is not a criticism, but indicates that the rating has been derived from fairly limited data. Additional race results may, in the near future, result in a nonsuspect rating which shows little or no change.

PHRF *(Performance Handicap Racing Fleets):* This is the most popular handicapping system for cruisers, and is based upon estimates of potential speed. The handicaps are given in seconds per nautical mile; a higher PHRF rating indicates a slower boat. In this book, the USYRU handicaps for 1983 were used. Normally they are given for various geographic areas with differing climatic conditions. In an attempt to smooth out the wide geographic variations that are listed, I have averaged the handicaps.

No rating shown: Ratings are frequently not available, but this should never condemn the boat. In some instances the manufacturer, the class, and the owners have no interest in racing. Also, ratings are based upon measurements, racing experience, or a combination of factors; and newer boats may not have had sufficient time or use to obtain a rating.

One-Designs / Small Boats

Optimist

Length: 7 ft. 9 in.
Beam: 3 ft. 8 in.
Draft: 2 ft. 9 in.
Weight: 77 lbs. (FRP hull)
Sail area: 35 sq. ft.
Hull: Wood or FRP
Spars: Wood or aluminum

Racing crew: 1
Rating: D–PN 138.0 suspect
First built: 1947
No. built: 250,000+ world
Designer: Clark Mills, modified
  by Axel Damgard

Pram bow. Spritsail. No stays.

With the Mirror Dinghy, the Optimist is the most widely used junior training and racing pram. The Optimist is IYRU controlled, and reached international status in 1973. There are class associations in 43 countries. There are many home-built boats in plywood, but the most recent races have been won by fiberglass boats. Flotation is required by class rules.

Shrimp

Length: 9 ft. 7 in.
Beam: 4 ft. 10 in.
Draft: 2 ft. 6 in.
Weight: 120 lbs.
Sail area: 50 sq. ft.
Hull: FRP
Spars: Aluminum

Racing crew: 2
Rating: None
First built: 1972
No. built: 340
Designers: Hubert Vandestadt
  and Fraser McGruer

Gunter rig.

A tender, rowboat, outboard, and small training dinghy, the Shrimp has an unusual gunter rig that helps in trailering or cartopping because the spars are short. If Shrimp is to be used as a tender the bow eye is relocated for better towing. The rudder and centerboard kick up. There are foam-filled buoyancy tanks. The sail is loose-footed.

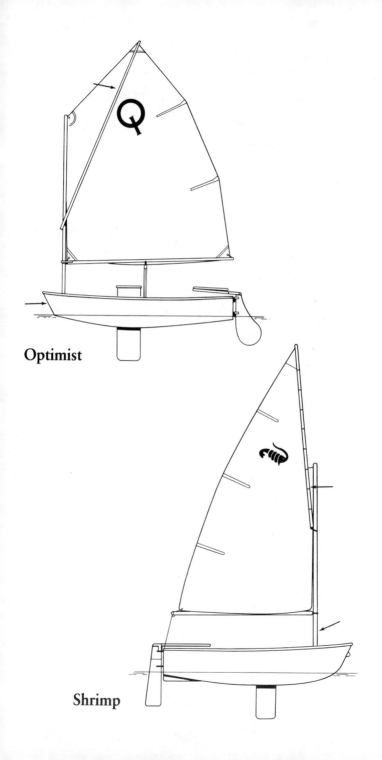

Optimist

Shrimp

International Moth

Length: 11 ft. maximum
Beam: 7 ft. 4 in. maximum
Draft: Varies
Weight: Varies; very light.
Sail area: 85 sq. ft. maximum
Hull: Open

Spars: Open
Racing crew: 1
Rating: D–PN 102.5
First built: 1928
No. built: 10,000 world,
  4,120 US

Designer: Individually designed. Evolved from designs by Len Morris (Australia) and Captain Joel Van Sant (USA) in 1928–1929.

Identification is difficult because almost any hull shape except multihull is allowed in this open developmental class. Single-hander.

This is a boat for nonconformists. Build one. If you don't like the way it sails, redesign it and build another. The Moth is under International Yacht Racing Union control. It issues building permits, and also controls one-design fleets. In the development class new designs, construction, and materials are encouraged. Hull designs are often skiff or scow, and there has been a tendency to add wings for hiking leverage. The wings extend the beam, which now averages about 3 ft. 10 in. Weight may be very low, and appears to average 50–60 lbs. In addition to the US, there are International Moth Class Associations in Europe, New Zealand, Japan, and Colombia.

Sundancer

Length: 11 ft.
Beam: 3 ft. 6 in.
Draft: 2 ft. 3 in. (scaled)
Weight: 52 lbs. (hull only)
Sail area: 60 sq. ft.
Hull: Cryolac, foam core

Spars: Aluminum
Racing crew: 350 lbs. maximum
Rating: None
First built: 1982
No. built: 1000
Designer: Ray Kosteneuli

Sleeved. Cat rig, loose-footed. Unusual foredeck. Unstayed mast. Yellow hull.

The Sundancer is very light and easily car-topped. Oarlocks are provided. Boom vang. Wood trim. The mast is unstayed, and the loose-footed main sleeved. There are 14 inches of freeboard.

International
Moth

Sundancer

Blue Crab

Length: 11 ft. 1 in.
Beam: 5 ft. 2 in.
Draft: 2 ft. 9 in.
Weight: 205 lbs.
Sail area: Main, 65 sq. ft.;
   jib, 23 sq. ft.
Hull: FRP

Spars: Aluminum
Racing crew: 2
Rating: D–PN 114.8 suspect
First built: 1972
No. built: 800
Designer: Harry R. Sindle

Shrouds aft of mast. Loose-footed main. Traveler quite high above transom.

Blue Crab is a beginner's boat. It is dry and easily rigged, and it can be sailed by one person. For its size, it is a light boat, and may be car-topped or trailered. Capacity is three adults. The transom is reinforced, and additional brackets are not required for an outboard. Blue Crab may be rowed; when not sailing, it has a capacity of five adults.

Skunk

Length: 11 ft. 1 in.
Beam: 5 ft. 5 in.
Draft: 2 ft. 6 in.
Weight: 190 lbs.
Sail area: Main, 50 sq. ft.;
   jib, 38 sq. ft.
Hull: FRP

Spars: Aluminum
Racing crew: 2 or 3
Rating: None
First built: 1966
No. built: 1050
Designers: Hubert Vandestadt
   and Fraser McGruer

Gunter rig. Recessed foredeck. Bigger than Shrimp, and has jib.

Skunk is a light, easily transported boat. Because of the gunter rig, all spars will fit inside the boat. There are no stays. The Super Skunk is marconi rigged and has an extra 10 sq. ft. of mainsail. Besides sailing, the Skunk may be used for fishing, as an outboard, or as a rowboat. The transom is reinforced and there is a motor clamp pad. There are oarlocks and a skeg. The recommended maximum horsepower is five. The mahogany rudder and the fiberglass centerboard kick up. There is storage under the foredeck.

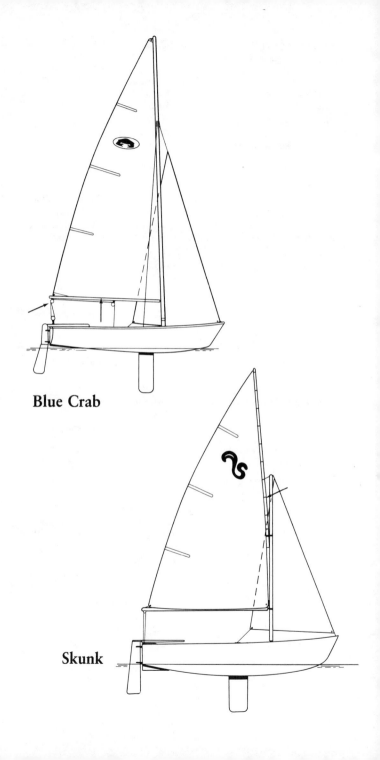

Blue Crab

Skunk

Sandpiper 100

Length: 11 ft. 4 in.
Beam: 4 ft. 10 in.
Draft: Not avail.
Weight: 110 lbs. (hull only)
Sail area: Main, 80 sq. ft.;
jib, 20 sq. ft.
Hull: Cryolac, foam core

Spars: Anodized aluminum
Racing crew: 580 lbs. maximum
Rating: None
First built: 1970
No. built: Not avail.
Designer: A. Kostanecki

Jib halyard runs to mast head. Mast set well forward. Loose-footed main.

Sandpiper is an auxiliary boat capable of being used for sailing, for rowing, or with an outboard. (Maximum four horsepower). There is an aluminum mounting plate for the outboard and removable oarlocks. The rudder kicks up and there is a hiking stick on the tiller. The hull material, Cryolac, is uncommon in sailboats although recently it has begun to be used in the manufacture of canoes.

International Penguin

Length: 11 ft. 5 in.
Beam: 4 ft. 8¾ in.
Draft: 3 ft. 9 in.
Weight: 180 lbs.
Sail area: 72 sq. ft.
Hull: Plywood or FRP

Spars: Spruce or aluminum
Racing crew: 1 or 2
Rating: D–PN 112.9
First built: 1938
No. built: 7000 +
Designer: Philip L. Rhodes

Hard chine. Cat. Loose-footed sail. Plumb bow. Racing boats have window. Stayed mast. Possible hood over fore portion.

The Penguin, very actively raced in the East, is not necessarily simple. The drawing shows a shock cord to the forestay, a mast turning handle below it, and a spray hood lowest of all. There is a boom vang and also a Cunningham. There are both down- and outhauls, and lever stay adjustment. Stay tangs allow for mast rotation, and the mast itself is bendy. There are active racing fleets in New England, Long Island Sound, and New Jersey. In addition to professionally built boats, many Penguins are built at home.

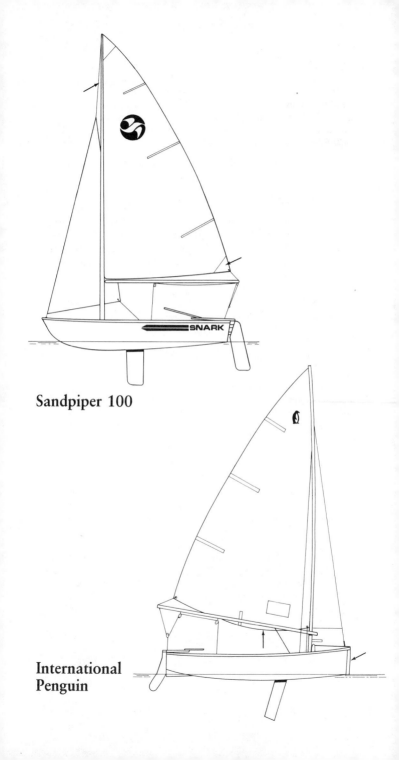

Sandpiper 100

International
Penguin

Echo

Length: 11 ft. 10 in.
Beam: 4 ft. 11 in.
Draft: 2 ft.
Weight: 140 lbs.
Sail area: Main and jib, 92 sq. ft. total
Hull: FRP

Spars: Aluminum
Racing crew: 2
Rating: None
First built: Not avail.
No. built: Not avail.
Designer: Not known

Significant sheer. Vertical stern. Mid-boom sheeting. Single shroud, no jumper.

A straightforward beginner's boat, the Echo has been designed for versatility and may also be rowed, or powered (with a maximum of five horsepower outboard). Oarlock sockets are built in, and there is a pad for the motor. A rowing seat runs athwartship. The rudder and daggerboard are mahogany. The former kicks up. The mast is two-piece for car-topping. There is a storage compartment and an optional whisker pole.

Butterfly

Length: 12 ft.
Beam: 4 ft. 6 in.
Draft: 1 ft. 3 in. (hull only)
Weight: 137 lbs. (hull only)
Sail area: 75 sq. ft.
Hull: FRP

Spars: Aluminum
Racing crew: 1 or 2
Rating: D–PN 108.0
First built: 1960
No. built: 8600
Designer: John Barnett

Reverse sheer of both top of deck and gunwale. No jib, but forestay and shrouds. Considerable roach to sail.

Butterfly is designed as a car-topper, so in addition to the normal one-piece anodized rotating mast, a two-piece mast is offered. Two people or three good friends would be reasonable capacity. Sail control has a fixed outhaul, but there is a boom vang and a downhaul. Stays are adjustable. The boat is unsinkable, with foam flotation. Rudder kicks up and there is a snubber for the mahogany daggerboard. Handrails are mahogany, and there is a vinyl rub-rail. The main runs up the mast on a track, but it is sleeved over the boom.

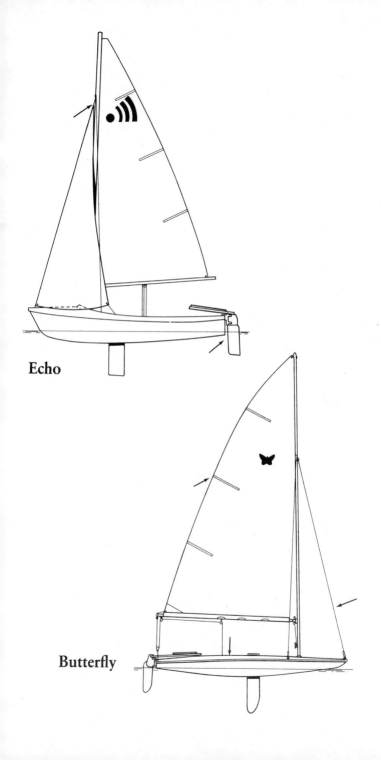

Echo

Butterfly

Howmar Twelve

Length: 12 ft. 2 in.
Beam: 5 ft.
Draft: 2 ft. 6 in.
Weight: 160 lbs.
Sail area: Main, 60 sq. ft.; jib, 30 sq. ft.; spinnaker, 86 sq. ft.
Hull: FRP

Spars: Anodized aluminum
Racing crew: 2
Rating: None
First built: 1981
No. built: 200
Designer: Sparkman and Stephens

Straight bow. Jib window. Loose-footed. Distinct sheer forward of mast.

Roomy for its size, the Howmar Twelve is a racer, trainer, and daysailer. The hull's light weight makes for easy car-topping. The boat has internal seating, is self-bailing, and has foam flotation. There is a dry storage locker under the forward seat. Capacity is 480 lbs. The main is loose-footed and has an adjustable outhaul. Both rudder and centerboard are polyurethane. Options include a vang, hinged mast step, hiking straps, and a mounting block for an outboard. The sharp bow cuts through waves, and with its broad aft lines, the Howmar Twelve will plane.

Beetle Cat

Length: 12 ft. 4 in.
Beam: 6 ft.
Draft: 2 ft.
Weight: 450 lbs.
Sail area: 100 sq. ft. approx.
Hull: Oak, cedar

Spars: Fir
Racing crew: 2
Rating: D–PN 100.2 suspect
First built: 1921, approx.
No. built: 3000 est.
Designer: The Beetle family

Gaff-rigged cat. Wood hull and spars. Main sheeted to elevated rod—or traveler—on transom. Typical Cape Cod rudder. Note bow.

Look for the Beetle Cat on the south and east of Cape Cod, in Buzzards Bay, and in Narraganset Bay. There are also fleets on Long Island. Competition, especially for Juniors, is stiff. The Beetle is an excellent, stable training boat. Since 1946 the boat has been built (in wood only) by the Concordia Company. Fastenings are bronze, and the deck is canvas-covered. There are no seats. The boat is offered complete, although sidestays and a clew outhaul are optional.

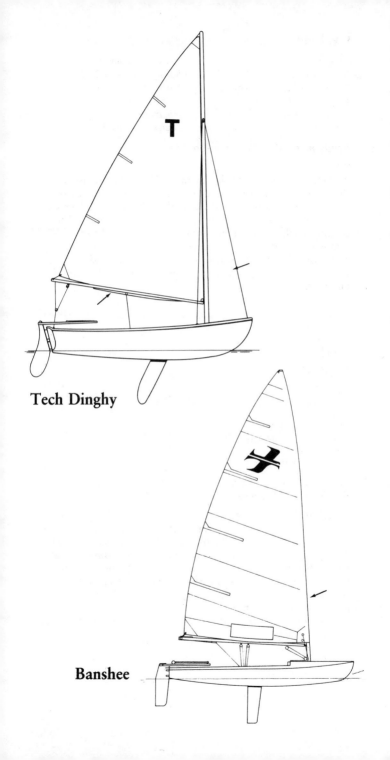

Tech Dinghy

Banshee

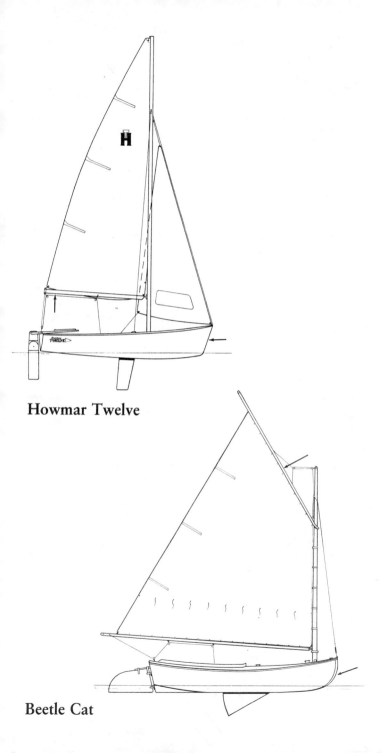

Howmar Twelve

Beetle Cat

Widgeon

Length: 12 ft. 4 in.
Beam: 5 ft.
Draft: 3 ft. 6 in.
Weight: 318 lbs.
Sail area: Main and jib, 90 sq. ft. total
Hull: FRP

Spars: Aluminum
Racing crew: 2
Rating: D–PN 121.6
First built: 1964
No. built: 5040
Designer: Robert Baker

Bow almost plumb. Note sheer line. Loose-footed main. Bow eye.

Widgeon is light and responsive and accelerates quickly. It is raced, but probably the main use has been as a trainer. The transom has been designed to carry an outboard with a recommended maximum of four horsepower. The mast is sealed, and there is foam flotation, so the boat is self-rescuing. There is a bow eye for mooring and trailering. Some of the options available include an outhaul and boom vang, compartment doors for the bow stowage, and a tiller extension. The centerboard is fiberglass and weighs 15 lbs. The rudder kicks up. There is seating for four.

Puffer

Length: 12 ft. 6 in.
Beam: 5 ft. 9 in.
Draft: 2 ft. 6 in. (scaled)
Weight: 160 lbs. (hull only)
Sail area: Main, 55 sq. ft.; jib, 35 sq. ft.
Hull: FRP

Spars: Aluminum
Racing crew: 1–3 (450 lbs.)
Rating: D–PN 116.1
First built: 1972
No. built: Not avail.
Designer: AMF

Open cockpit. Loose-footed main. Spoon bow. Rudder at noticable angle away from transom. Adjustable jib leads.

Puffer may be sailed or rowed, so she comes with oar locks. There is also a motor mount. Seats are molded into the double hull, and there is foam under the benches in case both hulls are holed. The rudder kicks up. There are hiking straps, a boom downhaul, and an outhaul. The centerboard and the rudder are mahogany.

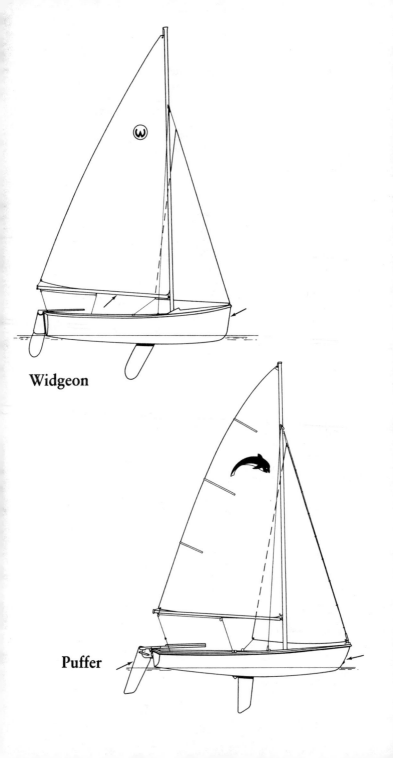

Widgeon

Puffer

Tech Dinghy

Length: 12 ft. 8 in.
Beam: 5 ft. 2 in.
Draft: 6 in. board up
Weight: 250 lbs. (hull only)
Sail area: 72 sq. ft.
Hull: FRP

Spars: Aluminum
Racing crew: 2
Rating: D–PN 109.0 suspect
First built: 1962
No. built: Not avail.

Designer: Halsey Herreshoff after initial design by Massachusetts Institute of Technology.

Cat, loose-footed main, has forestay. Note sheeting. Recessed foredeck, cross seat.

The original design of the Tech Dinghy was by MIT, for use in the Charles River Basin as either a trainer or a collegiate racer. About twenty years ago Halsey Herreshoff and the MIT sailing director, Hatch Brown, redesigned her a little faster, drier, and more forgiving. There is a lever to operate the FRP centerboard. The traveler, outhaul, and boom vang are adjustable, with the latter leading to the maststep casting. MIT has sold the original boats, and if you see a wood model, it may well be one of the originals.

Banshee

Length: 13 ft.
Beam: 4 ft. 11 in.
Draft: 2 ft. 6 in.
Weight: 120 lbs. (hull only)
Sail area: 88 sq. ft.
Hull: FRP

Spars: Aluminum (two-piece)
Racing crew: 1
Rating: D–PN 94.5
First built: 1969
No. built: 8000
Designer: Richard L. Reid

Spoon bow. Unstayed mast. Four battens. Loose-footed sail.

A high-performance boat designed for car-topping. Maximum capacity is two, or in a pinch, three. Sail control includes a vang and a Cunningham and an adjustable outhaul. The unstayed, nonrotating mast pivots fore and aft, raking aft when going to weather and forward when running. The loose-footed sail slips over the mast and has a window. The daggerboard is adjustable fore and aft, allowing the boat to be balanced when the sail is reefed around the mast. Rudder kicks up. Banshee is unsinkable, with foam flotation. Racing rules govern the hull, spars, and sail. Modifications are allowed to running rigging, including sail shaping. Originally designed for San Francisco Bay, Banshee now has more than fifty fleets in five countries. A Banshee T modification with a reduced sail area of 73 sq. ft. is available for extra stability.

Cyclone

Length: 13 ft.	*Spars:* Aluminum
Beam: 4 ft. 11 in.	*Racing crew:* 1 or 2
Draft: 2 ft. 10 in. (scaled)	*Rating:* D–PN 95.4
Weight: 148 lbs.	*First built:* 1972
Sail area: 74 sq. ft.	*No. built:* 2350
Hull: FRP	*Designer:* Frank Butler

Bendy mast. Short forestay. Loose-footed main. Mid-boom sheeting.

A planing dinghy with a bendy mast. There is an unusually short forestay. For ease of car-topping, the mast may be ordered in two pieces. Both the centerboard and the rudder are fiberglass. A beaching rudder is available as an option. The cockpit is self-bailing, there are hiking straps, and foam flotation is provided. Control includes an outhaul, a Cunningham, and a vang. A sail window is optional. A hatch leads to a forward compartment. Sheets are adjusted with a full-width cockpit traveler.

Gryphon

Length: 13 ft. 1 in.	*Racing crew:* 1
Beam: 5 ft.	*Rating:* Manufacturer est. D–PN
Draft: 2 ft. 6 in.	85–90
Weight: 120 lbs.	*First built:* 1980
Sail area: 82 sq. ft.	*No. built:* 50
Hull: Graphite fiber with PVC foam core	*Designer:* Team. Evolved from Banshee.
Spars: Graphite fiber	

Lever boom vang. Rudder head perforated. Main loose-footed. Bendy mast. Maximum beam well aft.

A high-technology boat designed to sell against Banshee, Laser, and Finn. The extremely light weight is due to the use of carbon fiber in the mast, hull, and foils. The mast is tapered and unstayed. There are dual controls for the vang, traveler, outhaul, and Cunningham. The foot and leech tension may be adjusted by single controls. There are hiking straps, a daggerboard slot gasket, and a beaching rudder. The traveler is curved. Flotation is provided by the PVC core of the sandwich hull, which is stiff. Because of its light weight, the Gryphon accelerates quickly.

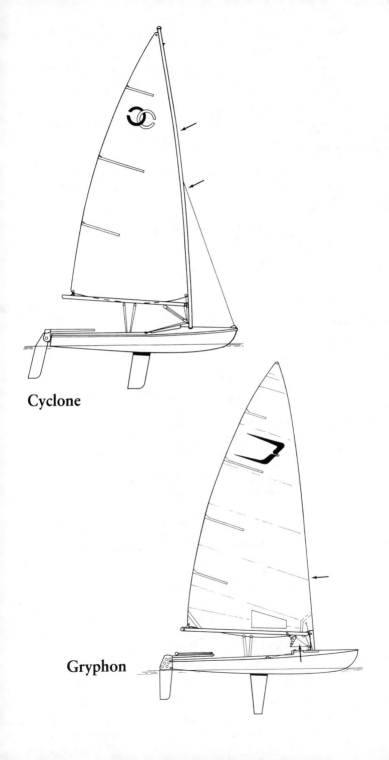

Cyclone

Gryphon

Spindrift

Length: 13 ft. 4 in.
Beam: 5 ft. 2 in.
Draft: 3 ft.
Weight: 205 lbs.
Sail area: Main, 68 sq. ft.;
   jib, 32 sq. ft.
Hull: FRP

Spars: Aluminum
Racing crew: 2
Rating: D–PN 112.8 suspect
First built: 1964
No. built: 620
Designer: Hubert Vandestadt

No spreaders. Straight bow. Splash rail. Mid-boom sheeting.

Spindrift is available completed in kit forms, and can also be built of wood, from scratch. In fiberglass the deck is a foam sandwich. Crew capacity is four. There is foam flotation in the mast and in buoyancy tanks fore and aft. Both the centerboard and the rudder kick up. There is a boom vang and jiffy reefing. This is a planing dinghy.

Blue Jay

Length: 13 ft. 6 in.
Beam: 5 ft. 2 in.
Draft: 3 ft. 9 in.
Weight: 275 lbs. min.
Sail area: Main, 62 sq. ft.; jib, 28
   sq. ft.; spinnaker, 110 sq. ft.
Hull: Plywood

Spars: Aluminum
Racing crew: 2 or 3
Rating: D–PN 110.7
First built: 1949
No. built: 6500
Designer: Sparkman and Stephens

Fractional rig. Both jib and main set fairly high. Splash rail. Shrouds slightly aft of mast.

This was originally designed as a junior trainer that would allow for a spinnaker, but many boats are now owned and raced by adults. The rig is relatively short, increasing stability. In line with the original design intent, class rules require anchors, PFDs, bailing equipment, and a paddle to be carried on board while racing. Flotation is optional. Cockpit seats are not permitted, but an adjustable outhaul and hiking straps may be used. The last information available indicated more than 140 fleets, with the majority located on the coasts, including Florida, and also in the Great Lakes. Large numbers are found in San Francisco and on Long Island Sound.

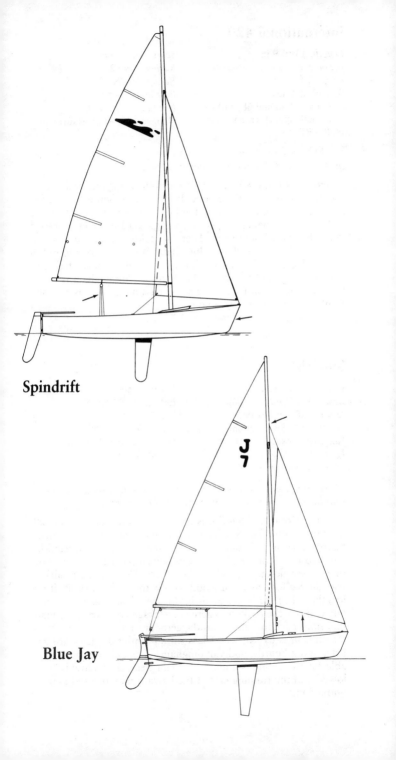

Spindrift

Blue Jay

International 420

Length: 13 ft. 9 in.
Beam: 5 ft. 5 in.
Draft: 3 ft. 2 in.
Weight: 220 lbs.
Sail area: Main and jib, 110 sq.
ft. total; spinnaker, 95 sq. ft.
Hull: FRP

Spars: Aluminum
Racing crew: 2
Rating: D–PN 97.5
First built: Not avail.
No. built: Not avail.
Designer: Christian Maury

Cockpit extends forward of mast and has splash rail. Foredeck quite elevated. Spoon bow, vertical transom.

A light, fast trapeze boat suited for both racing and training, the 420 comes in both options. It is a one-design, governed for international competition by the IYRU. The racing model has a roller traveler, bailers, tapered mast, gasket for the centerboard, and a five-part boom vang. There are hiking straps and hull inspection ports, as well as a downhaul. Windows are allowed in the jib. Flotation lies in the hollow seat tanks. The centerboard is mahogany, and the rudder kicks up. A Cunningham is optional, as are a mast gate and a compass mount. Construction results in a relatively rigid boat.

Sunfish

Length: 13 ft. 10 in.
Beam: 4 ft. 1 in.
Draft: 2 ft. 8 in. (scaled)
Weight: 129 lbs. (hull only)
Sail area: 75 sq. ft.
Hull: FRP
Spars: Aluminum

Racing crew: 1
Rating: D–PN 105.5
First built: 1955
No. built: Over 200,000
Designers: Alex Bryan and
Cortlandt Heyniger

Most common board boat. Lateen rig. Racing boats have very low boom, others may not. Straight sheer at rail.

Like the Hobie, the Sunfish is truly ubiquitous and is found all over the world. The Sunfish was chosen as the "breakthrough board" boat in *Sail* magazine's tenth-anniversary poll. Sunfish has also been honored by *Fortune,* which picked her as one of the 25 best designed products in the US. The original model was the Sailfish, made in wood, and without the cockpit. It was lengthened to the Super Sunfish, the same length as the Sunfish, but without the cockpit. There is a storage compartment, foam flotation, cockpit bailer, and daggerboard retention line. Sail attachment is by sail sets. Class rules prohibit daggerboard gaskets, jibing boards, and Cunninghams. The only option available for use racing is a mainsheet jam cleat. A window is allowed and the running end of the halyard may be used as a boom vang.

International 420

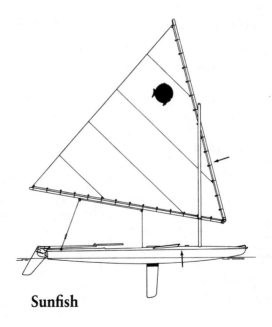

Sunfish

Laser (Laser M)

Length: 13 ft. 10¼ in.
Beam: 4 ft. 6 in.
Draft: 2 ft. 8 in. (scaled)
Weight: 130 lbs. (hull only)
Sail area: 76 sq. ft.; M, 60 sq. ft.
Hull: FRP
Spars: Aluminum

Racing crew: 1
Rating: D–PN 92.3
 98.0 (M; suspect)
First built: 1971
No. built: 105,000
Designer: Bruce Kirby

Long, straight spoon bow. Bendy, unstayed mast with sleeved sail. Loose-footed sail. Note angles on rudder.

The Laser M is the same boat as the Laser, but with a modified rig. The Laser has a 20 ft. mast and 76 sq. ft. of sail. The Laser M is designed for lighter crews or heavier weather: the top half of the two-piece mast is replaced with a shorter section and the replacement sail has an area of 60 sq. ft. If the conversion is not made, you can reef the Laser by wrapping the sail around the mast two or three times before attaching it to the boom. (Best done on shore.) Like most boats of this type, the Laser capsizes easily, but floats so high that when it is righted there is no water in the cockpit. (The Laser II, not shown, has a jib; a spinnaker and trapeze are optional.)

Force 5

Length: 13 ft. 10½ in.
Beam: 4 ft. 10 in.
Draft: 6 in. (centerboard up)
Weight: 145 lbs. (hull only)
Sail area: 91 sq. ft.
Hull: FRP

Spars: Aluminum
Racing crew: 1 or 2
Rating: D–PN 95.4
First built: 1972
No. built: 15,000 est.
Designer: Fred Scott

Mono rig. Unstayed mast. Mast slips through main. Four battens. Crew sits well forward.

The Force 5 is a "hot" boat. The normal racing crew is one, but two may be needed to hold her down. The main slips over the three-piece, unstayed mast. Sail control includes an eight-part boom vang, a Cunningham, outhaul, and traveler. All boat controls can be reached from both sides of the boat. She is self-bailing, has positive foam flotation and full-length hiking straps. The rudder kicks up. All fittings are stainless steel, aluminum, or plastic. Only minor modifications are allowed for racing, including a sail window, inspection ports, etc. The use of lever vangs or removal of any foam flotation is specifically disallowed.

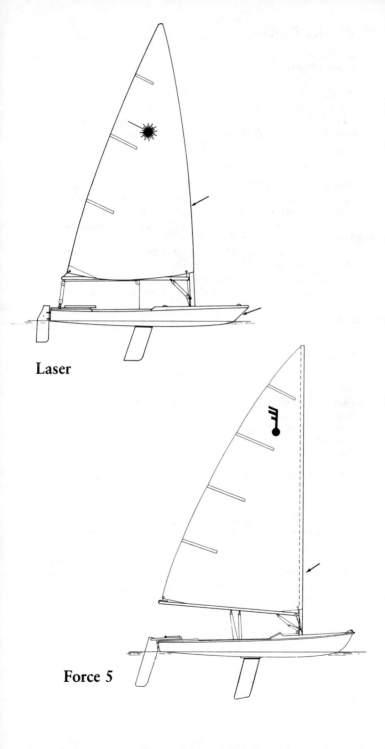

Laser

Force 5

Rhodes Bantam

Length: 14 ft.
Beam: 5 ft. 6½ in.
Draft: 4 ft. 2 in.
Weight: 325 lbs.
Sail area: Main, 77.25 sq. ft.;
   jib, 46.5 sq. ft.
Hull: Wood or FRP (balsa core)

Spars: Wood or aluminum
Racing crew: 2
Rating: D–PN 98.3
First built: 1945
No. built: 1400
Designer: Philip Rhodes

Vertical bow. Shrouds somewhat aft of mast. Considerable sheer. Fractional rig. Undecked.

This undecked planing one-design was originally intended for home construction in wood. Later construction has used FRP, balsa core with flotation tank, and foam-in-place flotation. Wood boats are competitive with FRP, as the minimum weight is controlled. Note the plumb bow. The hull is an arc-bottomed chine. Capacity is four adults. Spinnakers with an area of 135 sq. ft. are available. There is a strong class association, maintaining strict one-design racing rules. Fleets are in Kansas, Missouri, Ohio, Michigan, Pennsylvania, New York, and Virginia.

Cheshire

Length: 14 ft.
Beam: 6 ft. 2 in.
Draft: 2 ft. 1 in.
Weight: 185 lbs.
Sail area: Main, 105 sq. ft.;
   jib, 30 sq. ft.
Hull: FRP

Spars: Anodized aluminum
Racing crew: 1
Rating: D–PN 80.0 suspect
First built: 1963
No. built: 500
Designer: Frank Meldau

Two symmetrical hulls with exaggerated elliptical shape. Pivoting centerboards. Three cross members. Six full-length battens. Distinctive rudder head.

The Cheshire catamaran predates the Hobie, and has been in production for almost twenty years. The pivoting centerboards are unique to the Cheshire and its sister, the Isotope. The boards are easier to retract than dagger boards. There are three cross members, with the aft supporting the traveler, the middle the mast, and the forward the forestay. Hulls are stiff, as there is an internal tubular frame. The Cheshire is raced single-handed, but can accommodate three adults.

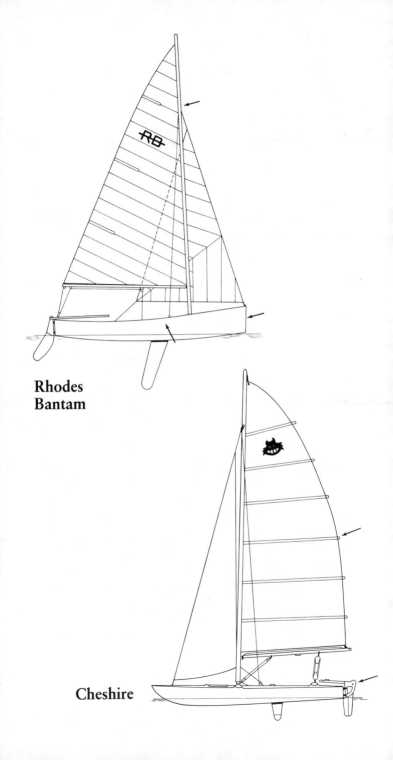

Rhodes Bantam

Cheshire

GP-14

Length 14 ft.	*Hull:* FRP, foam, and balsa
Beam: 5 ft.	*Spars:* Aluminum
Draft: 3 ft.	*Racing crew:* 2
Weight: 293 lbs. (hull only)	*Rating:* D–PN 101.3
Sail area: Main, 82 sq. ft.; jib, 30 sq. ft.; genoa, 44 sq. ft.; spinnaker, 81 sq. ft.	*First built:* 1950
	No. built: 13,000
	Designer: Jack Holt

Hard chine. Note lines of foredeck. Main stops well short of boom end. Wood seats and thwarts. High freeboard.

Relatively dry, with high freeboard, GP–14 is used both as a daysailer and as a highly competitive racer. Used for daysailing, capacity is four adults. Racing, she is light and responsive. In the United States most fleets are found in the mid-Atlantic states; in Canada, on the Great Lakes. There are large fleets overseas in Great Britian, Ireland, South Africa, and Australia.

Hobie 14

Length: 14 ft.	*Spars:* Aluminum
Beam: 7 ft. 8 in.	*Racing crew:* 1 or 2
Draft: 8 in.	*Rating:* D–PN 87.2
Weight: 240 lbs.	*First built:* Middle 1960s
Sail area: Main and jib, 118 sq. ft. total	*No. built:* Over 100,000, all lengths
Hull: FRP and foam	*Designer:* Hobie Alter

Catamaran. Full-length battens. Asymmetrical hulls.

The Hobie 16 and 18 (not shown) are faster and perhaps more popular, but the Hobie 14 was the first. Hulls are asymmetrical, with no boards. The trampoline or "wing" is elevated above the hulls. The boat is very fast, having been clocked at over 24 MPH. The sail is shaped by full battens, which themselves can be formed. The jib has roller furling as an option on the Turbo TJ model. Hobies are, with Sunfish, found at resorts all over the world. There are racing fleets to match. There are regional area, national, and world championships. The development history is interesting. Hobie Alter's first love was surfboards. He pioneered the substitution of foam for balsa wood cores, and he used the combination again when he first began venturing into catamarans in the mid-1960s.

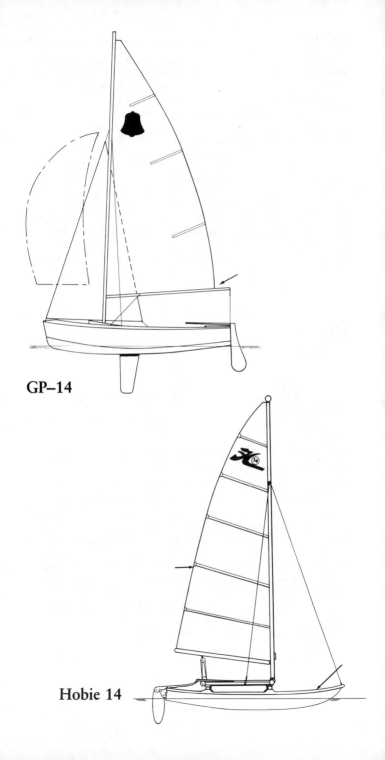

GP–14

Hobie 14

Javelin

Length: 14 ft.
Beam: 5 ft. 8 in.
Draft: 3 ft. 10 in.
Weight: 524 lbs.
Sail area: Main and jib, 125 sq. ft. total
Hull: FRP

Spars: Hard anodized aluminum
Racing crew: 2
Rating: D–PN 111.8
First built: 1962
No. built: 4900
Designer: Uffa Fox

Small daysailer. Curved transom. Sharp bow. Big cockpit.

A beamy, stable small daysailer. Javelin has an unusually large (nine-foot) cockpit, a gear locker under the seats, and a lockable storage compartment under the deck. She is self-bailing and self-rescuing. The transom is reinforced to take outboards up to eight horsepower. The fiberglass rudder kicks up. The galvanized steel centerboard is, at 49 lbs., fairly heavy and a definite aid to stability. Freeboard is quite high, and a molded-in splash rail helps keep the boat dry.

Lido 14

Length: 14 ft.
Beam: 6 ft.
Draft: 4 ft. 3 in.
Weight: 310 lbs.
Sail area: Main, 76 sq. ft.; jib, 35 sq. ft.
Hull: FRP

Spars: Anodized aluminum
Racing crew: 2
Rating: D–PN 100.9
First built: 1960
No. built: 4830
Designer: W. D. Schock

High freeboard. Deck line. Loose-footed main. Spoon bow. Gold anodized spars and rudder head.

Child's boat, racer and sailer. The Lido 14 evolved from the earlier Lehman 14 via a rather complete redesign including sheer, seats, foredeck, and sail plan. The cockpit length allows for six adults on full-length seats. The seats, with a bow compartment, provide flotation. Only limited modifications are allowed for racing, as the intention is to keep Lido as a simple, limited boat. Both rudder and centerboard are FRP foam sandwich construction. The latter is not pivoted, but is suspended by two stainless steel straps. There is a 2:1 outhaul and boom vang, and a pad eye for a whisker pole on the mast. Options include the whisker pole and hiking straps. A very strong association exists, particularly in southern California.

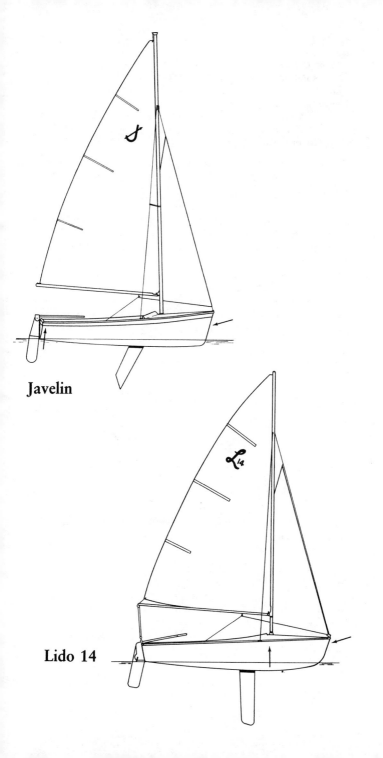

Javelin

Lido 14

Jet 14

Length: 14 ft. 1 in.
Beam: 4 ft. 8 in.
Draft: 4 ft. 2 in.
Weight: 285 lbs. minimum
Sail area: Main, 75 sq. ft.; jib, 38 sq. ft.; spinnaker, 150 sq. ft.
Hull: FRP or wood

Spars: Wood or aluminum
Racing crew: 2
Rating: D–PN 100.5
First built: 1955
No. built: Over 1000
Designer: Howard V. Siddons

Plumb bow. Partially decked. Sharp entry and long waterline. Rigged like Snipe. Hull same as International 14, but decked.

The Jet 14 was developed when molds for an International 14, designed by Uffa Fox, became available. She is fast, going well to windward. The long flat run of the hull and the light weight allow her to plane. There may be either a traveler or a head knocker on the boom. Two cut-outs may be made on the foredeck for spinnaker storage. Usually there is one near the forestay or two outboard of the mast. Size is restricted. A lever vang, not shown, is permitted, as is a jib window. Flotation is required, and with the FRP boats tanks are built in. Spinnakers were allowed in 1971. Fleets are in New York, New Jersey, Maryland, and Ohio. The 14 is often seen with both spinnaker and jib up, except in light air.

Trac 14

Length: 14 ft. 1 in.
Beam: 7 ft. 6 in.
Draft: Unknown
Weight: 195 lbs.
Sail area: Main, 119 sq. ft.; jib, 29 sq. ft.
Hull: FRP

Spars: Hard-coated aluminum
Racing crew: 2
Rating: D–PN 81.0 suspect
First built: 1980
No. built: Not avail.
Designer: Windrush Yachts (Australia)

Catamaran. Seven battens. Mainsail window. High boom. No trapeze. Trampoline even with top of hulls.

Trac 14 is manufactured by AMF under license from Australia, where it is the most popular catamaran. The jib has roller furling. The outhaul is adjustable, and there is a three-part downhaul. In a novel feature to assist transportation, the hulls fold under the trampoline to reduce the beam to just over six feet. Each hull has a compartment. The single tiller has an extension long enough for hiking. There is no trapeze. Mast rake may be adjusted under way using tweaker lines.

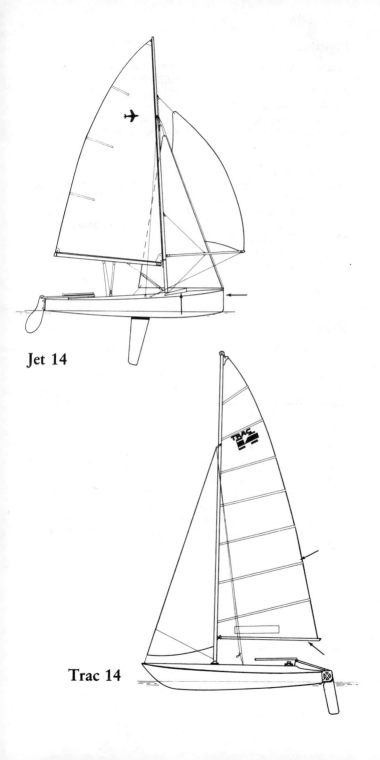

Jet 14

Trac 14

Phantom

Length: 14 ft. 1½ in.
Beam: 4 ft. 5 in.
Draft: 2 ft. 10 in.
Weight: 120 lbs. (hull only)
Sail area: 84.5 sq. ft.
Hull: FRP

Spars: Aluminum
Racing crew: 1
Rating: D–PN 103.7 suspect
First built: 1977
No. built: 9000
Designer: Jack Howie

Lateen-rigged board boat. Sail luff and foot sleeve over spars.

In order to reduce the common tendency of sailboards to submarine downwind, the designer gave Phantom a sharp forward entry and a high bow design. The coaming is molded in, and the halyard leads through it to the cockpit. There are hiking straps and a storage compartment in the cockpit. Spars and the tiller are hard-coated aluminum. Both the luff and the foot of the sail sleeve over the spars, reducing aerodynamic drag and distributing stress evenly.

Rascal

Length: 14 ft. 5 in.
Beam: 6 ft.
Draft: 3 ft.
Weight: 400 lbs.
Sail area: Main, 72 sq. ft.; jib, 49
  sq. ft.; spinnaker, 160 sq. ft.
Hull: FRP and balsa core

Spars: Aluminum
Racing crew: 2
Rating: D–PN 107.8
First built: 1961
No. built: 3000
Designer: Ray Greene

Sheer. High bow. Recessed foredeck. Jib window.

Sail magazine termed Rascal a "breakthrough boat" as the boat designed for the first-time buyer. Mast, boom, and rudder head are black hard-coated aluminum. The mast is on a tabernacle, and is filled with foam for flotation. Jib tracks are adjustable. There is an aft storage locker that can be locked, and also a bow locker. The centerboard trunk is enclosed. Trim is teak.

Phantom

Rascal

Dolphin Sr.

Length: 14 ft. 6 in.
Beam: 4 ft. 3 in.
Draft: 1 ft. 6 in.
Weight: 170 lbs.
Sail area: 85 sq. ft.
Hull: FRP

Spars: Aluminum
Racing crew: 1
Rating: D–PN 105.3
First built: 1969
No. built: 7100
Designer: Glen Cororran

Board boat with high freeboard. Lateen rig. Integral, molded splash rail at mast step.

Dolphin is a lateen-rigged cat board boat, slightly longer than most. Capacity for reasonable sailing is two adults. The daggerboard is fiberglass, as is the lower portion of the kick-up rudder. The rudder head is aluminum. There is a small compartment molded into the hull just aft of the mast. The cockpit has hiking bars.

Skipjack

Length: 14 ft. 7 in.
Beam: 5 ft. 3 in.
Draft: 3 ft. 6 in.
Weight: 320 lbs.
Sail area: Main, 82 sq. ft.; jib, 43 sq. ft.; spinnaker, 125 sq. ft.
Hull: FRP

Spars: Aluminum
Racing crew: 2
Rating: D–PN 93.2
First built: 1966
No. built: 800
Designers: Carter Pyle and Harry Sindle

Full-length battens. Undecked, but wide gunwales. Spreader quite low. Bendy rig. Large roach.

The Skipjack's design combines ideas from the Finn hull, Mobjack (wide side decks, flat cockpit floor), and Flying Dutchman (single spreader, mid-boom sheeting). The U.S. Naval Academy immediately ordered twenty. The Skipjack rides high, with the cockpit floor above the water line so transom bailers can be used, and no cockpit cover is necessary at anchor. The full-length fiberglass battens support the full roach. They should also make you stop and think about when and how you use the bar traveler. There is a downhaul and vang, and adjustable jib leads. Simple roller reefing is possible on the boom. The boat may be rigged as a cat by having the mast moved into one of several choices of step. The centerboard must be aluminum but choice of material for the rudder is optional.

Dolphin Sr.

Skipjack

Finn

Length: 14 ft. 9 in.	*Spars:* Aluminum
Beam: 4 ft. 10 in.	*Racing crew:* 1
Draft: 2 ft. 3 in.	*Rating:* Olympic; D–PN 94.8
Weight: 319 lbs.	*First built:* 1949
Sail area: 115 sq. ft.	*No. built:* Not avail.
Hull: FRP	*Designer:* Rickard Sarby

Mono rig with unstayed, bendy mast. Bow and transom almost vertical. Mid-boom sheeting.

Finn is an Olympic boat, and has been since 1952. The mast is unstayed. The main sheet is a three-part system with a curved traveler. The outhaul has a 6:1 mechanical advantage, and there are dual controls for the inhaul. Other gear which may be controlled from either side of the boat includes the Cunningham, centerboard, and 30:1 lever boom vang. The centerboard is aluminum, and its anodized coating is impregnated with Teflon. Flotation tanks, three bailers, and adjustable hiking straps assist in safety, and there are inspection ports for the double hull.

Scaffie

Length: 14 ft. 9 in.	*Spars:* Spruce
Beam: 5 ft. 9 in.	*Rating:* None
Draft: 1 ft. 3 in.	*First built:* 18th century
Weight: 460 lbs.	*No. built:* Unknown
Sail area: 100 sq. ft.	*Designer:* John Watkinson
Hull: FRP	

Standing lug sail. Mast sharply raked. Bilge fins. No centerboard. Lapstrake hull. Red sails.

The Drascombe Scaffie is a design that has been used in coastal sailing for over 200 years. Scaffies have been built for many years in England, and they are now also built in Maine. The loose-footed lug sail is carried on an unstayed mast. Since there is no centerboard trunk the cockpit has a lot of space, and with a tent, the Scaffie is used for cruising. A three-horsepower outboard may be fitted through the rounded stern. Rowing positions are provided. Other Drascombe types include a Longboat, with mizzen; a Coaster with the same hull but with a cabin; and several other designs. All are lapstrake in appearance and all have red sails. All have foam flotation.

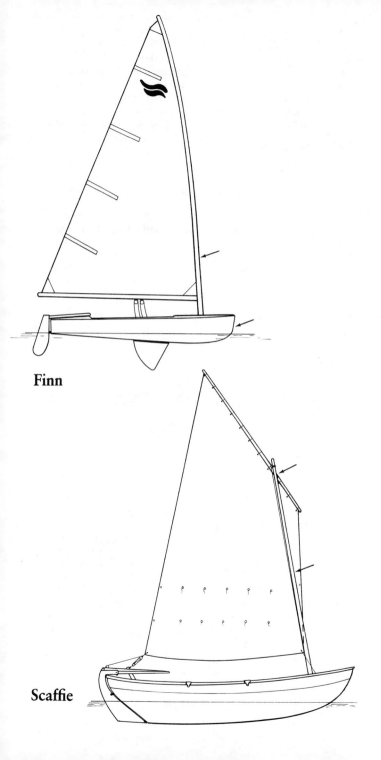

Finn

Scaffie

Designers Choice

Length: 14 ft. 10½ in.
Beam: 5 ft. 1 in.
Draft: 3 ft.
Weight: 315 lbs.
Sail area: Main, 82 sq. ft.; jib, 38 sq. ft.
Hull: FRP

Spars: Hard-coated aluminum
Racing crew: 900 lbs. max.
Rating: None
First built: 1979
No. built: 1000
Designer: Sparkman and Stephens

Sharp bow, planing hull aft. Rudder head and spars black. Hull seats plus thwart. Loose-footed main. Undecked.

This is a combination boat, meant for training, racing, or general sailing. The Designers Choice has curved sections forward and is relatively dry. With flat surfaces aft, she planes. Spars are anodized with a grooved mast luff and a loose foot. There is an outhaul, vang, and Cunningham. The cockpit sole is above waterline, so the scuppers may be left open at anchor or at dock. There is foam flotation. A stowage locker is under the afterdeck. Optional equipment includes a spinnaker and all necessary gear, a motor mount, and hiking straps.

Albacore

Length: 15 ft.
Beam: 5 ft. 4 in.
Draft: 4 ft. 5 in.
Weight: 240 lbs.
Sail area: Main, 90 sq. ft.; jib, 35 sq. ft.
Hull: FRP and wood

Spars: Aluminum
Racing crew: 2
Rating: D–PN 92.3
First built: Early 1950s
No. built: 7700
Designer: Uffa Fox

Fractional rig. Four battens. Plumb bow. Foredeck flares up. Unusual jib cut.

The basis for design of this sloop-rigged planing boat was a hot-molded plywood one-design, Swordfish. Construction was originally by the Fairey organization, manufacturers of the World War II Mosquito bomber. Standard features include a 4:1 boom vang, centerboard slot gaskets, and hiking straps. The rudder kicks up. Foam flotation is included. The maximum crew recommended for daysailing is four. Options include Elvstrom bailers, Barber haulers, a 10:1 vang, Harken package, and simple or remote Cunningham. There are active racing fleets in Connecticut, Pennsylvania, New Jersey, Maryland, Virginia, New York, and Illinois, with a total association membership of about 300.

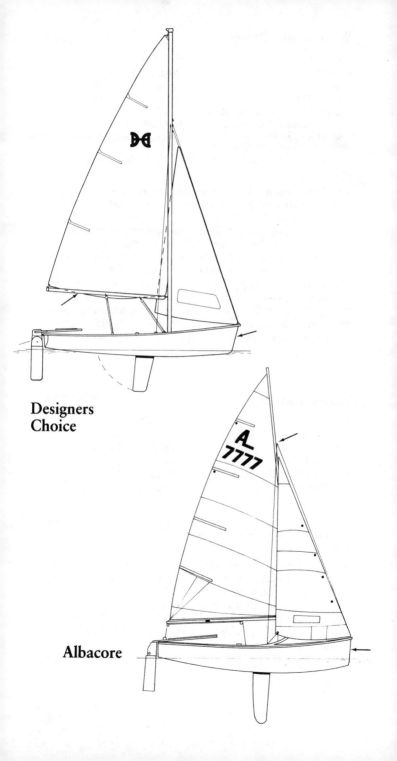

**Designers
Choice**

Albacore

West Wight Potter

Length: 15 ft.
Beam: 5 ft. 6 in.
Draft: 3 ft.
Weight: 475 lbs.
Sail area: Main, 68 sq. ft.; jib, 23 sq ft.; genoa, 43 sq. ft.; spinnaker, 85 sq. ft.

Hull: FRP
Spars: Aluminum
Racing crew: 1 or 2
Rating: D–PN 138.0
First built: 1966
No. built: 2000
Designer: Stanley T. Smith

Distinctive. Three battens, with top full length, give an angular roach.

The Potter was originally built in plywood with a gunter rig. Herb Stewart used one for a fiberglass plug, and modified the rig to marconi. With the top batten full length, appearance is somewhat similar to a gaff rig. The mast and its two shrouds are mounted on the cabin roof. There are three molded-in skegs, which reduce tipping or heeling, with or without sail. There are two 6-ft., 6-in. bunks in the cabin. The companionway hatch, which like all trim is mahogany, folds down into the cockpit, making a small table. An outboard bracket is standard and will carry a two-horsepower motor. The Potter has foam flotation and is self-righting and self-bailing. Options include a genoa, a pulpit, railings, and a cockpit tent.

Coronado 15

Length: 15 ft. 4 in.
Beam: 5 ft. 8 in.
Draft: 3 ft. 6 in.
Weight: 385 lbs.
Sail area: Main and jib, 139 sq. ft. total
Hull: FRP

Spars: Aluminum
Racing crew: 2
Rating: D–PN 91.1
First built: 1970
No. built: 3300
Designer: Frank Butler

Low freeboard. Spoon bow. Considerable sheer. Controllable mast that bends under sail; fractional forestay. Trapeze. High boom.

The planing hull is self-bailing and there is also flotation. There is a forward compartment, with hatch. Spars are black anodized aluminum; rigging, stainless steel. Control assists are an outhaul, boom vang, and mainsheet traveler. An optional barney post (binnacle) with compass may be ordered, as may a trapeze, a beaching rudder, and sail windows in both sails. Hiking straps are standard.

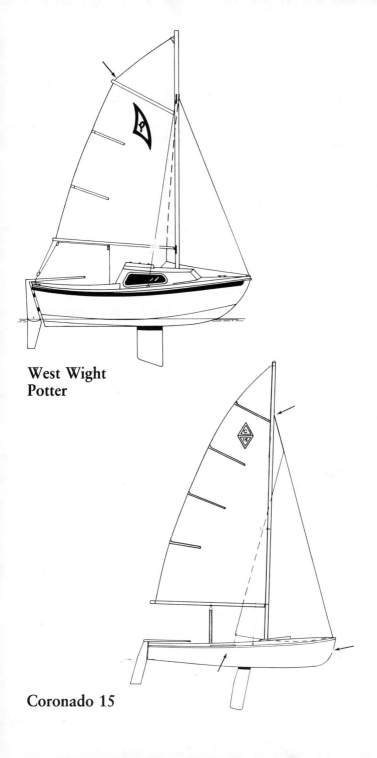

**West Wight
Potter**

Coronado 15

470

Length: 15 ft. 5 in.
Beam: 5 ft. 6 in.
Draft: 3 ft. 2 in.
Weight: 260 lbs. minimum
Sail area: Main, 97 sq. ft.; jib, 40 sq. ft.; spinnaker, 140 sq. ft.
Hull: FRP

Spars: Aluminum
Racing crew: 2
Rating: Olympic; D–PN 87.0
First built: 1963
No. built: Unknown, but in thousands
Designer: Andre Cornu

Significant mast rake. Top batten full length. Possible windows in main and jib. Tiller passes through opening in transom.

The 470 is an Olympic boat, internationally controlled by the IYRU. The first use in the Olympics was in 1976. Flotation is in the hollow seats and in the mast, which causes the boat to float high when capsized. (Don't sit on the capsized hull or the 470 will turtle.) There are hiking straps and a trapeze. The spinnaker has an uphaul, a downhaul, and guy twings. Various mechanical assists are available for the boom vang. Spars are anodized and tapered. Controls for the Cunningham are dual. There are Barber haulers for the jib and a traveler for the main. Both jib and main have windows. Elvstrom bailers are provided. Although this is not true for most boats, on the 470 the spinnaker pole is best carried at an upward angle, especially in heavy air. There are fleets in more than 45 countries.

US 1

Length: 15 ft. 5 in.
Beam: 4 ft. 7 in.
Draft: 2 ft. 6 in.
Weight: 190 lbs.
Sail area: 90 sq. ft.
Hull: FRP

Spars: Aluminum
Racing crew: 1
Rating: D–PN 91.7
First built: 1973
No. built: 300
Designer: Ralph Kupersmith

Cat. High aspect ratio. Sharp bow, rounded deck. Loose-footed main.

US 1 fleets are in Missouri, Ohio, Florida, Pennsylvania, and Texas. Modifications allowed include two bailers, centerboard gaskets, four inspection ports, and redesign and modifications of sheeting, the vang, Cunningham, traveler, outhaul, rudder and tiller controls, and centerboard controls. Crew is limited to one, or two not to exceed 270 lbs. An experiment during which the two-piece mast could be changed to three-piece has been repealed. Both mast and boom are foam-filled. The centerboard and the rudder pivot, which is unusual in a singlehander. Production boats come with dual Cunningham and outhaul control.

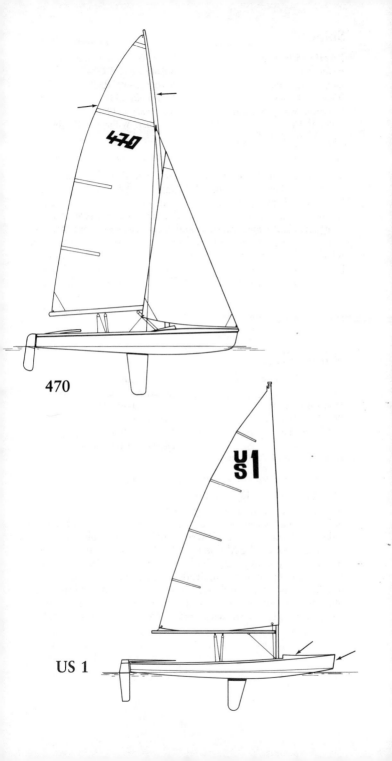

470

US 1

Snipe

Length: 15 ft. 6 in.	*Spars:* Wood or aluminum
Beam: 5 ft.	*Racing crew:* 2
Draft: 3 ft. 3 in.	*Rating:* D–PN 93.8
Weight: 381 lbs.	*First built:* 1931
Sail area: Main, 90 sq. ft.; jib, 38 sq. ft.	*No. built:* 25,080
Hull: Wood or FRP	*Designer:* William F. Crosby

Significant sheer. Angled transom. Concave curve to rudder.

The International class Snipe has over 800 fleets located on five continents. The class is found throughout the United States and has seven districts, with governors located in Massachusetts, Missouri, Illinois, Florida, Pennsylvania, and northern and southern California. International racing measurements are restrictive. Loose-footed sails and spinnakers are not allowed. Jib windows are permitted. If a chevron appears on the sail, the boat has won a championship. Gold chevron indicates World; Silver, European; Red, National; Blue, Junior National; Black, Fleet.

Windmill

Length: 15 ft. 6 in.	*Spars:* Aluminum
Beam: 4 ft. 8 in.	*Racing crew:* 2
Draft: 4 ft. 2 in.	*Rating:* D–PN 90.2
Weight: 198 lbs.	*First built:* 1953
Sail area: Main, 85 sq. ft.; jib, 34 sq. ft.	*No. built:* 4900
Hull: FRP and PVC foam	*Designer:* Clark Mills

Vee bottom, hard chine. Sheer appears cobled. Sail windows.

The Windmill is a high-performance sloop that can be built from plans or from a kit, or purchased complete. She is very light and planes quickly. Class rules are strict, and neither spinnakers nor trapezes are allowed. With a double hull and closed-cell foam, the Mill is unsinkable. This type of construction also results in a very rigid boat. The 2:1 outhaul is internal and the 4:1 boom vang leads to the skipper. The Cunningham has a 4:1 purchase. Jib fairleads may be adjusted, as may the traveler. There is an Elvstrom bailer. Almost all sailing equipment is standard, with options for such items as a trailer or compass.

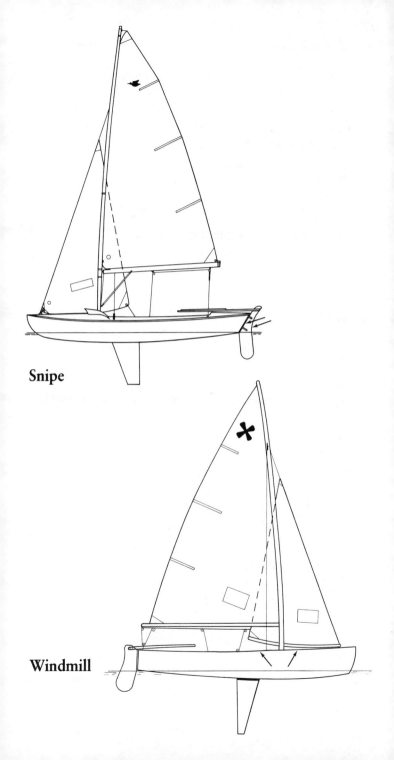

Snipe

Windmill

Invitation

Length: 15 ft. 7 in.
Beam: 5 ft.
Draft: 3 ft. (board up)
Weight: 180 lbs. (hull only)
Sail area: 90 sq. ft.
Hull: FRP
Spars: Aluminum

Racing crew: 1 or 2
Rating: D–PN 92.5 suspect
First built: Not avail.
No. built: Not avail.
Designer: Bombardier Research Center

Coble sheer for top of deck, with reverse sheer forward, normal sheer aft. Sail wraps around mast and is loose-footed.

A boat designed for ease in car-topping, with two-piece mast and overhanging two-inch gunwale to assist lifting. The loose-footed sail slips over the mast. Control includes adjustable outhaul, vang, and Cunningham. Safety provisions feature foam flotation, hiking straps, and vacuum bailer. The rudder kicks up. Invitation is a one-design with rigid class rules.

Bullseye

Length: 15 ft. 8½ in.
Beam: 5 ft. 10 in.
Draft: 2 ft. 5 in.
Weight: 1350 lbs.
Sail area: Main, 104 sq. ft.; jib, 30 sq. ft.; genoa, 60 sq. ft.; spinnaker, 100 sq. ft.
Hull: Wood before 1950, FRP since

Spars: Aluminum
Racing crew: 2 or 3
Rating: D–PN 114.1
First built: 1914
No. built: 2000 wood, 800 FRP
Designer: N. G. Herreshoff

High bow. Distinctive transom. Wood combings. Possible jib boom.

A New England classic, designed stiff and heavy for the short, choppy seas of Buzzards Bay. The Bullseye's original wood construction has been updated to FRP, and flotation tanks added under the cockpit floor and in the bow. The jib is self-tending and roller-reefing. In addition to the cuddy, there is a lazarette with teak hatch. Teak is also used elsewhere for trim. Rigging and hardware are stainless steel or bronze. The full keel incorporates 750 lbs. of lead. Lines are traditional. The Bullseye has active fleets concentrated in Massachusetts, but also in Maine, New Jersey, Florida, and Long Island Sound.

Invitation

Bullseye

Apollo

Length: 15 ft. 9 in.
Beam: 5 ft. 11 in.
Draft: Unknown
Weight: 300 lbs.
Sail area: Main, 90 sq. ft.;
 jib, 39 sq. ft.
Hull: FRP

Spars: Aluminum
Racing crew: 2 or 3
Rating: D–PN 92.3
First built: Not avail.
No. built: Not avail.
Designer: Manufacturer

Straight bow, rudder mounting. Jib not on forestay. Overhang at stem.

This one-design has an active racing class. It is designed to carry two to four people comfortably in a large cockpit. Halyards are internal and the mast step is hinged. Sail control includes end-boom sheeting, outhaul, vang, and Cunningham. Both main and jib have leech lines. Rudder and centerboard kick up. Traveler is full width with dual controls. There are a storage bin, hiking straps, and two Elvstrom vacuum bailers. Spinnaker, whisker pole, and jiffy reefing are options. Modifications permitted for racing are minor, with the intention to keep Apollo a true one-design class.

Bombardier 4.8

Length: 15 ft. 10 in.
Beam: 5 ft.
Draft: 3 ft. 10 in.
Weight: 300 lbs. (hull only)
Sail area: Main, 82 sq. ft.; genoa,
 56 sq. ft.; spinnaker, 140 sq. ft.
Hull: FRP

Spars: Aluminum
Racing crew: 2
Rating: None
First built: Not avail.
No. built: Not avail.
Designer: Bombardier Research
 Center

Gunwale wraps around bow. Mast step elevated. Shrouds aft of mast. Mid-boom sheeting.

The 4.8 is a daysailer large enough to sit four. It has polyurethane flotation. Control includes adjustable outhaul, boom vang, Cunningham, and a roller-furling genoa. The genoa leads are adjustable. Both rudder and centerboard flip up. Hiking straps are adjustable, and there is a forward storage compartment. The vacuum bailer operates at low speeds and may be left open when the boat is moored.

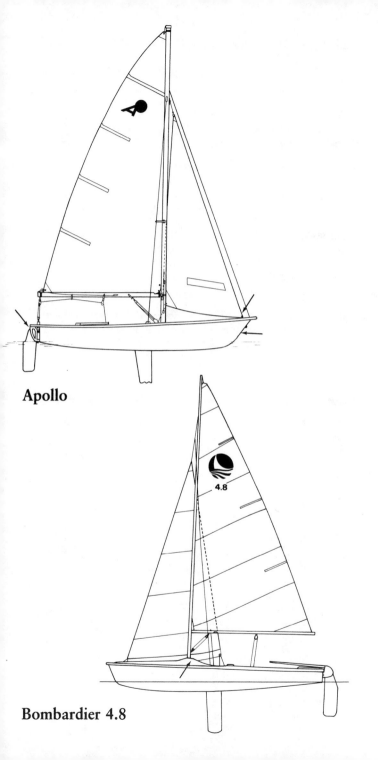

Apollo

Bombardier 4.8

Doughdish (Herreshoff 12½)

Length: 15 ft. 10 in.
Beam: 5 ft. 10 in.
Draft: 2 ft. 6 in.
Weight: 1500 lbs.
Sail area: Main, 109 sq. ft.; jib, 31 sq. ft.; spinnaker, 125 sq. ft.
Hull: FRP or wood

Spars: Sitka spruce
Crew: 1–4
Rating: D–PN 117.4
First built: 1914
No. built: 420
Designer: N. G. Herreshoff

Small, gaff-rigged. Jib boom. Coaming. Spoon bow, angled transom. Mast hoops. Strong sheer.

Buzzards Bay, under the hook of Cape Cod, has strong southwest winds and a short, steep chop. This boat was designed to cope with those conditions. It is very similar to the Bullseye, but the Bullseye has a cuddy and less displacement. Since the new version of the original boat is FRP, there are no frames or visible seams. An H Class Association has been formed to preserve activity and interest, and a class championship is conducted each year. Today's hull is sandwich construction, with an Airex core. Trim is teak, and is used for seats, the coaming, sheer strake, and elsewhere. To counteract the fixed keel with its 735 lbs. of lead, there is positive flotation of foam behind bulkheads. If you see an FRP boat it is the Doughdish. If it's wood, it is a Herreshoff 12½.

Wayfarer

Length: 15 ft. 10 in.
Beam: 6 ft. 1 in.
Draft: 3 ft. 10 in.
Weight: 365 lbs.
Sail area: Main, 95 sq. ft.; jib, 30 sq. ft.; genoa, 46 sq. ft.; spinnaker, 125 sq. ft.

Hull: Wood or FRP
Spars: Wood or aluminum
Racing crew: 2
Rating: D–PN 92.2
First built: 1957
No. built: 7500
Designer: Ian Proctor

Double chine visible when heeled. High-aspect centerboard. High freeboard forward.

There appears to be something about the Wayfarer that makes people want to cruise long distances. It has been sailed across the North Sea, from Scotland to Iceland, and elsewhere. It is particularly popular in Canada and in Britain, where it is a well-known instructional boat. The boat will plane. There are removable floorboards inside the nine-foot-long open cockpit, where six adults can sit. The double chine provides inherent stability, and there are large buoyancy compartments fore and aft that double as watertight storage lockers. The mast pivots and the centerboard and rudder retract. Yearly championships are held for the US, Canada, and North America. A world championship is held every two years.

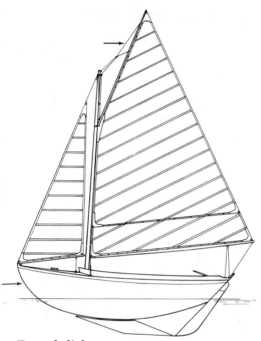

**Doughdish
(Herreshoff 12½)**

Wayfarer

Balboa 16

Length: 16 ft.
Beam: 7 ft. 5 in.
Draft: 2 ft. 5 in.
Weight: 1000 lbs.
Sail area: Main, 52 sq. ft.; jib, 65
    sq. ft.; genoa, 98 sq. ft. (150%)
Hull: FRP

Spars: Anodized aluminum
Racing crew: 2
Rating: None
First built: 1980
No. built: Not avail.
Designer: W. Shad Turner

Masthead rig. Straight bow. Very slight reverse counter. Straight line from foredeck to coach-roof. Backstay.

This daysailer is designed for recreation rather than racing, and offers overnight accommodation for four in one double and two quarter berths. The mast step is hinged, which adds to the ease of trailering. Standard equipment includes ice chest, Plexiglas sliding hatch, and carpeting. The cockpit is self-bailing. Total ballast is 400 lbs., and the maximum recommended outboard power is six horsepower. Considering the number of berths below, the cockpit is quite large. The manufacturer suggests the Balboa 16 for beginners.

Comet

Length: 16 ft.
Beam: 5 ft.
Draft: 3 ft.
Weight: 265 lbs. min. (hull only)
Sail area: Main, 110 sq. ft.;
    jib, 25 sq. ft.
Hull: New boats, FRP

Spars: Aluminum
Racing crew: 2
Rating: None
First built: 1932
No. built: 4100
Designer: C. Lowndes Johnson

Jumper stay instead of headstay optional. Spoon bow. Running backstays. Window in main optional.

An older design, the Comet has many modern features. The bottom is flat and the afterbody is broad. She planes. The Comet is a one-design with rigid controls on size, shape, and materials. Minor modifications through the years have kept her up to date. These include self-bailers, a full-width traveler, sail windows, and side tanks making the boat self-rescuing. There is a vang, which leads to the cockpit. The backstays have slides and are adjustable. There are two rigging options. The first uses three stays, the second, which has a jumper and backstays, seven. The centerboard, which may be of various metals, has a drum control.

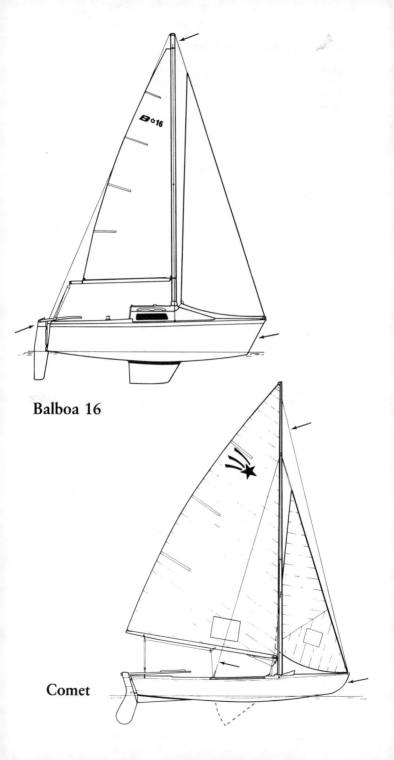

Balboa 16

Comet

International Contender

Length: 16 ft.
Beam: 4 ft. 8 in.
Draft: 4 ft. 8 in.
Weight: 230 lbs.
Sail area: 120 sq. ft.
Hull: FRP
Spars: Aluminum

Racing crew: 1
Rating: D–PN 91.4
First built: 1969
No. built: 300 US, Canada;
   1500 world
Designer: William Miller

Five battens. Heavily raked mast. Trapeze. Mono rig.

The Contender was designed by Australian Bill Miller to replace the Finn in Olympic competition. So far it hasn't; but as can be seen by the rating, it is a little faster. Contender is a single-handed trapeze boat, with active fleets throughout the United States and Canada. There is a boom vang for control off the wind.

Isotope

Length: 16 ft.
Beam: 7 ft.
Draft: 2 ft. 6 in.
Weight: 275 lbs.
Sail area: Main, 140 sq. ft.;
   jib, 45 sq. ft.
Hull: FRP

Spars: Aluminum
Racing crew: 1
Rating: D–PN 75.0
First built: 1964
No. built: 700
Designer: Frank Meldau

Catamaran. Eight full-length battens. Jib window. Elongated spoon bow. Considerable rocker. Three cross members.

Sister to the Cheshire, the Isotope is two feet longer and five Portsmouth numbers faster. Two sail options are available. When rigged for a total of 200 sq. ft., Isotope has a D–PN of 76.2. The mast rotates, rudders kick up, and the centerboards are self-tending. There are two storage hatches. A trapeze and mast limiter are optional. Hulls are exaggerated ellipses, and symmetrical. Racing crew is normally one; cruising, three. There is positive flotation and a righting bar.

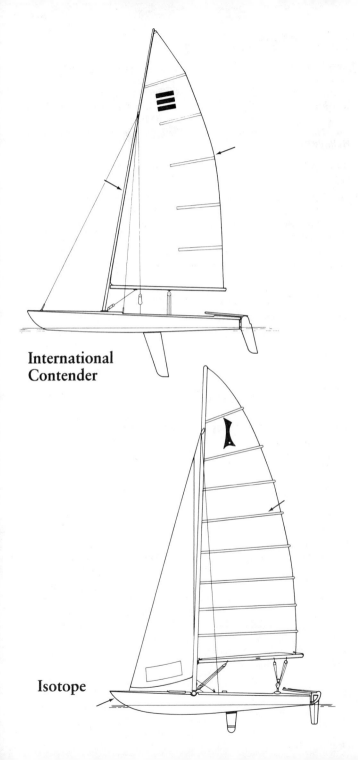

International Contender

Isotope

Leeward 16

Length: 16 ft.
Beam: 6 ft. 3 in.
Draft: 3 ft. 9 in.
Weight: 650 lbs.
Sail area: Main, 95 sq. ft.; jib, 45 sq. ft.; genoa, 73 sq. ft.
Hull: FRP

Spars: Anodized aluminum
Racing crew: 2
Rating: None
First built: Not avail.
No. built: Not avail.
Designer: Luger Industries

Bow eye for trailering. High boom. Cuddy angular, with FRP mast tabernacle on top. Curve at back of rudder.

Luger Industries builds kit boats ranging in length from 8 feet to 30 feet. The Leeward 16 is typical. It is delivered without sails and requires 10 to 15 hours to complete. There is a hinged tabernacle fitting for the mast, so that you can lower it for trailering by loosing the forestay. The boom allows for roller reefing of the main. An optional motor mount will carry a two- to seven-horsepower outboard. Sails, trim molding, and running lights are other options. Jib sheets, main sheets, and centerboard control lead to within reach of the tiller. Foam flotation is recommended. All fittings are either stainless steel or anodized aluminum.

M–16

Length: 16 ft.
Beam: 6 ft.
Draft: 2 ft. 8 in.
Weight: 440 lbs.
Sail area: Main, 107.25 sq. ft.; jib, 39 sq. ft.
Hull: FRP or cedar

Spars: Aluminum or wood
Racing crew: 2
Rating: D–PN 92.7
First built: 1957
No. built: Not avail.
Designer: Melges Boat Works, Henry McKee

Scow. End-boom sheeting. Sail windows. Hull sheer almost straight; deck has reverse sheer.

The M–16 scow is raced on the East Coast, in the Southeast, and in the Southwest, but most boats are to be found in the Midwest. There are bilgeboards and dual rudders and tillers. As with most scows, the amount of control possible is extensive. There is a boom vang and a Cunningham. There are Barber haulers and a traveler for the jib. The stern-mounted main traveler is controllable. Spars may not be tapered. Other limiting specifications are issued by the Inland Lake Yachting Association, which holds a championship regatta with sixty to ninety competitors.

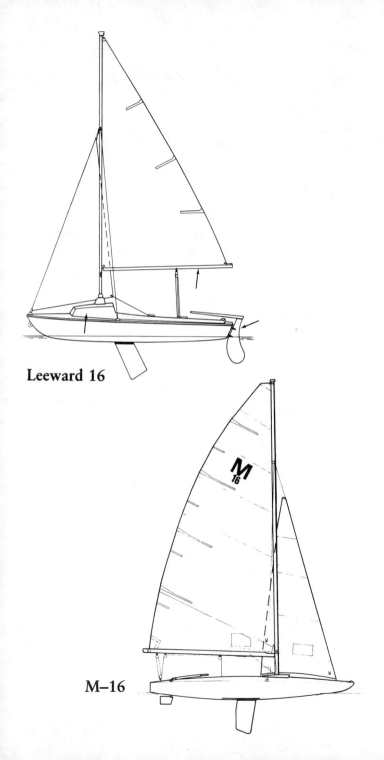

Leeward 16

M–16

MC

Length: 16 ft.	*Spars:* Anodized aluminum
Beam: 5 ft. 8 in.	*Racing crew:* 1–3
Draft: 3 ft.	*Rating:* None
Weight: 420 lbs.	*First built:* 1970
Sail area: 135 sq. ft.	*No. built:* 750
Hull: FRP	*Designer:* Harry C. Melges, Sr.

Scow. Mono rig with no jib. Rake to mast. Reverse sheer.

Singlehander? Catboat? Scow? Well, it has bilgeboards. The MC can be sailed singlehanded, but it is a big boat and will easily carry more. High aspect ratio. There are a traveler, Cunningham, vang, hiking straps, and adjustable outhaul. Trim is mahogany. There are many options, most of which involve hardware or repositioning control leads, such as a boom vang lead to the skipper. The MC is perhaps not quite as athletic as most singlehanders. There is plenty of mechanical advantage, with the outhaul 3:1, the traveler 2:1 and the vang 12:1. The mainsheet is four-part. An association was founded in 1972 and has 21 fleets, some of which are located in Texas, Georgia, Oklahoma, Missouri, Nebraska, North Carolina, Michigan, Wisconsin, and Iowa.

X Boat

Length: 16 ft.	*Spars:* Aluminum
Beam: 6 ft. 1 in.	*Racing crew:* 2
Draft: 2 ft. 7 in.	*Rating:* D–PN 114.2
Weight: 500 lbs.	*First built:* Not avail.
Sail area: Main, 85 sq. ft.;	*No. built:* Not avail.
jib, 24.75 sq. ft.	*Designer:* Melges Boat Works
Hull: FRP	

Stern bar traveler. Spoon bow. Angled transom.

The X Boat was designed as a low-performance training boat for junior programs. With the exception of the boom vang, sail control is minimal so as to emphasize handling skills. There are two sets of hiking straps. Melges builds this boat and it is common in the Midwest.

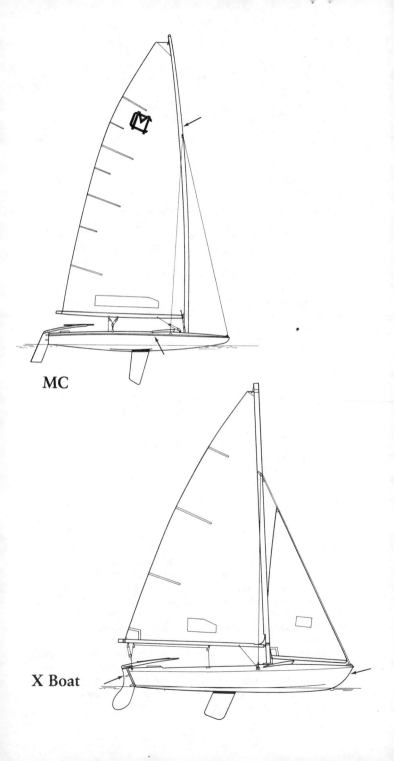

MC

X Boat

Rebel

Length: 16 ft. 1 in.
Beam: 6 ft. 6 in.
Draft: 3 ft. 4 in.
Weight: 700 lbs.
Sail area: Main, 120 sq. ft.;
    jib, 46 sq. ft.
Hull: FRP, some balsa core

Spars: Hard-coated aluminum
Racing crew: 2 minimum
Rating: D–PN 97.5
First built: 1948 approx.
No. built: 5000
Designer: Ray Greene

Straight sheer. Full foredeck. Full-length seats. Black (hard-coated) spars. (Class plans show sheer; manufacturer's drawings do not.)

Rebel was the first production sailboat built in fiberglass. Acceptance was fast, and there have been annual national regattas since 1952. The cockpit will seat eight, and there is lockable storage aft, in addition to the cuddy. There is foam flotation in the bow and under the seats. The mast rotates. Jib tracks are adjustable, and the rudder kicks up. Options include a mast rotation bar, a boom vang, Cunningham, whisker pole, cockpit bailers, and hiking straps. The centerboard is steel and weighs 110 lbs.

International Fireball

Length: 16 ft. 2 in.
Beam: 4 ft. 8½ in.
Draft: 4 ft. ½ in.
Weight: 175 lbs.
Sail area: Calculated as triangles:
    main, 87.5 sq. ft.; jib, 35.5
    sq. ft.; spinnaker, 140 sq. ft.
Hull: Wood or FRP

Spars: Aluminum, steel
Racing crew: 2
Rating: D–PN 86.4
First built: 1964
No. built: 125,000 world,
    13,000 US
Designer: Peter Milne

Overhanging bow with angled bend. Low freeboard, but not a board boat. Trapeze.

Fireball is a high-performance dinghy, not as fast as an International 505 or Flying Dutchman, but allowing a great deal of latitude in the positioning and adoption of all gear except sails and hull. This scow-shaped boat was originally built in wood, but fiberglass was allowed in 1966. IYRU International status was granted in 1970. Major fleets are in the UK, South Africa, France, Sweden, Australia, Canada, and the USA, with smaller numbers in many other countries. The (usually) high-cut jibs and the spinnaker are small enough so that many successful racing crews have had women members. (Adoption of a trapeze in 1965 limits this somewhat.) In addition to jib cut and lead, mast adjustments has seen considerable development. Mast chocks and struts have both been used, but many recent champions have dropped the strut.

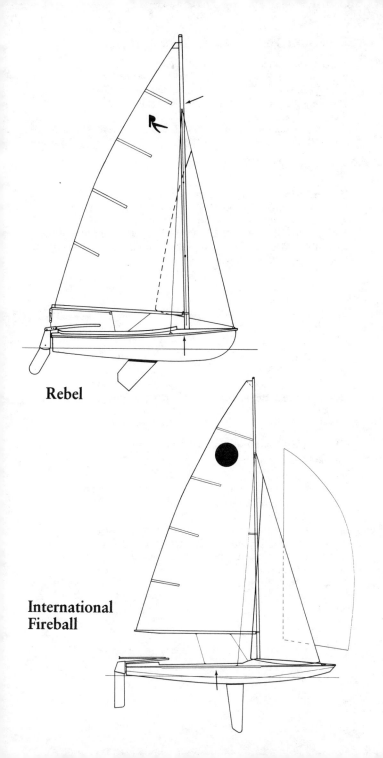

Rebel

**International
Fireball**

Precision 16

Length: 16 ft. 3 in.
Beam: 6 ft. 8 in.
Draft: 3 ft. 8 in.
Weight: 3901 lbs.
Sail area: Main, 97 sq. ft.; jib, 58 sq. ft.; spinnaker, 162 sq. ft.
Hull: FRP

Spars: Aluminum
Racing crew: 2
Rating: None
First built: 1981
No. built: 64
Designer: Steve Seaton

Undecked. Long bow, considerable sheer. Aluminum rudder head. Mid-boom sheeting.

The Precision 16 is a new boat currently being sold in Florida. The aspect ratio approximates 2.3 to 1. The boat has a double hull and 10 cubic feet of foam flotation. The cockpit is self-bailing. Precision planes in a breeze. The centerboard and the kick-up rudder are foam-filled FRP. Trim is teak, and there are two storage compartments.

Tanzer 16

Length: 16 ft. 4 in.
Beam: 6 ft. 2 in.
Draft: 2 ft. 9 in.
Weight: 450 lbs.
Sail area: Main, 100 sq. ft.; jib, 35 sq. ft.; genoa, 45 sq. ft.; spinnaker, 205 sq. ft.

Hull: FRP
Spars: Aluminum
Racing crew: 3
Rating: D–PN 99.9
First built: 1963
No. built: 1550
Designer: Johann Tanzer

Four battens. Spoon bow. Vertical transom. Possible over-nighter configuration with cuddy.

Before a name change the Tanzer 16 was known as the Constellation. She is sold both as a one-design and as an over-nighter. The latter has a cuddy with two bunks and an optional boom tent, and the mast is stepped on the cabin roof instead of on the keelson. The Tanzer 16's wide beam and low center of gravity aid stability. Both the aluminum centerboard and the rudder kick up. There is a roller-reefing boom, with vang. Storage for the daysailer consists of a lazarette compartment, side compartments in the cockpit, and a shelf under the foredeck. Trim is oiled teak. There is foam flotation. The Tanzer will plane.

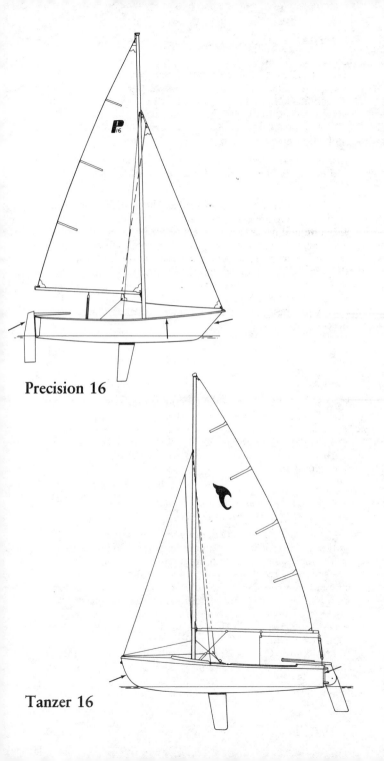

Precision 16

Tanzer 16

International 505

Length: 16 ft. 7 in.
Beam: 4 ft. 3 in.
Draft: 4 ft. 10 in.
Weight: 220 lbs. minimum
Sail area: Main, 100 sq. ft.; jib,
50 sq. ft.; spinnaker, 225 sq. ft.
Hull: Plywood or FRP

Spars: Aluminum
Racing crew: 2
Rating: D–PN 81.0
First built: 1953
No. built: Over 7,000
Designer: John Westall

Fast dinghy with end-boom sheeting to traveler. Curved rudder and foredeck. Flat bottom. Transom often open with tiller through.

The length translates to 5.05 meters. She is an International boat and there are extensive (but often liberal) rules for construction and measurement. Centerboard and rudder shapes may vary; but they must have similar profiles on both sides, and the centerboard cannot project below the hull when raised. Rigging may be modified, but the mast cannot be permanently bent. A trapeze is normal. Sail dimensions are rigid. The 505 has buoyancy compartments. Major fleets are in the San Francisco and Chesapeake areas, but there are more than thirty fleets in all.

G–Cat

Length: 16 ft. 8 in.
Beam: 8 ft.
Draft: 1 ft. 1 in.
Weight: 340 lbs.
Sail area: Main, 150 sq. ft.;
jib, 60 sq. ft.
Hull: FRP

Spars: Aluminum
Racing crew: 2
Rating: D–PN 77.0 suspect;
previously 76.5
First built: 1970
No. built: Over 1000
Designer: Hans Geissler

Catamaran. Symmetrical hulls. No daggerboards. Forestay attached well aft. Full battens.

G–Cat is an unusual catamaran with symmetrical hulls and without daggerboards. Also unusual is the trampoline forward of the mast, upon which an optional tent may be pitched for cruising. (To avoid pitch-poling, remove the forward trampoline in heavy weather.) The hulls are a deep vee section to resist leeway. The boat has substantial rocker that puts lateral resistance well below the center of effort, making the boat pivot easily about the middle. The mast rotates. Shrouds go to chain plates on the hull, while the forestay leads to a bridle. Other control consists of outhaul, downhaul, and main sheeting to a traveler on the aft cross beam. Rudders kick up for beaching. The G–Cat comes in two sizes, 5.0 meters and 5.7 meters. The "number built" figure above reflects production for both types.

International 505

G–Cat

Day Sailer

Length: 16 ft. 9 in.
Beam: 6 ft. 3 in.
Draft: 3 ft. 9 in.
Weight: 628 lbs.
Sail area: Main, 102.5 sq. ft.; jib, 48.75 sq. ft.; spinnaker, 213.5 sq. ft.

Hull: FRP
Spars: Aluminum
Racing crew: 2
Rating: D–PN 99.8
First built: 1958
No. built: 11,500
Designer: Uffa Fox

Jumper strut is forward of mast. Cuddy. High aspect ratio. Lower jumper strut raked aft of mast.

The original Day Sailer was designed in 1958 for George O'Day, who produced the boat until 1978. Since then, the boat has been produced by both Bangor Punta and Spindrift. The former calls their boat Day Sailer I; the latter, Day Sailer II. There is no difference in the hull or sails, but there are minor differences in the cuddy. Day Sailer is a relatively dry boat, with high freeboard and a sharp bow entry. The large cockpit seats six adults. Standard and optional equipment vary with the manufacturer but may include storage lockers, a lazarette for the outboard or for storage, and an ice box. Sail control includes adjustable sheet leads, boom vang, and Cunningham. Safety features provided are foam flotation, foam-filled spars, a cockpit drain, and a kick-up rudder. There is a strong class association, with more than one hundred fleets.

Dolphin 17

Length: 16 ft. 9 in.
Beam: 6 ft.
Draft: 4 ft. 3 in.
Weight: 725 lbs. (800 for Model C)
Sail area: Main and jib, 160 sq. ft. total; 130 sq. ft. for Model C

Hull: FRP
Spars: Aluminum
Racing crew: 2
Rating: D–PN 96.2
First built: 1973
No. built: 740 (open and cabin)
Designer: Glen Cororran

Jib independent of stay. Two sidestays with one jumper strut. Splash rail molded in. Possible cuddy with one window for Model C.

In addition to the open design, there is a cabin model available. As might be expected, it is slightly heavier and has a reduced sail area. Capacity in either model is six adults; the cabin model sleeps two. The Dolphin 17 has covered storage on both sides of the mast and also has aft storage. The cockpit is self-bailing. The kick-up rudder and the centerboard are fiberglass. The mast is stayed, and there is both a fore- and a backstay. The traveler is adjustable and there is a boom vang.

Day Sailer

Dolphin 17

Cape Cod Cat

Length: 17 ft.
Beam: 7 ft. 11 in.
Draft: 4 ft. 10 in. (centerboard); or 1 ft. 11 in. (keel)
Weight: 2200 lbs.; ballast 500 lbs.
Sail area: 250 sq. ft.
Hull: FRP
Spars: Painted aluminum
Rating: None
First built: Not avail.
No. built: Not avail.
Designer: Charles Wittholz

Traditional lines. Typical (Cape Cod) rudder. Plumb bow. Gaff rig. Mast hoops. High coamings.

A modern version of the classic catboat found near Cape Cod, this cat is produced in fiberglass. Both a keel version and a centerboard version are available, with sales to date giving a two-to-one preference to the keel, undoubtedly because there is then no trunk in either cockpit or cabin. The cockpit is self-draining, with room to seat six adults. There are bunks for two and space for a sink, shelves, lockers, head, and stove. A diesel or gasoline inboard engine may be installed. Alternatively, an outboard may be mounted. While indigenous to the Cape, the boat may also be found in the Great Lakes, the West Coast, and Florida.

Marsh Hen

Length: 17 ft.
Beam: 6 ft.
Draft: 3 ft.
Weight: 650 lbs.
Sail area: 150 sq. ft.
Hull: FRP
Spars: Aluminum
Rating: None
First built: 1980
No. built: 40
Designer: Reuben Trane

Spritsail rig. With canvas dodger up she is distinctive. Unusual rudder. Mast unstayed. Double-ended.

Hull shape has evolved from working boats of the Chesapeake, and the rudder and spritsail rig are also traditional. The Marsh Hen was designed as a pocket cruiser. The dodger, which unlike a boom tent allows sailing when it is raised, is standard. There is provision for rowing, but that is not the prime intention. There are a portable toilet, a built-in ice chest, and six lockers for stowage. The tiller is teak, there is flotation, and the fully open cockpit is self-bailing.

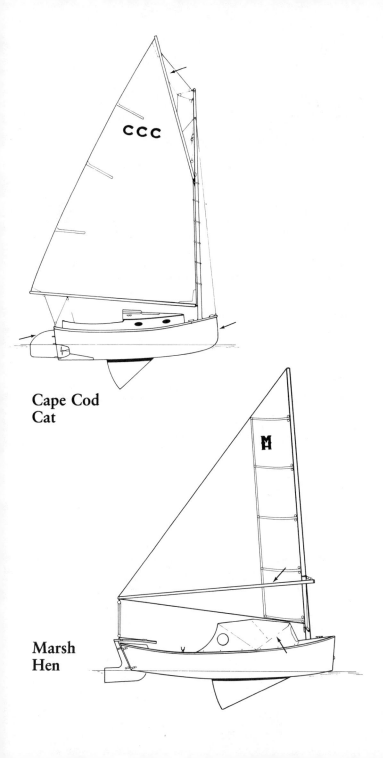

Cape Cod Cat

Marsh Hen

Nacra 5.2

Length: 17 ft.
Beam: 8 ft.
Draft: 2 ft. 6 in.
Weight: 375 lbs.
Sail area: Main, 170 sq. ft.;
   jib, 50 sq. ft.
Hull: FRP

Spars: Anodized aluminum
Racing crew: 2
Rating: D–PN 73.8
First built: 1975
No. built: 2500
Designer: Tom Roland

Catamaran. Nine full-length battens. Plumb bow. Jib bridle well aft. Daggerboards. Symmetrical hulls.

The 5.2 has evolved from Tom Roland's designs for the Alpha 18, Roland 36, and Nacra 5.5. Sister ships are the 5.5 and 5.8. The hulls are wide at the bottom and narrow at the top to create extra buoyancy. Adjustments include mast rotation, trapeze wires, shroud tension, outhaul, and jib luff and main downhaul. The daggerboards and rudders are fiberglass. There are fleets in Australia, Europe, Japan, and the United States. In spite of the high aspect ratio, the center of effort is low.

Thistle

Length: 17 ft.
Beam: 6 ft.
Draft: 4 ft. 6 in.
Weight: 515 lbs. (hull only)
Sail area: Main, 136 sq. ft.; jib,
   55 sq. ft.; spinnaker, 220 sq. ft.
Hull: FRP

Spars: Aluminum
Racing crew: 3
Rating: D–PN 83.0
First built: 1945
No. built: Over 3600
Designer: Gordon K. Douglass

Sharp vertical bow. Undecked. Wood cross members forward of mast. Round bilges. Three spreaders.

The Thistle was influenced by English dinghy design, and has a similarity to the International 14, another racing dinghy with a plumb bow and flat run. Originally, boats were of molded wood. Racing crew is three, but the Thistle will carry six. She will fit into a garage. Thistle has a lot of sail and a lot of speed. Class rules are strict. Gear which may be technically legal but which provides an advantage is not allowed. There is built-in flotation. The centerboard operates off a drum. Decks and seats are sandwich construction. The tall rig is supported by three diamonds and sidestays. There are more than 150 local fleets of this planing boat.

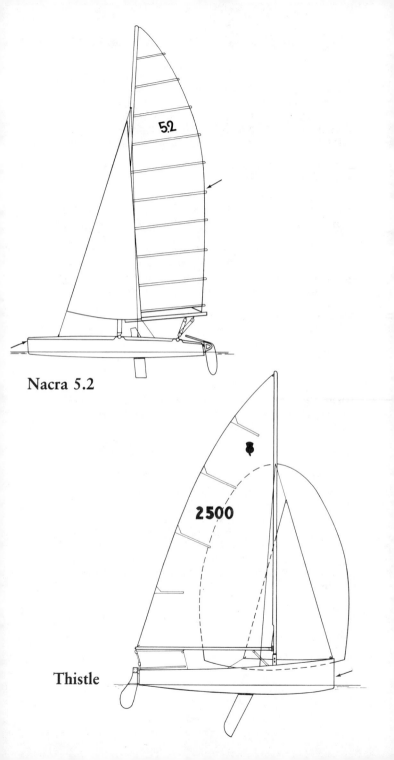

Nacra 5.2

Thistle

Vagabond 17

Length: 17 ft.
Beam: 7 ft. 3 in.
Draft: 4 ft. 2 in.
Weight: 950 lbs.
Sail area: Main, 82 sq. ft.; jib, 65 sq. ft.; genoa, 87 sq. ft.; spinnaker, 210 sq. ft.

Hull: FRP
Spars: Anodized aluminum
Racing crew: 2
Rating: None
First built: Not avail.
No. built: Not avail.
Designer: Ron Holder

Wide beam. Pulpit. Backstay. Two windows. Rudder and keel have high aspect ratio.

A little overnighter, the Vagabond 17 will sleep four in two quarter berths and a split vee berth. There is a galley sink and water storage. A bulkhead runs halfway across the cabin, giving some privacy to a head. There is a bridled backstay. Handrails are of teak. When the 150-percent genoa is used, optional winches are available. The keel swings down and locks into place, with a lifting wire going through a hole in the cabin sole. The bow pulpit is stainless steel, and there is foam flotation.

Siren

Length: 17 ft. 2 in.
Beam: 6 ft. 8 in.
Draft: 4 ft. 3 in.
Weight: 750 lbs.
Sail area: Main and jib, 145 sq. ft. total
Hull: FRP

Spars: Aluminum
Racing crew: 2 or 3
Rating: D–PN 107.0 suspect
First built: Not avail.
No. built: Not avail.
Designer: Hubert Vandestadt

High boom with end sheeting. Large cabin windows.

Daysailer and weekender. There are berths for two, but an optional tent will provide shelter for two more in the cockpit. The ice box is molded in, as is a tank which may be converted to a head. An alcohol stove is optional. There is a well for outboards up to seven horsepower. The cockpit is seven feet long and self-bailing. Trim is mahogany. The mast step is hinged, and there are a boom vang and jiffy reefing. Siren has foam flotation.

Vagabond 17

Siren

Buccaneer

Length: 18 ft.
Beam: 6 ft.
Draft: 3 ft. 10 in.
Weight: 500 lbs.
Sail area: Main, 114 sq. ft.; jib, 61 sq. ft.; spinnaker, 178 sq. ft.
Hull: FRP

Spars: Aluminum
Racing crew: 2 minimum
Rating: D–PN 88.1
First built: 1968
No. built: 4000
Designer: J. R. Macalpine-Downie

Four battens. Medium spoon bow. Continuous curve from rudder through head to tiller. Straight sheer.

Buccaneer, originally built by Chrysler, is a big boat with a 7-ft., 3-in. cockpit, seating six. The boat was designed to be easy to sail and maintain. The hull is planing, with the wide beam well aft and a lean bow. Standard controls include adjustable jib fairleads and roller furling for the jib. Optional controls are a vang, jib hauler, and spinnaker launching tube. All controls lead to the cockpit. There is an enclosed lazarette as well as an under-deck storage compartment. Trim is wood. The anodized aluminum spars are foam filled, and there are two suction bailers. Mooring eyes may be used for lifting. Both rudder and centerboard kick up and both are fully adjustable. Racing is under North American Yacht Racing Union or local rules. Safety equipment is required.

Geary 18

Length: 18 ft.
Beam: 5 ft. 5 in.
Draft: 1 ft. 4 in. (centerboard up)
Weight: 525 lbs.
Sail area: Main and jib, 200 sq. ft. total
Hull: FRP or wood

Spars: Aluminum or wood
Racing crew: 2
Rating: D–PN 91.9
First built: 1929
No. built: 1450
Designer: Ted Geary

Full roach. Hard chine, flat bottom. Decked. Looks flat. Trapeze. Inboard rudder.

The Geary was designed in 1928 as a club racer; it was originally built of cross-planked cedar, then plywood, and now of FRP. A trapeze has been allowed but not a spinnaker. The Geary's stability comes from her beam, as the centerboard is quite light. A whisker pole is used downwind, and she will plane. Vangs are used. When the Geary is FRP, a balsa core is common. The centerboard is aluminum and the rudder FRP.

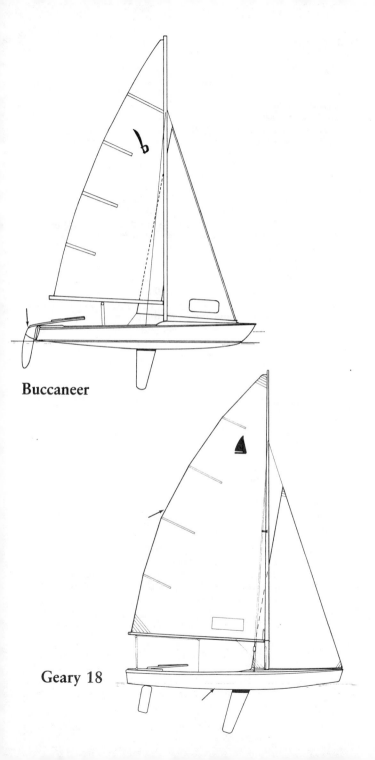

Buccaneer

Geary 18

Interlake

Length: 18 ft.
Beam: 6 ft. 3 in.
Draft: 4 ft. 7 in.
Weight: 650 lbs.
Sail area: Main, 125 sq. ft.; jib,
    50 sq. ft.; spinnaker, 200 sq. ft.
Hull: FRP, balsa core

Spars: Aluminum
Racing crew: 2 or 3
Rating: D–PN 91.4
First built: 1932
No. built: 1250
Designer: Francis Swiesguth

Hard chine. Sharp bow. Forward flare. Considerable rocker. Medium aspect ratio.

Interlake was designed for Sandusky Bay, Ohio, known for its short chop. She will plane fairly readily. The bow and sheer are classic, and the forward flare throws spray down, keeping her dry. She was originally built in wood, but fiberglass was allowed in 1955. Interlake is one of the older one-design classes in the United States. Sandwich construction with a balsa core is used for the hull and deck, and there is foam flotation. The boom is roller reefing, has a vang, and uses a bridle for a traveler. The centerboard winch has a 10:1 mechanical advantage. While there are fore- and sidestays, there are no jumpers or backstays. Storage is in pan lockers under the foredeck. There are hiking straps. Rudder and centerboard are of fiberglass.

Mercury

Length: 18 ft.
Beam: 5 ft. 4 in.
Draft: 3 ft. 1 in.
Weight: 1175 lbs.
Sail area: Main, 121 sq. ft.;
    jib, 56 sq. ft.
Hull: Wood or FRP

Spars: Wood or aluminum
Racing crew: 2
Rating: None
First built: 1938
No. built: 1060
Designer: Ernest Nunes

Backstay. Note counter and transom. Rudder not visible. Long spoon bow. Hard chine. Two jumpers, with topmost raked forward.

This classic-design, full-keel sloop is usually found on the Northeast or the West Coast. There is no ballast, and the keel must weigh at least 675 but not more than 700 lbs. Until 1952 hulls were of wood; since then, of fiberglass. Plans are available for home construction, as are FRP hulls. For the West Coast boat there is an active association. Flotation is not required; but preservers, bilge pump, and other safety equipment are necessary.

Cape Cod Shipbuilding makes a Mercury with the same winged insignia on the sail, but with the letters CC instead of M. This very different Mercury was designed by Sparkman and Stephens, is 15 ft. long, has a single sail with an area of 119 sq. ft., and is available with either keel or centerboard.

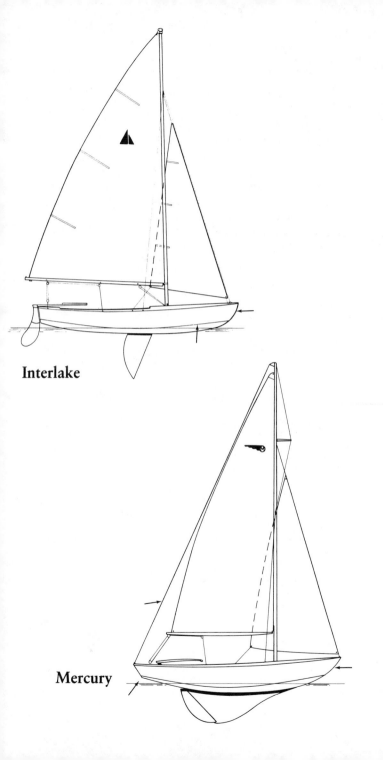

Interlake

Mercury

Prindle 18

Length: 18 ft.
Beam: 7 ft. 11 in.
Draft: 7 in.
Weight: 335 lbs.
Sail area: Main, 170 sq. ft.;
   jib, 48 sq. ft.
Hull: FRP

Spars: Aluminum
Racing crew: 2
Rating: D–PN 74.1 suspect
First built: 1978
No. built: 2000
Designer: Geoff Prindle

Two asymmetrical hulls. Nine battens. No centerboards or daggerboards. Mesh trampoline. Single or double trapeze. Lots of rocker.

The Prindle fleet consists of the 18, 16, and 15. The 16 was the first. The beaching rudders have an adjustable tiller cross bar. The mast step is hinged. There are a 4:1 downhaul system, an outhaul, and mast rotation controls. The jib luff is zippered. Battens are foam and FRP, and halyards are internal. There are two trapezes. Rake of the spreaders is adjustable. All of the Prindles are actively raced.

Windrose 5.5

Length: 18 ft.
Beam: 8 ft.
Draft: 2 ft. 3 in.
Weight: 1500 lbs.
Sail area: Main, 82.5 sq. ft.; jib,
   69 sq. ft.; genoa, 94 sq. ft.

Hull: FRP
Spars: Aluminum
Racing crew: 2–4
Rating: None
First built: 1980
Designer: W. Shad Turner

Wide beam, wide transom. Straight bow. High boom. Comes close to a masthead rig.

Windrose is designed as a pocket cruiser and has bunks for four, with a double berth forward and two quarter berths. Space remains for cabin seating, shelf storage, and a head. This shoal-draft boat has 500 lbs. of ballast in the keel. The manufacturer claims that the special shape of the keel makes Windrose track unusually well. An outboard with six horsepower may be used. There is under-deck storage in the cockpit. The mast is stepped on the keelson and therefore comes down through the cabin just aft of the foredeck hatch.

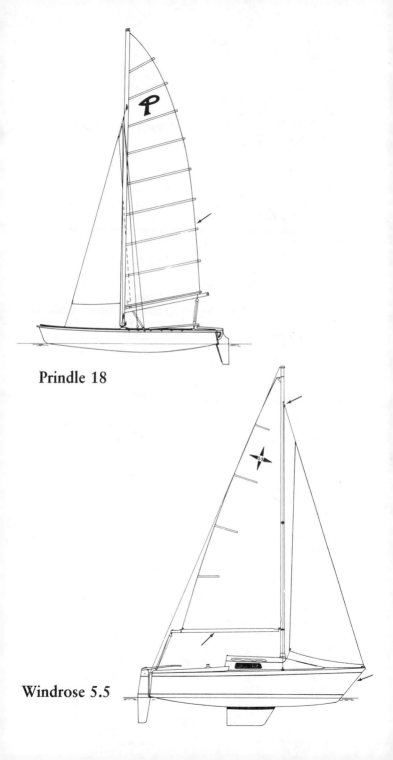

Prindle 18

Windrose 5.5

Y Flyer

Length: 18 ft. 2 in.
Beam: 5 ft. 8 in.
Draft: 4 ft.
Weight: 500 lbs. minimum
Sail area: Main, 110 sq. ft.;
   jib, 51 sq. ft.
Hull: Wood or FRP

Spars: Wood or aluminum
Racing crew: 2
Rating: D–PN 88.7
First built: 1952
No. built: 2600
Designer: Alvin Youngquist

Scow. Long bow. Counter. Bridle traveler. Centerboard rather than bilgeboards.

The Y Flyer has a hard chine and flat bottom, and is unusually stable. A slight heel reduces wetted surface dramatically, however, as may be seen from the rating. Sheer is reverse, but this is difficult to see in a boat with such low freeboard. Although there are two builders, the boat may also be built from plans using spruce and plywood. The centerboard is steel or aluminum. The mast can rotate, and the rig is flexible. The traveler may be moved amidships and bailers, barber haulers, transom flaps, and hiking assists may be used. Spinnakers are used in Canada, where there are fleets in Alberta, Manitoba, Ontario, and Quebec. US fleets are heavily concentrated in Indiana, Illinois, Ohio, Missouri, Georgia, and South Carolina, but are also in the Northeast, on the Pacific coast, and elsewhere.

Victoria

Length: 18 ft. 5 in.
Beam: 5 ft. 6 in.
Draft: 2 ft.
Weight: 1200 lbs.
Sail area: Main, 83 sq. ft.; jib, 51
   sq. ft.; genoa, 81 sq. ft.;
   spinnaker, 120 sq. ft.
Hull: FRP

Spars: Tapered, anodized
   aluminum
Racing crew: 1–3
Rating: None
First built: 1977
No. built: 1000
Designer: G. William McVay

Long counter. Pulpit. Keel. Traditional lines above water. Duplicate ports.

Victoria has two classes. One is for families and one for racing. The first has standard rigging and allows only main, jib, and genoa. The racing class permits adjustable backstay, boom vang, Barber haulers, and a spinnaker. The cockpit is six feet long and an optional boom tent is available. There are genoa tracks and winches. Below, there are two berths and a cooler. Roller reefing is standard, as are opening ports, a lazarette, and a boom crutch. An optional outboard bracket will carry a 4.5-horsepower motor. With her shallow-draft keel, Victoria is designed for trailering.

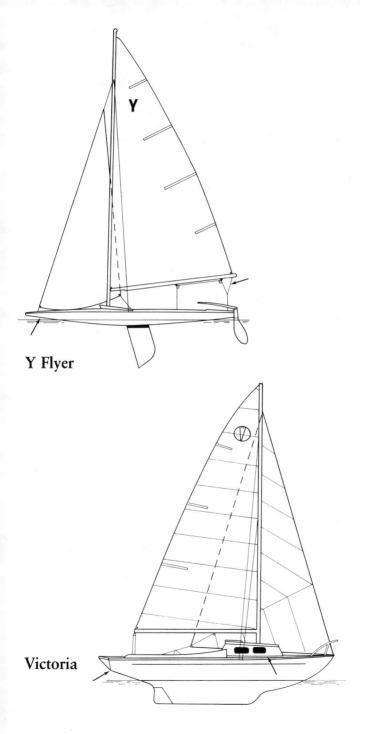

Y Flyer

Victoria

Typhoon

Length: 18 ft. 6 in.
Beam: 6 ft. 3½ in.
Draft: 2 ft. 7½ in.
Weight: 2000 lbs.
Sail area: Main and jib, 160 sq. ft. total

Hull: FRP
Spars: Anodized aluminum
First built: Not avail.
No. built: Not avail.
Designer: Carl Alberg

Heeled, look for full keel. Cuddy. Wood coamings. Diagonal end-boom sheeting. Cruiser bow.

There is a weekender version of this daysailer. The significant visual differences are an extension of the cabin aft and the addition of a round porthole and a top hatch for entry. The jib may be working or genoa. The weekender has a vee berth and two quarter berths, with room for an optional head. The boat has a 900-lb keel and is very steady. On the daysailer, seats are teak, as are the rub strakes and toe-rails. Both boats have balsa-cored decks and teak coamings and taffrails. Storage in the daysailer is in a forepeak locker, while in the weekender there are two cockpit lockers and cabin shelves. Both have a genoa track, winches, and cleats.

Appledore

Length: 19 ft.
Beam: 3 ft. 3 in.
Draft: 4 in. (board up)
Weight: 1000 lbs.
Sail area: Main and mizzen, 40 sq. ft. each

Hull: FRP
Spars: Aluminum
Racing crew: 1 or 2
Rating: None
Designer: Arthur E. Martin

Unmistakable two-masted sliding gunter rig. Double-ended hull. Full-length battens.

A very unusual design based upon sailing canoes, and intended for both sailing and rowing. The center of effort is quite low. Sails roll on booms for reefing. There is an anodized-aluminum kick-up rudder and a daggerboard. Deck and bulkheads are mahogany, with the latter providing flotation in conjunction with foam. Note the teak belaying pins. There are no halyards or stays, and the boat may be converted for rowing with sliding seats for two oarsmen.

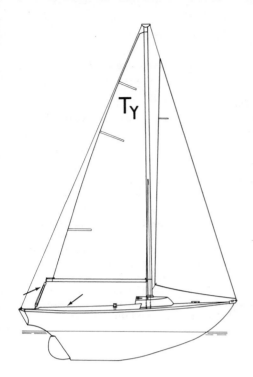

Typhoon

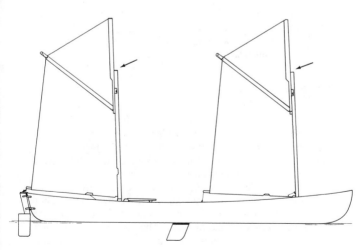

Appledore

Flying Scot

Length: 19 ft.
Beam: 6 ft. 9 in.
Draft: 4 ft.
Weight: 850 lbs.
Sail area: Main, 138 sq. ft.; jib, 53 sq. ft.; spinnaker, 200 sq. ft.
Hull: FRP, balsa core

Spars: Aluminum
Racing crew: 3
Rating: D–PN 90.0
First built: 1957
No. built: 3750
Designer: Gordon K. Douglass

Normal sheer at rail, but reverse sheer at deck. Very large cockpit. Big boat.

A big, fast centerboard boat, the Flying Scot has an unusual reverse sheer. Capacity is eight adults. With hard bilges and a slightly tunneled hull, stability is good. Rigging is relatively simple, and the class rules discourage complexity. Required or allowed are vangs and roller furling for the main. Specifically not allowed are hiking straps and trapezes, leech cords, Barber haulers, twings, and self-bailers. No mast adjustment is allowed while racing. The centerboard is heavy — 105 lbs. — so control usually includes a 6:1 assist. Foam flotation is provided under the seats, which have a drain to the transom. The boat is a one-design and all hulls are made from the same mold.

Lightning

Length: 19 ft.
Beam: 6 ft. 6 in.
Draft: 4 ft. 11 in.
Weight: 700 lbs.
Sail area: Main and jib, 177 sq. ft. total; spinnaker, 300 sq. ft.
Hull: Wood or fiberglass

Spars: Wood or aluminum
Racing crew: 3
Rating: D–PN 89.8
First built: 1938
No. built: Over 13,000
Designer: Olin Stephens

Raked mast. Permanent backstay. May have windows. If wood mast, there is a jumper stay from the head to the spreader. Long vee coaming.

Lightning may be bought complete, built from hull kits, or built from scratch. Most of the older boats are wood, but replacements are mostly FRP. If the boat is to be raced, rigid one-design specifications intended to keep costs within bounds must be met. Lightning is an International class, supervised by the IYRU. There are over 460 fleets in the US, Europe, Canada, and South America. The large cockpit holds five adults. There is a clear area forward of the centerboard and aft of the mast from which crew may handle sails. The backstay is permanent and lands at the chain plate off center, so as to clear the tiller. There is good freeboard and stability.

Flying Scot

Lightning

Mariner

Length: 19 ft. 2 in.
Beam: 7 ft.
Draft: 4 ft. 11 in.
Weight: 1250 lbs.
Sail area: Main and jib, 185 sq. ft. total
Hull: FRP; deck balsa core
Spars: Hard-coated aluminum
Racing crew: 2
Rating: None
First built: 1966
No. built: 4100
Designer: George O'Day

Backstay. Same hull as Rhodes 19. Cuddy. Two windows. Black headboard, mast, boom. Possible sail window in jib.

The Mariner, a very typical daysailer, was originally built by the O'Day Corporation, but since 1979 has been built by Spindrift. There is sharp bow entry and high freeboard; like the Rhodes 19, the Mariner can handle heavy weather. This capability is enhanced by the 210-lb centerboard. There is seating for six adults. The mast is deck mounted. In the cuddy are two forward berths, two quarter berths, under-berth storage, opening windows, space for a portable head, and teak trim. The cockpit is self-draining and has a storage compartment. A vang, 105-sq. ft. genoa, and spinnaker package are optional.

Rhodes 19

Length: 19 ft. 2 in.
Beam: 7 ft.
Draft: 4 ft. 11 in. (centerboard); or 3 ft. 3 in. (keel)
Weight: 1000 lbs. (centerboard); or 1240 lbs. (keel)
Sail area: Main, 112.5 sq. ft.; jib, 60.5 sq. ft.; spinnaker, 326 sq. ft.
Hull: FRP
Spars: Aluminum
Racing crew: 2
Rating: D–PN 97.4 (centerboard) or D–PN 99.0 (keel)
First built: 1959
No. built: 3000
Designer: Philip Rhodes

Triangular spreaders forward of mast, second set below. Backstay. Cuddy.

A *Sail* magazine "breakthrough boat" with tremendous influence upon sailing, the Rhodes 19 is the first popular daysailer. Centerboard and keel versions are available, with the former found mostly on lakes and the latter in coastal waters. The large cockpit will hold six to eight, while the cuddy can sleep two. There is a built-in ice box. The traveler is mounted on the stern. Jib leads are adjustable. In the centerboard model the rudder kicks up. In both, there is foam flotation. Optional features are a boom tent, boom vang, Cunningham, cockpit bailers, a tapered mast, a whisker pole, and a spinnaker package.

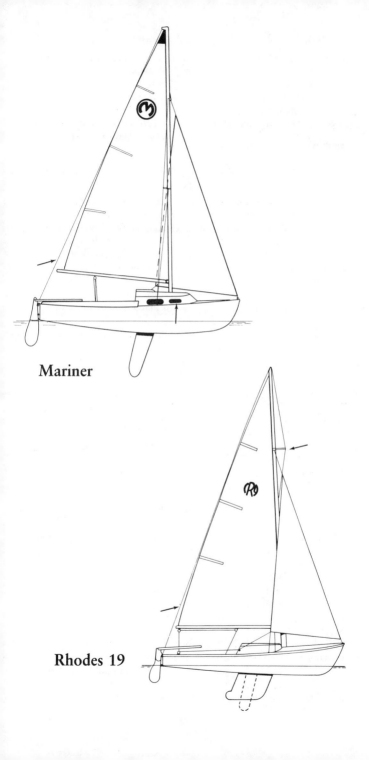

Mariner

Rhodes 19

Flying Dutchman

Length: 19 ft. 10 in.
Beam: 5 ft. 11 in.
Draft: 3 ft. 8 in.
Weight: 347 lbs. minimum
Sail area: Main, 116 sq. ft.;
   genoa, 84 sq. ft.; spinnaker,
   190 sq. ft.
Hull: Wood, FRP, composite

Spars: Optional, usually
   aluminum
Racing crew: 2
Rating: Olympic; D–PN 79.9
First built: 1951
No. built: 6500 world, 1400 US
Designer: Uus van Essen

Sharp spoon bow. Hull extends far aft of boom. Straight sheer. Trapeze.

The Flying Dutchman (FD) is the first trapeze boat selected for the Olympics. It is an International class boat, controlled by the IYRU. FD is a compromise between a "rule" boat and a strict one-design. Hull shape, centerboard and rudder, and sail plan are controlled. There are guidelines for standing and running rigging, layout, and cockpit size. There is a sharp, hollow bow which reduces pounding. Initial stability is high due to the hard bilges. She is fast, but not nervous. The boat is frequently built from hull kits, sometimes from plans. Fleets are scattered over the East Coast, Florida, Michigan, Texas, Washington, and California; there is also one in Green River, Wyoming.

C–Scow

Length: 20 ft.
Beam: 6 ft. 10 in.
Draft: 3 ft. 3 in.
Weight: 650 lbs. minimum
Sail area: 216 sq. ft.
Hull: FRP
Spars: Aluminum or wood

Racing crew: 2 or 3 (475 lbs.
   max.)
Rating: D–PN 81.0
First built: Early 20th century
No. built: 2000
Designer: Inland Yacht
   Association

Scow. No jib. Running backstays. Mast raked aft. Boom close to deck.

The C–Scow was first built early in the century. Sources differ, with one claiming 1906 and the other, 1923. As may be seen from the rating, this cat-rigged scow is fast. Scows were developed in the Midwest, but the C–Scow can also be found in Texas and California. There is extensive control. Forestays may be adjusted while the boat is sailing; a lever aft of the vang track is used, and of course the backstays must be released. Sidestay adjustment is by turnbuckle, but the mast may not be pulled to windward while sailing. There is an adjustable ball-bearing traveler. The boom vang leads to a radial recessed track. The double-ended 6:1 outhaul and Cunningham also control shape. These boats are one-design, with strict control of hull shape. They have polystyrene foam flotation.

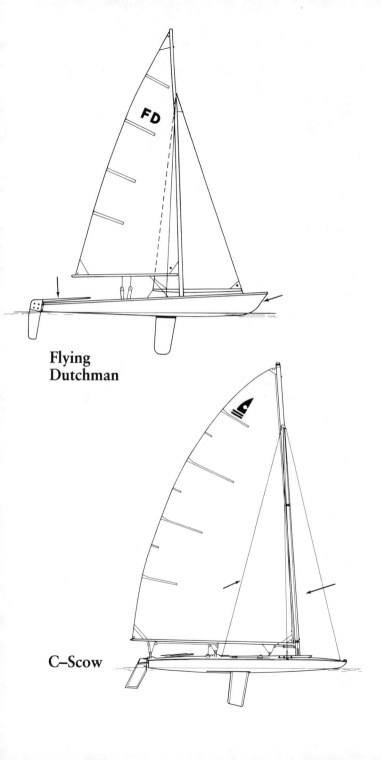

Flying Dutchman

C–Scow

Flying Fifteen

Length: 20 ft.
Beam: 5 ft.
Draft: 2 ft. 6 in.
Weight: 697.4 lbs. minimum
Sail area: Main, 100 sq. ft.;
  genoa, 50 sq. ft.; spinnaker,
  150 sq. ft.

Hull: FRP or wood
Spars: Aluminum
Racing crew: 2
Rating: D–PN 91.0
First built: 1948
No. built: 2900
Designer: Uffa Fox

Long spoon bow. Unusual counter. Rudder post well forward of stern.

The Flying Fifteen is an ultra-light-displacement keel boat that has been clocked at 16 knots. The cockpit is self-bailing, and there is airbag flotation. She became an International class in 1981. The majority of boats are in the UK, Australia, New Zealand, South Africa, and Hong Kong. In the US, fleets are in San Francisco, Maine, and Connecticut. Class rules require positive buoyancy, hiking straps, and other safety equipment. Instrumentation and mast adjustment under way are not allowed. Championships must be sailed on tidal waters. All controls lead to the cockpit just forward of the traveler. Included are sheets, Cunningham, vang, down- and outhaul, and spinnaker sheet and guy. Roller furling for the jib is available.

Highlander

Length: 20 ft.
Beam: 6 ft. 8 in.
Draft: 8 in. (centerboard up)
Weight: 830 lbs.
Sail area: Main and jib, 225 sq.
  ft. total; spinnaker available,
  used for racing.

Hull: FRP
Spars: Aluminum
Racing crew: 3
Rating: D–PN 84.8
First built: 1951
No. built: Not avail.
Designer: Gordon K. Douglass

Three jumper struts. Reverse sheer similar to Flying Scot. Jib window possible. Curved rudder.

The Highlander evolved from the same designer's dinghies and from the Thistle. It predates the Flying Scot (also by Gordon Douglass) and was originally built of molded plywood. The bow is similar to the Thistle, while the reverse sheer foretells the Scot. The mast has a triple diamond-shroud system. While apparently heavy, the Highlander has a low length-to-displacement ratio of 69.8, and planes. The cockpit is 11 feet long and 5 feet wide, and will hold ten people. Wood is used for seats, foredeck rail, and elsewhere. Standing rigging is adjustable. Running rigging is simple and includes a vang, Cunningham, and centerboard adjustment with a high mechanical advantage. Fleets are mostly in Ohio, with others in Tennessee, Maryland, Massachusetts, Kentucky, North Carolina, and New York.

Flying Fifteen

Highlander

Tornado

Length: 20 ft.
Beam: 10 ft.
Draft: 2 ft. 7 in.
Weight: 279 lbs.
Sail area: Main and jib, 235 sq.
  ft. total
Hull: Wood

Spars: Aluminum
Racing crew: 2
Rating: Olympic; D–PN 66.5
First built: 1967
No. built: 3600
Designer: Rodney Marsh

Two symmetrical hulls. Trapeze. Very high aspect ratio. Very high jib. Ten battens in loose-footed main.

The Tornado is the only Olympic catamaran, having been in use since 1976. There are very few boats with lower Portsmouth numbers than this daggerboarder. No spinnaker is used. This International boat is self-rescuing. Hiking assists allowed are straps, usually used by the skipper, and a trapeze ridden by the crew.

Sirius

Length: 21 ft. 2 in.
Beam: 7 ft. 11 in.
Draft: 5 ft.
Weight: 2000 lbs.
Sail area: Main, 93 sq. ft.; jib,
  110 sq. ft.; genoa, 156 sq. ft.;
  spinnaker, 385 sq. ft.

Hull: FRP
Spars: Aluminum
Racing crew: 2 or 3
Rating: None
First built: 1976
No. built: 565
Designer: Hubert Vandestadt

Very high boom. Foremost cabin windows slightly smaller. Possible bow and stern pulpit. Note straight lines of rudder. Masthead rig.

The Sirius is built in Ontario and is mostly found on the Great Lakes. There are berths for five, a dinette, and a galley. Sink, five-gallon water tank, and pump are extra. The interior is finished, with hull and deck liners and teak trim. Sirius has a wide beam; and this, combined with the hard bilge and a retractable cast-iron keel, gives good stability. She is unsinkable and, if the keel is locked down, self-righting. There is a well for the anchor. In the cockpit is a compartment for a gas tank. A pop-top is standard. Rudder kicks up, and there are a boom vang, jiffy reefing, and topping lift.

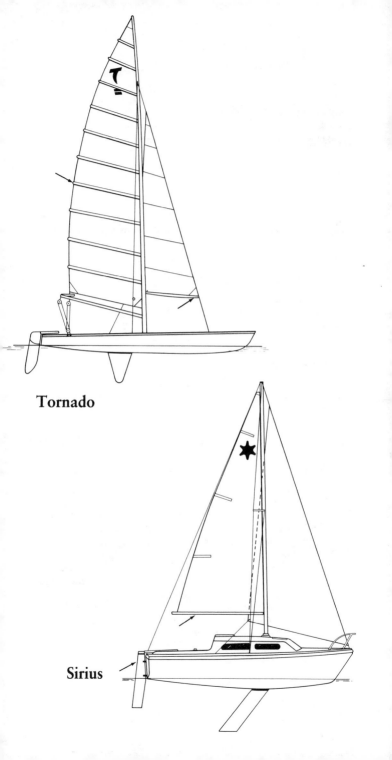

Tornado

Sirius

Santana 20

Length: 20 ft. 2½ in.
Beam: 8 ft.
Draft: 4 ft.
Weight: 1350 lbs.
Sail area: Main, 36 sq. ft.; jib, 109 sq. ft.; genoa, 149 sq. ft.; spinnaker, 359 sq. ft.

Hull: FRP
Spars: Aluminum
Racing crew: 3 or 4
Rating: D–PN 92.6
First built: 1976
No. built: 630
Designer: W. Shad Turner

Straight bow, counter, reverse transom. High aspect ratio. Stern support for lifeline. Distinctive deckhouse.

This large daysailer has a cabin with two opening windows that will sleep four. There is storage under the vee berth, also under the cockpit seats. The cabin has a liner and teak trim. Cockpit layout is split. Forward, controls for halyards and the vang lead to the top of the cuddy. There is a traveler, and aft is the helmsman's station. Note the size of the main in relation to the jib or genoa. Most fleets are on the West Coast, but some are also in Oklahoma, Indiana, Florida, and Texas. Sail the Santana 20 heeled about 7 degrees, and roll tack.

Atlantic City

Length: 21 ft. 3 in.
Beam: 9 ft. 6 in.
Draft: 5 ft.
Weight: 5,300 lbs.
Sail area: 350 sq. ft.
Hull: FRP

Spars: Wood
Rating: None
First built: 1982
No. built: Not avail.
Designer: Mark-O-Boats

Catboat, mast hoops, gaff rigged. Ports unusual shape. Typical plumb bow.

The basic design of this catboat is classic. Note the high coaming and the rudder design, typical of boats built for this part of the Atlantic coast. (For contrast, see Marshall 22 for a Cape Cod style rudder.) Below, there is an area for the galley and for a chart table and locker (all optional). The opposing settees can be used for berths, and each has a pilot berth above. A door isolates the head, forward, and a rope locker in the forepeak. Typically, the cockpit is large. With available options including a 12-horsepower diesel, cockpit table, marine head, and even a fireplace, the Atlantic City is ready for short cruises. Tiller steering, a bilge pump, and bronze hardware are standard.

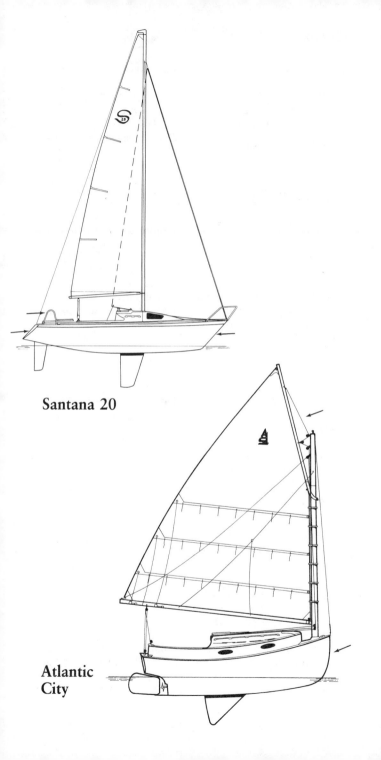

Santana 20

Atlantic
City

Tempest

Length: 21 ft. 11¾ in.
Beam: 6 ft. 5½ in.
Draft: 3 ft. 7 in.
Weight: 977 lbs.
Sail area: Main, 164 sq. ft.;
  jib, 82.78 sq. ft.; spinnaker,
  225 sq. ft.

Hull: FRP
Spars: Aluminum
Racing crew: 2
Rating: D–PN 77.5
First built: 1965
No. built: 850
Designer: Ian Proctor

Keel boat, rudder submerged. Aft deck. Note foredeck line down to hull at mast.

The International class Tempest was an Olympic boat in 1972 and 1976. As may be seen from the rating, she is fast. Tempest is a one-design, and class rules are strict. Trapezes are allowed. The mast's design and material are optional, but the mast may not rotate. Older boats have thicker, stiffer masts and, in addition to the diamond shrouds and spreaders found today, additional swept-back spreaders. Good racing boats are rigid, although this is not necessary in the deck, and are light at the ends. Windows are allowed in the jib and main, with size controlled. Tempests are often dry-sailed. There are three transverse bulkheads for flotation. Items prohibited include mast jacks, trim tabs, and more than two spinnakers. Only one person may use the trapeze, and safety equipment must be carried.

Ensign

Length: 22 ft. 6 in.
Beam: 7 ft.
Draft: 3 ft.
Weight: 3000 lbs.
Sail area: Main, 140 sq. ft.; jib,
  61 sq. ft.; genoa, 150 and 111
  sq. ft.; spinnaker dimensions
  restricted by class: leech and
  luff, 25 ft; foot from clew to
  clew, 15 ft.

Hull: FRP; deck balsa core
Spars: Anodized aluminum
Racing crew: 2 or more
Rating: D–PN 95.6
First built: 1962
No. built: 1755
Designer: Carl Alberg

Long spoon bow, counter, reverse transom. High coamings. Mast splits two shrouds fore and aft. End-boom sheeting.

There are more than 1700 Ensigns sailing in 47 fleets in 20 states. Fleets are concentrated in Long Island Sound, Massachusetts, Maine, the Great Lakes, and Texas. Ensign is the largest full-keel one-design class in the country. The cuddy has two berths, optional head, and 3-ft., 10-in. headroom. In the 8-ft., 8-in. cockpit are teak sole, seats, and coamings. Mast adjustments during racing are not permitted, except by the backstay, which is controlled with a turnbuckle. Roller reefing on the boom is allowed. There is a boom vang, and mid-boom sheeting is an allowed modification. Barber haulers, geared sheet winches, and internal halyards are not permitted.

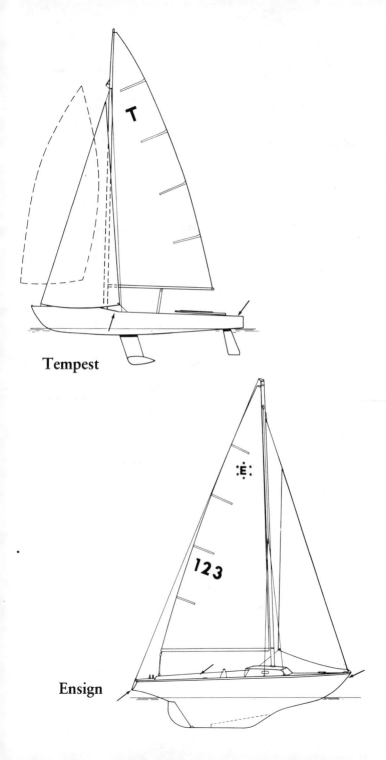

Tempest

Ensign

Star

Length: 22 ft. 8½ in.
Beam: 5 ft. 8¼ in.
Draft: 3 ft. 6 in.
Weight: 1480 lbs. minimum
Sail area: Main, 240 sq. ft.;
  jib, 78 sq. ft.
Hull: Wood or FRP
Spars: Wood or aluminum

Racing crew: 2
Rating: Olympic; D–PN 84.7
First built: 1911 (present length)
No. built: 6740
Designer: William Gardner in
  1906, Francis Swiesguth in
  1910

Inboard rudder. Small cockpit. Relatively low boom. Running backstays.

Roller reefing in the twenties and thirties. Vang very early, and circular vang in the fifties. Flexible rig in the thirties. Mast benders in the twenties. Now, almost everything is adjustable, and the Star rig must be fine-tuned very carefully. Adjustments include the traveler, backstays, low backstays, jib leads, and mast partners. There is a lever-operated mast bender. Most of these lead to amidships in the cockpit. The Star originally had a gaff or gunter rig which changed to marconi in 1921. The original wood hull changed to FRP in 1967; the spars to aluminum in 1971. Hull shape has changed very little, with the major change a lengthening from 18 feet to the present length in 1911. Measurement rules are extensive. There are about 160 fleets on five continents, with about 3000 boats actively racing. Buoyancy has been required since 1979.

Sonar

Length: 23 ft.
Beam: 7 ft. 10 in.
Draft: 4 ft.
Weight: 2160 lbs.
Sail area: Main, 153.55 sq. ft.;
  jib, 99 sq. ft.; spinnaker, 360
  sq. ft.

Hull: FRP
Spars: Aluminum
Racing crew: 3 or 4
Rating: None
First built: 1980
No. built: 250
Designer: Bruce Kirby

Large, keel daysailer. Sharp bow. Reverse transom. Backstay. Very large cockpit.

The Sonar was designed for the same market as the Etchells 22, Soling, Tempest, and Ensign. The basic concept was generated by a committee of the Noroton Yacht Club (Connecticut), then designed by Bruce Kirby. The cockpit is huge. Seven adults can sit in its eleven-foot length. The boat is very stable, with a 935-lb. keel. Notice that the rudder is inboard. Only three sails are allowed — main, jib, and spinnaker. There are three cockpit lockers and a locking cabin which is sometimes rigged for two berths. The tapered boom has internal slab reefing. Adjustment is with a 4:1 sheet, and there is a vang. Class rules prohibit hiking. Production figures for this new boat may be misleading; 60 were sold the first month it was approved.

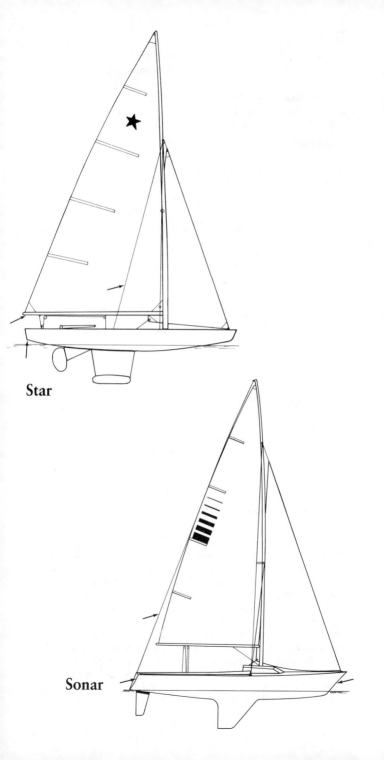

Star

Sonar

Balboa 24

Length: 23 ft. 7 in.
Beam: 8 ft. 4 in.
Draft: 2 ft. 11 in.
Weight: 2666 lbs. or 2800 lbs.
Sail area: Main, 115 (124.5) sq. ft.; jib, 105 (127) sq. ft.; genoa, 158 (190) sq. ft.; spinnaker, 360 (462) sq. ft.

Hull: FRP
Spars: Anodized aluminum
Racing crew: 2
Rating: D–PN 98.0 suspect
First built: 1980
Designer: W. Shad Turner

Masthead Rig. Bow pulpit, stern pulpit. Three windows. Straight bow, almost vertical transom.

Two rigs are available for this sloop. The first has a 26-ft, 6-in. mast; the taller rig has a 28-ft. mast and two hundred additional pounds of ballast. The latter is the better rig for racing. Both are equipped for cruising, with five berths, a galley with fixed ice chest and sink, separate head area with sink, and area for recessed alcohol stove. The boat opens up with a Plexiglas foredeck hatch and pop-top allowing six feet of head room. Storage includes an anchor locker, two cockpit lockers and a cockpit lazarette for gas can, under-berth storage, galley storage, shelves, and a hanging locker. Interior trim is teak. Safety items include a pulpit, lifelines, integral toe-rails and a stern pulpit.

110

Length: 24 ft.
Beam: 4 ft. 3 in.
Draft: 2 ft. 9 in.
Weight: 910 lbs.
Sail area: Main and genoa, 167 sq. ft. total; spinnaker, 200 sq. ft.

Hull: Plywood
Spars: Wood or aluminum
Racing crew: 2 or 3
Rating: D–PN 89.6
First built: 1939
No. built: 700
Designer: C. Raymond Hunt

Untraditional double-ender. Low freeboard, narrow hull. Vertical sides.

This fin-keeler was a breakthrough design of the late thirties. Recent rule changes, allowing a trapeze, enabled the 110 to win the Keel Division of the One-of-a-Kind Regatta in 1969. She points extremely well, planes on the flat bottom, and goes well downwind, but unless weight is kept well aft the bow tends to bury. Because of the very simple lines, the 110 is easy to build. In spite of her weight, which includes the 300-lb. keel, she is unsinkable. The most frequent racing crew is two. A third crew member has to fight the boom vang for space. Many boats have been fiberglassed. There is a roller-furling jib, a trapeze, and a spinnaker tube. The cockpit is small, and with the narrow beam, is difficult to work off the foredeck. Most boats are in New England, the West Coast, and the upper Midwest.

Balboa 24

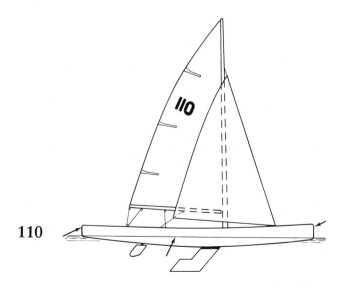

110

Raven

Length: 24 ft. 3 in.
Beam: 7 ft.
Draft: 5 ft. 4 in.
Weight: 1170 lbs.
Sail area: Main and jib, 300 sq. ft. total
Hull: FRP
Spars: Anodized aluminum
Racing crew: 3
Rating: D–PN 83.3
First built: 1949
No. built: Over 300
Designer: Roger McAleer

No visible tiller or rudder. Continuous curve to bow. Two spreaders. Adjustable jib leads.

Raven, originally in molded plywood, was a forerunner of today's planing boats. Construction was switched to FRP in 1951, and the Coast Guard Academy took the first eight. Coamings and centerboard trim remain in wood. The boom is fitted with roller reefing and a six-part outhaul. There are two self-bailers. Rule changes, most in 1970, allow for a one-piece aluminum centerboard, trapeze, full-width traveler on the large aft deck, and hiking straps.

Soling

Length: 26 ft. 11 in.
Beam: 6 ft. 3 in.
Draft: 4 ft. 3 in.
Weight: 2277 lbs.
Sail area: Main, 146 sq. ft.; jib, 87 sq. ft.; spinnaker, 340 sq. ft.
Hull: FRP
Spars: Aluminum
Racing crew: 3
Rating: Olympic; D–PN 83.9
First built: 1965
No. built: 3000
Designer: Jan Herman Linge

Backstay. Big sloop with no cabin. Long spoon bow. Long counter, reverse transom. Rudder not visible.

An Olympic class since 1972. The Soling is heavy, but she planes. There are active class associations in 35 countries, and about 750 Solings in the US. There are strict class rules covering more than 150 items. All boats are built from an official mold. The Soling is self-bailing, but it has been known to sink despite flotation compartments fore, aft, and below the floor. There is a cabin of sorts which may contain a galley and other types of storage. There are also storage lockers in the cockpit. While the Soling can be found almost anywhere in the US, because it is a keel boat it is most often found on the coasts or on large bodies of water. The areas listed for the US include the Atlantic, West, Midwest, South, Northwest, and Mideast. The International, one-design class is administered by the IYRU. About 950 Solings are members of the International Soling Association.

Raven

Soling

E Scow

Length: 28 ft.
Beam: 6 ft. 9 in.
Draft: 4 ft.
Weight: 965 lbs. (hull only)
Sail area: Main, 228 sq. ft.; jib, 95 sq. ft.; spinnaker, 550 sq. ft.
Hull: Wood or FRP

Spars: Aluminum, wood permitted
Racing crew: 2 or 3
Rating: D–PN 74.9
Designer: Evolved through many designs

Large scow. Rudder concealed. Bilgeboards. Windows in jib and main. Running backstays. Forestay attached well aft of bow.

This is a very fast and sophisticated boat with a long history of development. Scows probably evolved from sharpies, and the first scows were in evidence around 1895. E Scows were born at a meeting of the Inland Lake Yachting Association in 1923. Wood has been used for many years, but since 1976 FRP has predominated. Manufacturers now use sandwich construction. The E Scow has twin bilgeboards and rudders. Transom bailers are provided by both Johnson and Melges. Sail control is sophisticated. Main shape devices can include outhaul, downhaul, Cunningham, vang, and leech cord. Luff wire and downhauls are allowed for the jib. Other control includes radiused traveler and jib tracks. Artificial hiking assists other than hiking straps are not allowed. Fleets are found in Texas, Colorado, Wisconsin, Minnesota, Michigan, New York, and New Jersey.

Dragon

Length: 29 ft. 2 in.
Beam: 6 ft. 5 in.
Draft: 3 ft. 11 in.
Weight: 3740 lbs.
Sail area: Main, 135 sq. ft.; genoa 150 sq. ft.; spinnaker, 155 sq. ft.

Hull: Wood or FRP
Spars: Wood or aluminum
Racing crew: 3
Rating: D–PN 89.3
First built: 1928
No. built: 4500
Designer: Johan Anker

Long overhangs at bow and stern. Classic lines. Very high aspect ratio. Two jumper struts. Very small cabin. Narrow beam.

This fractional sloop-rigged keel boat has celebrated more than fifty years of international popularity. Originally built of pine and subsequently of mahogany, it is now built of both FRP and laminated wood. A major change was made in 1945, when spinnakers and genoas were allowed. Dragon then served as an Olympic boat from 1952 through 1972. It is maintained as a one-design class by the IYRU. Although there is a cuddy which was designed to sleep two, the elegant lines of the Dragon proclaim its use in international and national racing. There are over 288 Dragons registered in the United States and 130 in Canada. Fleets are at Rochester, Toledo, Cleveland, Chicago, Long Beach, Santa Barbara, San Francisco, and Seattle.

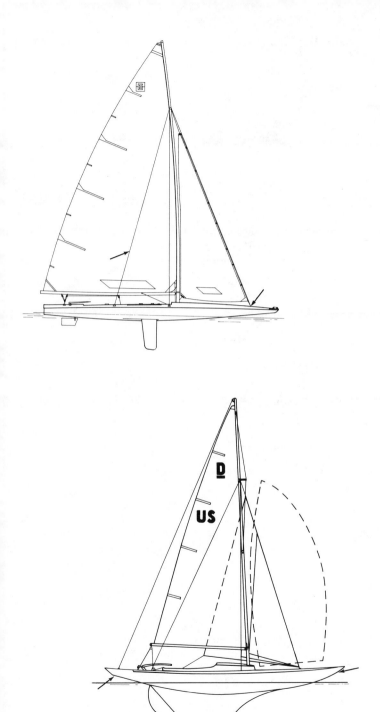

Shields

Length: 30 ft. 2½ in.	*Hull:* FRP
Beam: 6 ft. 5¼ in.	*Spars:* Aluminum
Draft: 4 ft. 9 in.	*Racing crew:* 3 or 4
Weight: 4600 lbs.	*Rating:* D–PN 83.8 suspect
Sail area: Main, 222 sq. ft.;	*First built:* 1963
jib, 138 sq. ft.; spinnaker,	*No. built:* 227
490 sq. ft.	*Designer:* Olin Stephens

Big, classic sloop. Note bow and especially the very long counter. Sheeting just aft of large cockpit. No cabin. No genoa.

This beautiful boat, while large, is used for daysailing and particularly for racing. Class rules are rigid. For example, only one suit of sails is allowed per year. Cape Cod Shipbuilding first built the Shields; then Chris Craft and Hinkley; and now, again, Cape Cod. This design was the concept of Cornelius Shields. As currently built, the Shields has teak coamings, toe-rails, handrails, floor grating, and cockpit seats. There is a console for halyard winches with cleats mounted vertically. There are flotation compartments under the seats, and in addition, there are watertight bulkheads fore and aft. The lead keel weighs 3080 lbs. The backstay has four-part tackle, the vang four-part, and the mainsheet three-part.

E 22 (Etchells 22)

Length: 30 ft. 6 in.	*Hull:* FRP
Beam: 6 ft. 11½ in.	*Spars:* Anodized aluminum
Draft: 4 ft. 6 in.	*Racing crew:* 3
Weight: 3400 lbs.	*Rating:* D–PN 84.8 suspect
Sail area: Main, 188 sq. ft.; jib,	*First built:* 1968
102 sq. ft.; spinnaker,	*No. built:* 500
400 sq. ft.	*Designer:* E. W. Etchells

Large boat, classic lines, long overhangs at bow and stern. High aspect ratio. Forestay fractional, well back from bow. Keel.

Big, fast, and stiff, and with an association that intends to resist complex mast and sail control mechanisms, the E 22 is designated for International competition by the IYRU. There are builders and classes around the world. The cuddy is for storage and there are no bunks. The Etchells 22 is for daysailing or for racing. An unusual feature of the cockpit is a control console, and the jib halyard (8:1), foreguy, topping lift, Cunningham (4:1), and mainsheet (4:1) lead to it. On the aft bulkhead of the cuddy are the coarse jib sheet (2:1), jib fine tune (6:1), Barber hauler (2:1), and spinnaker halyard. The backstay (6:1) is adjustable, as is the traveler. US fleets are in Long Island Sound, Seattle, Maine, Massachusetts, Detroit, Chicago, Minneapolis, San Francisco, and San Diego. In Canada, there are fleets in Toronto and Halifax.

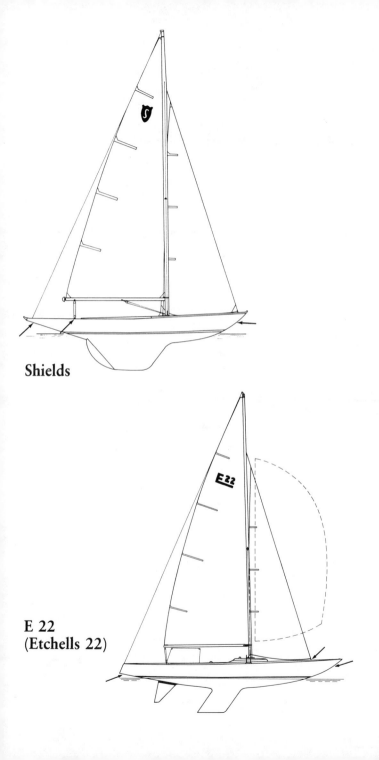

Shields

E 22
(Etchells 22)

Cruisers / Auxiliaries

Com-Pac 19

Length: 19 ft. LOA; 16 ft. 4 in. LWL	*Spars:* Anodized aluminum
Beam: 7 ft.	*Berths:* 4
Draft: 2 ft.	*Engine:* None
Displacement: 2000 lbs.	*Head:* Optional
Sail area: Main and lapper, 188 sq. ft.	*Galley:* Optional
Hull: FRP	*Water:* With galley
	Rating: None
	Designer: Bob Johnson

Cruiser bow. Deep sheer. Round ports. Long, diagonal end-boom sheeting. Short rig.

This little cruiser has berths for four, and with the optional head and galley it is self-contained. Com-Pac was first built in 1981; unlike its sister, the 23, it has not yet been rated.

When fitted, the galley is placed in the notch between the vee berths and the head goes at the bottom of the companionway.

The cockpit has two scuppers and two seat lockers as well as a gas-tank storage locker for the outboard if it is fitted. There is a large chain locker in the forepeak. Four bronze ports open, and additional ventilation is through a cowl vent on the fore-deck. The boom is fitted for an outhaul. Options include sheet and halyard winches, a genoa track, and pulpits.

Com-Pac 19

Falmouth Cutter

Length: 20 ft. 10 in. LOA;
   20 ft. 10 in. LWL
Beam: 8 ft.
Draft: 3 ft. 6 in.
Displacement: 7400 lbs.
Sail area: Main, 170 sq. ft.; jib,
   102 sq. ft.; staysail, 85 sq. ft.
Hull: FRP
Spars: Painted aluminum

Berths: 3
Engine: Yanmar 7 HP
Fuel: 23 gals.
Head: Portable
Galley: 2-burner, kerosene
Water: 30 gals.
Rating: None
Designer: Lyle Hess

Wide beam, wide transom. Bowsprit and boomkin. Boxy deck house. Plumb bow.

This cutter is designed and built for cruising. The first cutter was the "Renegade," somewhat larger and with a gaff rig. Larry Pardey asked for a similar but marconi-rigged boat and made the result, "Seraffyn," famous. The Bristol Cutter, larger at 28 feet, followed; and the latest design is the Falmouth. Beam is wide and displacement heavy. The keel is full and bilges are firm. Because of the wide beam there is a remarkable amount of space below.

The two quarter berths double as seats for the dinette. When it is not in use, the table slides aft under the cockpit. The gimbaled kerosene stove is to port with a chart table and ice box opposite. The starboard quarter berth is the seat for the navigation station. A hanging locker is forward. In the bow is a double bunk and the head. There is stowage below for sails and the ground tackle. A large hatch is above the forward cabin and is obvious in the profile view. There are also six bronze opening ports.

Bulwarks, taffrail, boomkin, and trim are mahogany. The fir bowsprit is the reefing type. It may be retracted to the deck (or "housed"), which shortens the boat by four feet. There are two winches on the mast for halyards and four at the cockpit for sheets. All deck fittings are bronze. A skylight is just aft of the mast, over the main cabin.

Falmouth Cutter

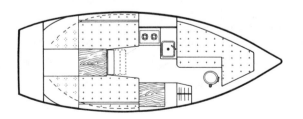

Catalina 22

Length: 21 ft. 6 in. LOA;
19 ft. 4 in. LWL
Beam: 7 ft. 8 in.
Draft: 3 ft. 6 in. (fixed keel) or
5 ft. (swing keel)
Displacement: 2490 lbs. (fixed) or
2250 lbs. (swing)
Sail area: main, 105 sq. ft.; 100%
foretriangle, 107 sq. ft.
Hull: FRP

Spars: Aluminum
Berths: 4 or 5
Engine: Outboard
Head: Optional, marine
Galley: Optional
Water: 7.5 gals.
Rating: D–N 99.0 (fixed keel);
99.2 (swing keel); PHRF 270
Designer: Frank Butler

Unlike other Catalinas, top of sail logo diamond is not shaded. Continuous taper to ports. End-boom sheeting angles back.

This boat was voted the best small cruiser for trailering in the *Sail* tenth-anniversary issue. There are over 11,000 Catalinas, with 70 racing fleets in 10 regions across the United States. Racing was originally restricted to main and genoa, but recent changes allow spinnakers. Racing divisions now include working jib, 150 percent genoa, and spinnaker.

There are vee berths forward which may be isolated with a privacy curtain. Space exists under the port berth for installation of a head. In the main cabin there is a dinette to port and a seat and galley to starboard. A fiberglass pop-top lifts to provide standing headroom. The galley is of molded fiberglass. It slides aft under the cockpit for stowage. A hatch on the foredeck provides light and air in the forecabin.

The cockpit is self-bailing. Trim is teak. Under the seats are two lockers. Winches are provided for the genoa sheets.

Catalina 22

Edel 665

Length: 21 ft. 10 in. LOA;
  18 ft. 2½ in. LWL
Beam: 8 ft. 2½ in.
Draft: 3 ft. 3 in.
Displacement: 2403 lbs.
Sail area: Main and jib,
  203 sq. ft.
Hull: FRP

Spars: Anodized aluminum
Berths: 4
Engine: Outboard
Head: Optional, recirculating
Galley: 1-burner propane
Water: Manual
Rating: None
Designer: Not stated

Very wide beam. Single, long portlight. Straight bow. Two blocks on boom. In port, may have pop-top.

The Edel was designed in Europe, where it was awarded "Boat of the Year" at the Paris Boat Show. While it is certainly capable of cruising, many appointments suggest this boat for daysailing and racing. There is a lifting eye built into the keel for dry-sailing, and she may be trailered.

A berth in the peak, a convertible settee, and a quarter berth sleep four. The portlights are fixed, but there is a hatch in the foredeck. A hydraulic pop-top is available for additional headroom. Woodwork is mahogany.

On deck there are jiffy reefing, a vang, a downhaul, genoa tracks and winches, and a traveler for the main. The cockpit has seat and coaming stowage. Some of the options are spinnaker gear, recirculating toilet, lift-up top, and winches.

Edel 665

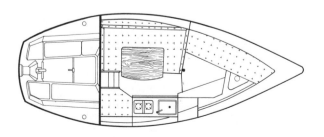

Alberg 22

Length: 22 ft. LOA; 16 ft. LWL
Beam: 7 ft.
Draft: 3 ft. 1 in.
Displacement: 3200 lbs.
Sail area: Main, 114 sq. ft.; jib,
   85 sq. ft.; genoa, 182 sq. ft.
Hull: FRP
Spars: Aluminum

Berths: 4
Engine: Outboard
Head: Standard
Galley: Butane
Water: 5 gals.
Rating: None
Designer: Carl Alberg

Masthead rig. Coamings. Two equal-size ports. Counter.

The 22 is a small boat which, because of its weight and full keel, feels and handles like a much larger boat. The masthead rig has a large sail plan.

There is a double berth forward and two quarter berths. In the galley there is a sink and a pump; the ice box is removable. Cabin trim is teak.

On deck are genoa tracks and fairleads and genoa turning blocks leading to winches. Halyards are internal and lead to two winches mounted on the cabin roof. There is jiffy reefing and a Cunningham. Taffrail and handrails are teak. There is an outboard well suitable for a five- or six-horsepower motor and lazarette storage for a five-gallon gasoline tank.

Alberg 22

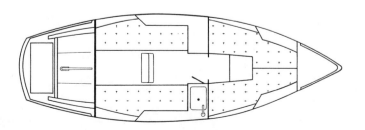

Marshall 22

Length: 22 ft. 2 in. LOA;
21 ft. 4 in. LWL
Beam: 10 ft. 2 in.
Draft: 3 ft.
Displacement: 5660 lbs.
Sail area: Cat main, 388 sq. ft.;
sloop main, 338 sq. ft.; sloop
jib, 100 sq. ft.
Hull: FRP

Spars: Aluminum
Berths: 4
Engine: Yanmar 21 HP
Fuel: Diesel, 19 gals.
Head: Marine
Galley: Optional, has sink
Water: 20 gals.
Rating: None
Designer: Breckenridge Marshall

Gaff-rig cat. Distinctive rudder shape. Mast hoops. May be a sloop, with long bowsprit and bobstay. Round bottom.

A cruising size of the traditional Cape Cod catboat, the 22 is also available as a sloop.

The port settee extends into the forepeak, and has storage below and behind. The head is to starboard and there is an opening hatch above. In the main cabin the galley is to port and the dropleaf table rests on the centerboard trunk. A second locker is in front of the starboard berth, which has the water tank below. (Photographs show a hanging locker forward of the galley and a counter extension that slides out from below the galley to rest on the centerboard trunk.) There are two ports in the forecabin and four in the main.

Rigging for this cat is simple, with only a forestay for the mast and a mainsheet. The boom and gaff are grooved for bolt ropes while the mast has hoops. A portion of the cockpit sole is raised to accommodate the engine. There is wheel steering. Standard equipment supplied includes a boat hook, foghorn, fire extinguisher, and life preservers.

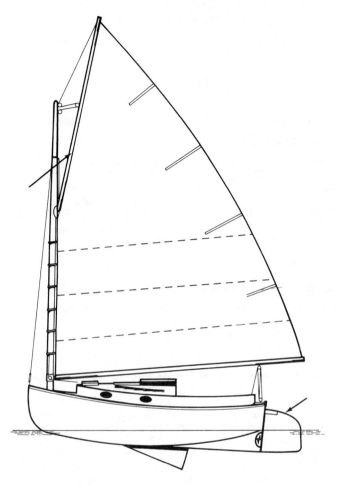

Marshall 22

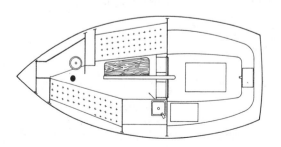

Cape Dory 22

Length: 22 ft. 4 in. LOA;
16 ft. 3 in. LWL
Beam: 7 ft. 4 in.
Draft: 3 ft.
Displacement: 3200 lbs.
Sail area: Main, 114 sq. ft.; jib,
102.25 sq. ft.; genoa, 183 sq.
ft.
Hull: FRP

Spars: Aluminum
Berths: 4
Engine: Yanmar 7½ HP
Fuel: Diesel, 13 gals.
Head: Optional, marine
Galley: 2-burner alcohol
Water: 24 gals.
Rating: PHRF 265 average
Designer: Carl Alberg

Masthead rig. End-boom sheeting. Long bow, short counter.

Cape Dory and Carl Alberg believe in full-keel design, strongly built. The rudder is attached directly to the keel, and the propeller is protected. The hull is beamy and the rig high-aspect. Lines are traditional.

There are berths for four, with a curtain giving some privacy between the main cabin and the vee berths. A marine toilet can be installed forward, under the vee-berth filler. The galley is split, with the sink and portable ice chest to port and the stove starboard. Counter tops are hinged. A hatch opens over the vee berth and there are four opening bronze ports. Joinery is teak, and the sole is teak and holly. An inboard diesel comes with the D model and is located behind the companionway ladder.

On the balsa-core deck rub strakes, taffrails, coamings, drop boards, and companionway framing are teak. There are fuel tank, sail, and lazarette lockers. The anchor rode has a roller and there are genoa tracks. The main is roller reefing and there are a topping lift and an adjustable outhaul.

Cape Dory 22

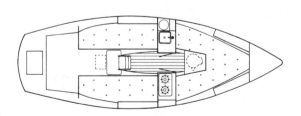

Achilles 24

Length: 23 ft. 9 in. LOA;
   20 ft. LWL
Beam: 7 ft. 1½ in.
Draft: 3 ft. 9 in. (fin keel)
Displacement: 2600 lbs.
Sail area: Main and 100%
   foretriangle, 210 sq. ft.
Hull: FRP

Spars: Aluminum
Berths: 4
Engine: Outboard
Head: Chemical
Galley: 2-burner alcohol
Water: 20 gals.
Rating: None
Designer: C. J. Butler

Single, very long window. Moderate beam and wetted-surface area. May have triple keel.

The Achilles was designed in England, where tides are extreme. The English like triple keels, so that when the tide goes out the boat will sit high and dry; Achilles has an optional triple keel. The manufacturer claims there is only a 3 percent drop in performance as opposed to the bulb-fin keel. Sail area is moderate.

There are two quarter berths and a vee berth. The chemical head is under the forward cushion of the latter. Ahead of the saloon the galley is split, with the double sink to port and the two-burner stove to starboard. Trim is teak.

The mast is stepped on the coach roof and does not penetrate the cabin. Jib/genoa tracks, two halyards, and two sheet winches are shown on the deck plan. In the forepeak there is a self-draining anchor well. All exterior timber is oiled teak. There are two seat lockers in the cockpit, and two lazarette storage compartments. An outboard is standard, but an inboard can be fitted beneath the cockpit sole.

Achilles 24

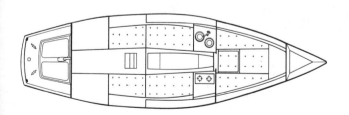

Seidelmann 245

Length: 24 ft. 2 in. LOA;
  20 ft. 6 in. LWL
Beam: 8 ft.
Draft: 4 ft. 5 in.
Displacement: 3000 lbs.
Sail area: Main and jib, 276 sq.
  ft. total
Hull: FRP
Spars: Aluminum

Berths: 4
Engine: Outboard
Head: Portable chemical
Galley: 1-burner alcohol
Water: 10 gals.
Rating: D–PN none. (Seidelmann
  25 is 92.0)
Designer: Bob Seidelmann

Rudder on transom. Straight bow. Seven-eighths rig. Sheer virtually straight.

This is a tall rig. The mainsail luff is 27 ft; the foot, 9.75 ft. The foretriangle base is 10.75 ft. and the height 27 ft. The Seidelmann, however, is meant to be trailered, so the mast is stepped in a tabernacle and there is a bow eye. With centerboard up, the draft is 1 ft. 11 in.

The galley has the stove to starboard, the sink to port, and the ice box under the ladder. Water tank loads from on deck. Both main-cabin berths have stowage under. The trim is teak; the sole, holly and teak. The table folds away against the bulkhead. Two of the four ports open. The chemical head is private, with a door. Forward are two vee berths with a hatch overhead.

Pulpits and liferails are standard. On-deck storage includes a cockpit locker and an anchor locker. The jib has track-mounted blocks and two winches. The halyard winch is mounted on deck. Outhaul and reef lines are internal, as are the halyards.

Seidelmann 245

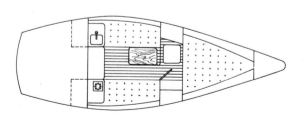

Capri 25

Length: 24 ft. 7 in. LOA;
19 ft. 2 in. LWL
Beam: 9 ft. 2 in.
Draft: 4 ft. 2 in.
Displacement: 2785 lbs.
Sail area: Main and 100%
foretriangle, 276 sq. ft.
Hull: FRP

Spars: Aluminum
Berths: 4
Head: Chemical
Galley: Sink, ice box
Water: Not stated
Rating: D–PN 83.6 average;
PHRF 169 average
Designer: Frank Butler

Masthead rig. Spoon bow. Vertical transom. Sheer almost straight.

This is a tall rig, with an aspect ratio of about 3 to 1. She is medium stiff, with a ballast/displacement ratio of 32 percent. The Capri is intended as a one-design racer.

The main cabin has two berths, the sink, and an ice box under the ladder. There is no table shown. Forward, the port berth extends over the chemical head and a storage locker. While the bulkhead is not full height, it can be extended for privacy. There is storage under the port and starboard settees in the main cabin.

The cockpit is split level, and the traveler extends across just in front of the tiller steering. There are lockers under both seats. Two winches are provided here, and two on the cabin roof for the halyards. Spinnakers are used, as is a boom vang.

Capri 25

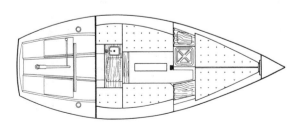

Bayfield 25

Length: 25 ft. LOA;
19 ft. 8 in. LWL
Beam: 8 ft.
Draft: 2 ft. 11 in.
Displacement: 3500 lbs.
Sail area: Total, 240 sq. ft.
Hull: FRP, balsa core
Spars: Aluminum
Berths: 4

Engine: 7.5 HP
Fuel: Diesel, 11.1 gals.
Head: Standard
Galley: 2-burner alcohol
Water: 20 gals.
Rating: D–PN 97.0 suspect;
PHRF 270
Designer: H. Ted Gozzard

Cutter, clipper bow. Slight counter. Hull, except cabin, similar to larger Bayfield 32. Masthead rig.

Bayfield calls this a pocket cruiser. Lines are traditional. Bayfield ornamentation is used.

All berths have storage under. Forward, there is a vee berth with optional filler. The starboard berth runs forward from the main cabin under a vanity and locker. The head is to port and has a 20-gallon holding tank. In the main cabin there are two settee berths, with lockers over and under. The alcohol stove stores under the starboard berth. Fresh water has a manual pump. Aft of the port berth is a hanging locker.

Above there are three lockers in the cockpit, and an anchor locker forward. Halyards are internal; the four-part mainsheet leads to a traveler; and there are slab reefing and a topping lift. Two single-speed cockpit winches are standard, a halyard winch is optional. There is tiller steering, with a wheel optional. The genoa track is aluminum and all deck trim is teak.

Bayfield 25

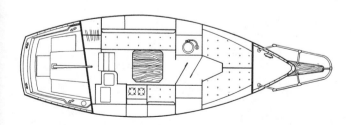

Merit 25

Length: 25 ft. LOA;
  20 ft. 6 in. LWL
Beam: 8 ft.
Draft: 4 ft.
Displacement: 3000 lbs.
Sail area: Main and jib, 285 sq.
  ft.
Hull: FRP
Spars: Aluminum

Berths: 4
Engine: Outboard
Head: Portable
Galley: Stove optional
Water: 5 gals.
Rating: PHRF 170 average;
  D–PN 84.0 suspect
Designer: Paul Yates

Fifteen-sixteenths rig. Smoked acrylic over the windows. Straight bow. Split backstay. Long slope from cabin roof to foredeck.

The accent is on racing rather than cruising. Wetted surface is low, lines aft are flat, the keel and rudder are high aspect. She planes.

To save space, the main-cabin berths extend slightly under the cockpit. Both have stowage under. The ice box serves as the companionway ladder. Forward of the berths a curtain gives privacy to the portable head. A sink and the storage for the galley are opposite. There is a steel mast support splitting the foot of the vee berth which has storage beneath. A hatch is above. Trim is teak.

There are lots of controls above. Two halyards, the spinnaker pole lift, and the outhaul are internal. There is an internal reefing system. The mainsheet is 4:1 and there are a mid-cockpit traveler and a Cunningham as well as a vang. The split backstay has a 4:1 adjuster. Jib tracks lead to two cockpit winches, and two winches on the cabin roof serve the halyards. In the cockpit are two lockers. Steering is tiller.

Merit 25

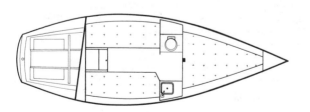

Dufour 1800

Length: 25.09 ft. LOA;
  22 ft. LWL
Beam: 8.9 ft.
Draft: 4.27 ft.
Displacement: 3968 lbs.
Sail area: Main, 152.9 sq. ft.; jib,
  100.1 sq. ft.; storm jib, 35.5
  sq. ft.
Hull: FRP
Spars: Aluminum

Berths: 4
Engine: Outboard well, or Volvo
  MD–5A
Fuel: Diesel, 6 gals.
Head: Chemical; marine optional
Galley: 2-burner
Water: 25.1 gal.
Rating: None
Designer: Laurent Cordelle-
  Dufour

Seven-eighths rig. Very high aspect ratio—over 3 to 1. One port well aft. Backstay adjustment tackle.

Dufour built France 3 and builds the Dufour 24, 27–1, and 31. The boats are fairly heavily built and are moderate displacement. Over 1000 boats have been built in four years. The wetted surface is low, but the waterline length is 88 percent of LOA.

Below, there are four berths. In the main cabin the port berth extends back under a navigation table. The starboard berth extends forward under the basin of the head. The dinette table can be stored under the starboard berth or may be moved into the cockpit. There is storage behind both berths and above and below the galley. The cross-boat head is private and has a hanging locker behind the WC. The fo'c'sle is lit and ventilated by a hatch. The bunk is full width.

There are tracks for both the main sheet and the jib. One winch serves the main and jib halyards and there are two more for jib sheets. The tiller has an extension. There are two seat lockers in the cockpit, which lock. A boom vang and four-part tackle on the backstay are standard.

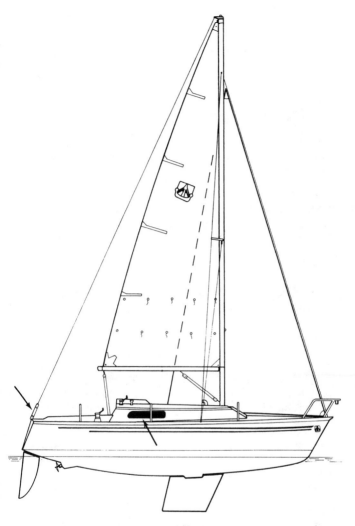

Dufour 1800

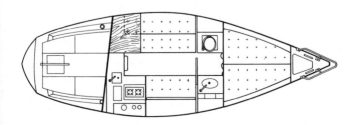

Cal 25

Length: 25 ft. 3 in. LOA;
  22 ft. LWL
Beam: 9 ft.
Draft: 4 ft. 6 in.
Displacement: 4500 lbs.
Sail area: Main, 133 sq. ft.;
  100% foretriangle, 181.5 sq. ft.
Hull: FRP
Spars: Painted aluminum
Berths: 5

Engine: Optional Universal
  11 HP
Fuel: Diesel, 12.5 gals.
Head: Chemical, marine optional
Galley: 2-burner alcohol optional
Water: 22 gal.
Rating: D–PN 90.0; PHRF 222
  average
Designer: William Lapworth

If boat is heeled, look for rudder mounting. Long slope to coach roof.

Bill Lapworth designs boats with long waterlines, spade rudders, and moderate to light displacement. The result is a compromise between a cruiser and a racer. There is a short keel option.

The galley spans the hull. To port is the stainless sink and the 4.5-cubic-foot ice box. The two-burner stove stores under the cockpit, sliding out for use. A counter extension also stores. The quarter berth could possibly be used as a double. Amidships the large dinette between two settee berths folds against the bulkhead when not in use. The head, forward of a sliding teak door, has a chemical toilet with a marine head as an option. There is a hanging locker and a vanity. The vee berth has a filler inset. Teak trim is used throughout. Ventilation is through a flush forward hatch and two opening ports in the head. Main cabin ports are fixed.

Halyards are internal, as are the double reef and outhaul. There are a topping lift and a boom vang, a traveler for the main, tracks for the jib and genoa, a winch for the halyard, and two genoa winches. A locker in the peak holds the anchor. The tiller, handrails, and slides for the hatch are teak.

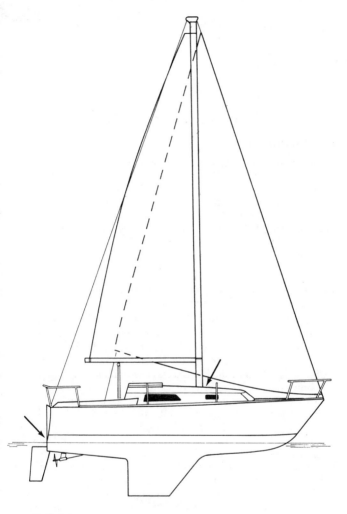

Cal 25

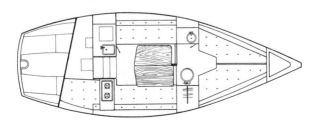

Beachcomber 25

Length: 25 ft. 4 in. LOA;
25 ft. 3 in. LWL
Beam: 8 ft.
Draft: 1 ft. 3 in. (board up)
Displacement: 5300 lbs.
Sail area: Main, 182 sq. ft.;
mizzen, 93 sq. ft.
Hull: FRP
Spars: Aluminum

Berths: 4
Engine: Optional, inboard or
outboard
Fuel: Diesel, 19 gals. (inboard)
Head: Portable
Galley: 2-burner alcohol
Water: 20 gal.
Rating: None
Designer: Walter Scott

*Cat-ketch or sloop. Plumb bow. High freeboard. Cat-ketch has
wishbone booms, roller-furling masts.*

The Beachcomber may be purchased either as a cat-ketch or as
a sloop. Designed in Florida and with 1400 lbs. of ballast in
the grounding shoe, it is intended to be extremely shallow
draft. Still, you'll have to put the board down for windward
work. Sails are controlled by sheet, clew outhaul, and topping
lifts only; there is no traveler or vang.

Below, to port there is a quarter berth. Starboard is an
L-shaped settee that converts to a berth. No masts below—they
both mount on the coach roof. The galley and a hanging locker
are across. The head has a teak door, storage space, and ventilation. Another hanging locker is to port. In the bow are vee
berths and a chain locker which may be reached from inside.

Both masts rotate, with sail-furling lines leading to the cockpit. The centerboard has four-part tackle, and it and the two-
part sheets lead to the cockpit. Masts are unstayed. There are
cockpit lockers, and a bimini top is optional.

Beachcomber 25

Parker Dawson 26

Length: 25 ft. 7 in. LOA;
  22 ft. 2 in. LWL
Beam: 8 ft.
Draft: 5 ft. 4 in.
Displacement: 5700 lbs.
Sail area: Total, 271 sq. ft.
Hull: FRP
Spars: Aluminum
Berths: 5

Engine: Outboard; inboard
  Yanmar 7.5 HP optional
Fuel: Diesel, 15 gals. (inboard)
Head: Portable standard;
  additional marine optional
Galley: 2-burner alcohol
Water: 25 gals.
Rating: None
Designer: Bob Finch

Aft cabin and rudder distinctive.

Parker Dawsons have crossed the Atlantic—singlehanded. The two cabins are unusual on a boat of this size, and since there is an optional cockpit tent, a third cabin is possible. The iron swing keel has a 50:1 worm gear control, and draft can be reduced to 1 ft. 8 in. The rudder is also adjustable and raises and lowers inside an aluminum frame to one of three draft settings.

The aft cabin has two bunks, its own sink, and space for either the portable head or a marine installation. It is reached from the cockpit. In the main cabin the galley is to port. The forward cabin has two berths, and since there are no bulkheads, it is part of the main cabin. To starboard, the head is under the settee, and when the table is removed, this settee makes into a berth. The four ports in the forward cabin are fixed. In the aft cabin, two are fixed and one opens.

The mast step is on the cabin trunk, and is hinged. Jiffy reefing is provided on the boom. Two winches are provided for sheets; one, for the jib halyard. There is storage for the anchor rode and a port-side cockpit seat locker.

**Parker
Dawson 26**

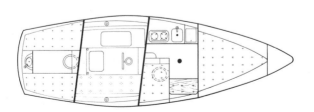

Freedom 25

Length: 25 ft. 8 in. LOA;
  20 ft. LWL
Beam: 8 ft. 6 in.
Draft: 4 ft. 6 in.
Displacement: 2900 lbs.
Sail area: 300 sq. ft.
Hull: FRP
Spars: Carbon fiber

Berths: 4
Engine: Optional diesel
Head: Standard
Galley: 2-burner
Water: Not stated
Rating: PHRF 182 average
Designer: Garry Hoyt

Catboat. Mast appears heavy. Full battens. Spinnaker pole fixed to bow pulpit, not mast.

This cat has distinctly modern lines, with a fin keel, flat sections aft, and a transom-mounted spade rudder. The mast is not stayed and the main is fully battened. This Freedom is designed to be sailed from the cockpit, singlehanded.

Below deck, colors are light, with ash and white predominating. The sole is teak and holly. There are two main-cabin berths, which extend under the cockpit; a private head; and a small galley. Forward are vee berths. A portable cooler is used for the ice chest.

The mast is designed as an airfoil, and rotates. You furl the main by dropping it into a cradle formed by lazy jacks, at which time the full battens fold somewhat like a venetian blind. The spinnaker pole rides through a sleeve mounted on the pulpit. When not in use it slides to one side and rotates back with one end on deck. In use, the spinnaker is raised from the cockpit. Since most of the load is taken by the "gun mount" fixing it to the pulpit, control of the sheet and guy does not require a winch.

Freedom 25

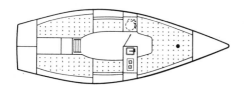

Pearson 26

Length: 26 ft. 1½ in. LOA;
   21 ft. 8 in. LWL
Beam: 8 ft. 8¼ in.
Draft: 4 ft.
Displacement: 5400 lbs.
Sail area: Main, 138 sq. ft.;
   100% foretriangle, 183 sq. ft.
Hull: FRP
Spars: Aluminum

Berths: 5
Engine: Outboard
Head: Optional, portable
Galley: Stove optional
Water: 22 gals.
Rating: PHRF 210 average;
   D–PN 89.1
Designer: William Shaw

Straight bow, vertical transom. Aft port is large. Vertical cabin roof aft leads to cockpit. No coaming.

This Pearson was designed in 1970 and has sold very well. Note how the rudder is cut away and the aft-slanting keel. Ballast/displacement ratio is 40 percent. Waterline is 83 percent of overall length.

A double folding door gives the forepeak privacy. There is a double berth and under-berth storage. A translucent hatch overhead gives light and air. Aft, the optional, portable WC is to port with a hanging locker opposite. A solid door isolates this area from the main cabin. There is a dinette with seats facing fore and aft which converts to a double berth. The settee opposite becomes a single. The galley lies across the hull with the sink to port, the optional stove to starboard, and the ice chest under the ladder.

In the cockpit there are two under-seat lockers and a well in the transom for the outboard. A separate locker holds the gas tank. There is also storage for the anchor in the forepeak. The main cabin has four fixed ports. The backstay is adjustable and there are two winches for sheeting and a topping lift. Genoa tracks are on the rail.

Pearson 26

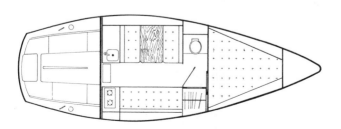

Yamaha 26

Length: 26 ft. 2 in. LOA;
21 ft. LWL
Beam: 9 ft. 2 in.
Draft: 5 ft. 1 in.
Displacement: 4349 lbs.
Sail area: Main and 100%
foretriangle, 330.6 sq. ft.
Hull: FRP
Spars: Aluminum
Berths: 3–5

Engine: Yanmar 7.5 HP
Fuel: Diesel, 6.6 gals.
Head: Standard
Galley: 1-burner
Water: 18.5 gals.
Rating: IOR 19.2 approximate;
PHRF for Yamaha 25 about
217
Designer: Yamaha

Stern distinctive, with reverse curve to counter and unusual transom curve. Beam is midships. Bow is straight. Long slope to cabin roof. Small foretriangle.

Many aspects of the Yamaha 26 are unusual, and it almost appears that the designers decided to throw out all traditional ideas and design for function only.

The vee berth forward is full width over the water tank, and must be considered standard. The head, to starboard, is also normal. In the main cabin, the stove stores in the port quarter berth and slides out for use. Seat backs can be used to convert the entire cabin into one big berth that is level with the quarter berths, so it is difficult to say just how many can sleep aboard. There is a hanging locker and fresh- and salt-water footpumps. A small table over the starboard seat can be used as a chart table and stowed when not in use.

The cockpit is large, although the traveler crosses it. There is a notch in the transom which accepts a permanently mounted swimming ladder. Two primary and two secondary winches are outboard of the coaming, and there are two multipurpose winches on the coach roof. The genoa tracks are inboard and recessed. Spinnaker gear is standard.

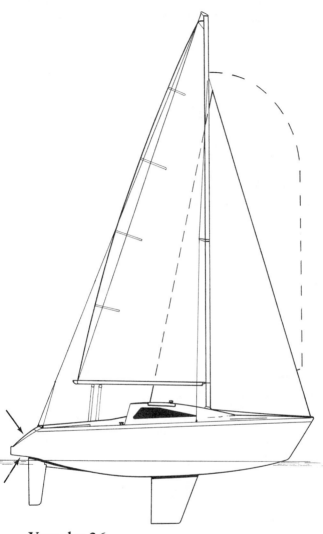

Yamaha 26

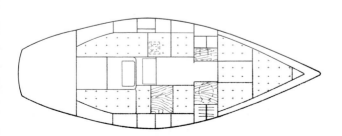

Tanzer 26

Length: 26 ft. 4 in. LOA;
22 ft. 6 in. LWL
Beam: 8 ft. 8 in.
Draft: 3 ft. 10 in.
Displacement: 4350 lbs.
Sail area: Main, 143 sq. ft.; jib,
117 sq. ft.; 165% genoa, 265
sq. ft.; spinnaker, 500 sq. ft.
Hull: FRP
Spars: Aluminum

Berths: 5
Engine: Outboard; inboard
optional
Fuel: 12 gals. (inboard)
Head: Portable or marine
Galley: 2-burner alcohol
Water: 15 gals.
Rating: PHRF 216 average for
inboard model
Designer: Johann Tanzer

Transom-mounted rudder. Split backstay. Self-tacking jib. Single long port.

This is a combination boat, for racing or cruising. The cockpit is large, so she is also a daysailer, with capacity for six or more. With a fairly high ballast/displacement ratio, she can be expected to be stiff.

The forward cabin has a double berth and a hatch above. It is separated from the head by a folding door. The head is to port, with a hanging locker; it, in turn, is separated from the main cabin by a door. The large settee converts to a double, and there is a quarter berth in the main cabin. The table folds against the bulkhead for stowage. The galley is to starboard.

The cockpit is self-bailing and has a sail locker and a locker for the outboard gas tank. There is also an anchor locker. The mast is mounted on the cabin roof and the step is hinged. Tracks for the jib sheets are mounted on the toe-rail, and the traveler for the main is on the bridge deck. There is also a translucent hatch over the main cabin, and a forward-facing opening port lights and ventilates the head.

Tanzer 26

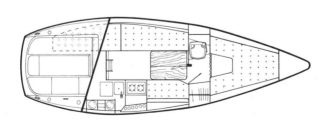

Stiletto

Length: 26 ft. 10 in. LOA;
   24 ft. LWL
Beam: 13 ft. 10 in.
Draft: 4 ft.
Displacement: 1100 lbs.
Sail area: Main, 230 sq. ft.; jib,
   106 sq. ft.; genoa, 159 sq. ft.;
   spinnaker, 750 sq. ft.
Hull: FRP and honeycomb

Spars: Coated aluminum
Berths: 4
Engine: Outboard
Head: Portable
Galley: Space and storage
   allocated
Water: 25 gals.
Designer: Bill Higgins

*Cruising catamaran. Full-length battens and very full roach.
Cabin windows unusual.*

Stiletto is available in either a cruising or a racing configuration. The racing version is heavier and has additional sails, sheet winches, and a 6:1 downhaul. A spinnaker package and pivoting centerboards are available for either model.

The starboard hull contains a double berth, the galley, and storage. Both hulls have a Lexan skylight and a forward hatch for light and ventilation. The port hull also has a double berth, and to give more space a tent is available for complete enclosure of the bridge deck. Access to either hull is through the skylights, which slide forward. The head is in the port hull.

The headsails may be roller furling. Jiffy reefing, a halyard winch, sheet winches, and a small cruising mainsail are also optional. Stiletto breaks down for trailering. The bridge deck and mast can be removed and the hulls telescope to a beam of 7 ft. 11½ in.

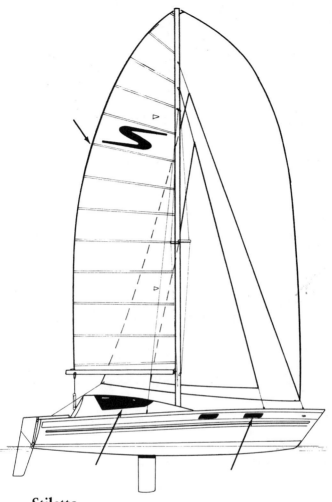

Stiletto

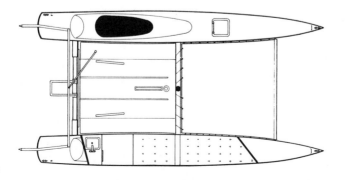

Hotfoot 27

Length: 27 ft. LOA; 22 ft. LWL
Beam: 9 ft. 4 in.
Draft: 5 ft. 6 in.
Displacement: 3600 lbs.
Sail area: Main and jib, 346 sq.
   ft. total
Hull: FRP, foam core
Spars: Aluminum

Berths: 4
Engine: Outboard
Head: Chemical
Galley: 1-burner alcohol
Water: 12 gals.
Rating: None
Designer: Douglas Hemphill

Single trapezoidal port. Note shape of rudder. Bent mast. Running backstays.

The Hotfoot is a new design which is selling well in Victoria, BC and starting to move south. Keel and rudder are both deep to assist to windward, often a problem with boats this light. The running backstays are unusual. The manufacturers feel that they are needed for shaping the sail, not for keeping the rig up.

In the main cabin, there are two berths both of which extend aft. To starboard, the galley with stove and sink is kept under the cockpit and slides forward for use. On the opposite side, the chart table is stored the same way. The head and the vee berths are forward of the bulkhead. The head is on the port side.

Some of the standard sailing equipment, such as all spinnaker gear, the outboard-motor bracket, and a compass, are unusual, as is the headfoil. There are two primary winches and two halyard winches. An outboard can be mounted in the starboard lazarette. When it is not in use, the motor swings up and a hinged flap covers the hull opening. The outhaul is internal and 4:1. The vang is 8:1 and has double leads, and the backstay is adjustable. All controls lead to the cockpit.

Hotfoot 27

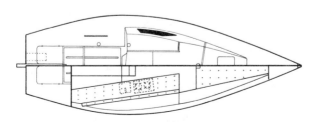

Express

Length: 27 ft. 3 in. LOA;
23 ft. 9 in. LWL
Beam: 8 ft. 1 in.
Draft: 4 ft. 6 in.
Displacement: 2450 lbs.
Sail area: Main and jib, 276 sq.
ft. total
Hull: Vinylester, S-glass, foam,
balsa core

Spars: Hard-coated aluminum
Berths: 4
Engine: Outboard
Head: Portable
Galley: Available
Water: Not stated
Rating: PHRF 130 average
Designer: Carl Schumacher

*Reverse sheer. Aspect ratio almost 3 to 1. Reverse transom.
Flare forward.*

The Express is designed for racing and perhaps for overnighting. The bow is fine, but there is a flare forward to prevent digging in downwind. The waterline is long. V-sections allow for planing; and because this is an ultra-light-displacement boat, the large rudder helps prevent skittering.

Below, accommodations are for the racing crew of four. There is a vee berth forward with chemical toilet beneath. Aft of the full bulkhead are a navigation table and the galley. The seats in the main cabin are not convertible to berths, but two additional quarter berths are aft. The sole is teak and holly.

All lines lead to the cockpit. There is lots of mechanical advantage with the mainsheet 4:1, traveler 2:1, outhaul 4:1, backstay 16:1, vang 12:1, and Cunningham 3:1. There are two single-speed winches. A good part of the rig design evolved from these winches, as most of the power is intended to be in the main, where it can be dumped quickly. There is a foredeck hatch.

Express

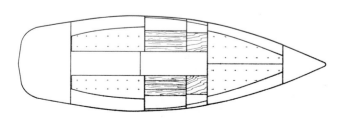

Sea Sprite 27

Length: 27 ft. 11 in. LOA;
  20 ft. LWL
Beam: 8 ft. 10 in.
Draft: 4 ft. 3 in.
Displacement: 7600 lbs.
Sail area: Main, 183 sq. ft.; jib,
  149 sq. ft.; 150% genoa, 233
  sq. ft.; spinnaker, 540 sq. ft.
Hull: FRP

Spars: Anodized aluminum
Berths: 5
Engine: Universal 11 HP
Fuel: Diesel, 12 gals.
Head: Standard, shower
Galley: 2-burner alcohol
Water: 45 gals.
Rating: PHRF 232 average
Designer: A. E. Luders, Jr.

Seven-eighths rig. End-boom sheeting. High bow. Note transom.

There are three Sea Sprites. The others are the 23 and the 34. Luders designed the 34, Carl Alberg, the 23. All are displacement boats and all have a full keel.

The vee berth occupies most of the forward cabin, but there is storage. The head lies across the boat and has a hanging locker, storage locker, and optional pressure water. In the main cabin the double berth is to starboard. Shelves are behind both berths. At the companionway the stove and sink are to port; the ice box doubles as a table for navigation. Pressure water is also available for the galley. Bulkheads and trim are teak. There is a translucent forward hatch and four opening ports. A second midships hatch is also an option.

Deck trim, handrails, toe-rails, coamings, and taffrail are teak. The traveler is just aft the cockpit and there are genoa tracks. The boom has jiffy reefing and a topping lift. One winch is mounted on the mast and two for genoas at the cockpit. The tiller is laminated wood. Options include a vang, spinnaker gear, main halyard winch, wheel steering, and roller-furling gear.

Sea Sprite 27

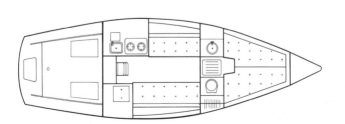

Albin Cumulus

Length: 28 ft. 1 in. LOA;
  22 ft. 3 in. LWL
Beam: 9 ft. 3 in.
Draft: 5 ft. 3 in.
Displacement: 7055 lbs.
Sail area: Main, 172 sq. ft.; jib,
  193 sq. ft.; genoa, 285 sq. ft.;
  spinnaker, 645 sq. ft.
Hull: FRP
Spars: Polyurethane-coated
  aluminum

Berths: 5
Engine: Yanmar 12 HP
Fuel: Diesel, 9.24 gals.
Head: Standard
Galley: 3-burner alcohol
Water: 25 gals.
Rating: PHRF 197 average
Designer: Peter Norlin

*Straight bow. Reverse transom, with rudder following same
line. Very high-aspect main; ⅞ rig.*

Cumulus has a sharp bow, short keel, and rudder mounted
well aft.

The companionway leads directly into the galley. To con-
serve space, the galley work area is behind the stairs. To starboard is a quarter berth. Just forward is the saloon. Settees on
both sides double as bunks, and the table folds for passageway.
The head crosses the boat, with a hanging locker to port. Forward is a vee berth and a well for foresails, anchors, or fenders. A bulkhead with door is just forward of the saloon. There
are 24 lockers, drawers, and storage areas. Finish is teak. There
is an acrylic hatch over the vee berths and two ventilators.

The deck has a nonslip surface and bow and stern pulpits.
The spinnaker, main, and genoa halyards are internal, and lead
to jam cleats and two winches. There are also two self-tailing
primary winches. Both the mainsheet and the boom vang are
four-part. The spinnaker has a track and car, as does the
genoa. There is jiffy reefing with a dual track. A tiller is used.
The cockpit has compartments for sheets and winch handles,
and also has two storage lockers.

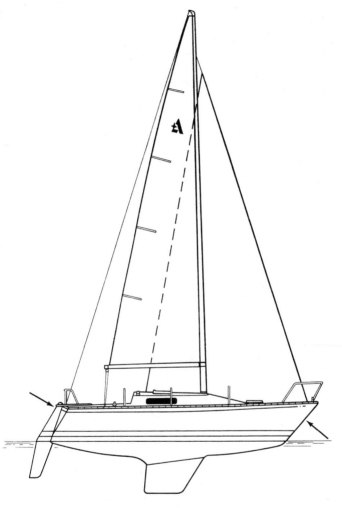

Albin Cumulus

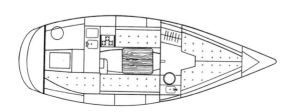

Sabre 28

Length: 28 ft. 5 in. LOA;
22 ft. 10 in. LWL
Beam: 9 ft. 2 in.
Draft: 4 ft. 8 in. (standard) or
3 ft. 10 in. (shoal)
Displacement: 7800 lbs.
Sail area: main, 168 sq. ft.; jib,
234 sq. ft.; 150% genoa, 351
sq. ft.
Hull: FRP

Spars: Aluminum
Berths: 6
Engine: Westerbeke 13 HP
Fuel: Diesel, 20 gals.
Head: Standard
Galley: 2-burner alcohol
Water: 20 gals.
Rating: D–N 92.1 suspect;
PHRF 200 average
Designer: Sabre Design Team

Straight bow, vertical stern. Ports generally increase in size moving aft. Sheeting is to coach roof. Normal sheer.

A modern performance cruiser, Sabre has low wetted surface and a fin keel. A shoal-draft model is offered.

There are berths for two in the forecabin, a single and a double to port in the main cabin, and a quarter berth. Storage in the bow cabin is in two drawers, two lockers, and storage bins. The head has a hanging locker. The forecabin has a translucent hatch, the head has a Dorade (self-draining) ventilator. A door separates the forecabin from the head. The table folds against the bulkhead. In the galley the stove is recessed. A cutting board fits above. Galley stowage is in four drawers and lockers and a cabinet.

The cockpit is over seven feet long. There are two lockers and a storage bin. There is a control pedestal with wheel. Teak is used for toe-rails, handrails, coaming caps, and other trim. There is a foredeck anchor well. In addition to the foredeck hatch, there are four opening ports, four fixed ports, and a hatch over the main cabin. Halyards for the main and genoa are internal and lead to mast winches. The genoa track is on the toe-rail and leads to two-speed winches on the coaming. The traveler is on the cabin top. There is a winch for the mainsheet, two sets of jiffy-reefing gear, and an internal outhaul and topping lift.

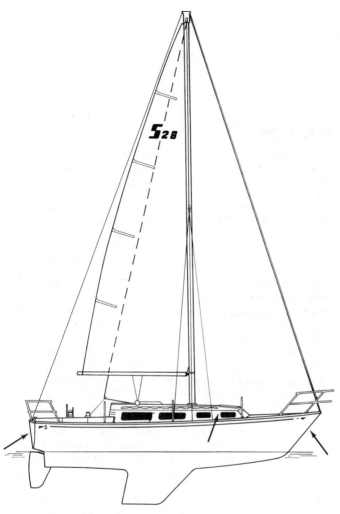

Sabre 28

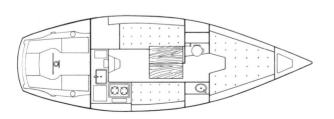

C & C 29

Length: 28 ft. 6 in. LOA;
  22 ft. 4 in. LWL
Beam: 9 ft. 6 in.
Draft: 5 ft. 3 in.
Displacement: 6500 lbs.
Sail area: Main, 176.72 sq. ft.;
  100% foretriangle, 218.5 sq. ft.
Hull: FRP
Spars: Aluminum

Berths: 6
Engine: Yanmar 12 HP
Fuel: 20 gals.
Head: Standard, shower
Galley: Variable, to be chosen
Water: 32 gals.
Rating: D–PN 88.0 suspect;
  PHRF 174 average
Designer: C & C Design Group

Aspect ratio over 3 to 1. Some counter, reverse transom. Single trapezoidal port.

The hull is long and narrow, with volume carried into the ends of the boat. Design is modern. The keel is quite large and the rudder has no skeg. Displacement is quite light.

The quarter berth, while quite large, is a single. Across, the galley has a sink and top-loading ice box. There are several stove options, and the layout can be varied. The dinette table folds against the forward bulkhead, allowing room for a double berth to port. The settee opposite is also a berth. The head has a dual-purpose door which can isolate either the entire area or just the WC. The vee berth is a double and has a hatch over.

All halyards lead back to the cabin top. The coaming around the T-shaped cockpit is high. The cockpit, with pedestal steering, has a seat locker to starboard. The traveler is recessed into the bridge deck. Genoa tracks are inboard for narrow sheeting angles. A second hatch over the main cabin, four fixed lights, and a vent admit light and air below. There is an anchor locker.

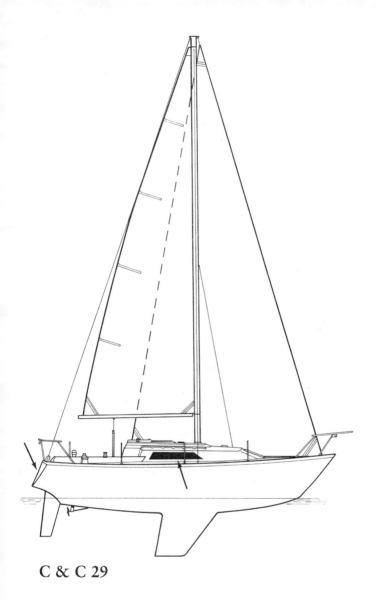

C & C 29

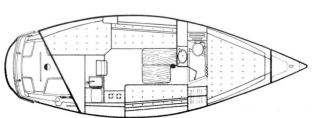

Triton

Length: 28 ft. 6 in. LOA;
20 ft. 6 in. LWL
Beam: 8 ft. 3 in.
Draft: 4 ft.
Displacement: 8400 lbs.
Sail area: Sloop with 100%
foretriangle, 362 sq. ft.; yawl
with 100% foretriangle, 400
sq. ft.
Hull: FRP

Spars: Anodized aluminum
Berths: 4
Engine: Universal Atomic 30 HP
Fuel: 15 gals.
Head: Standard
Galley: 2-burner LPG
Water: 15 gals.
Rating: D–PN 97.9 (sloop);
PHRF 246
Designer: Carl Alberg

*Yawl or sloop. Double jumper stay. Long spoon bow. Counter.
Two-level coach roof. Yawl has boomkin.*

The Triton was one of the first—if not the first—stock FRP
boats and was first built in 1950. It is popular, with more than
700 boats found all over the country. The design is displacement, with a full keel.

Cabin layout is traditional. The galley spans the hull at the
companionway. The ice box is to port and is front loading.
The sink can be covered and its top used for a chart table.
There are berths port and starboard, with shelves behind and
drawers under. Access to the forward cabin is through the
head, which can be closed off from both cabins. There are
shelves, hanging locker, and a linen locker. The vee berths in
the forward cabin have shelves behind, stowage under, and a
hatch above. Trim is teak below, mahogany above.

The cockpit has tiller steering, two seat lockers, and a lazarette. Coamings and rails are wood. There are a genoa track
and roller reefing. In the forepeak is a large anchor locker.

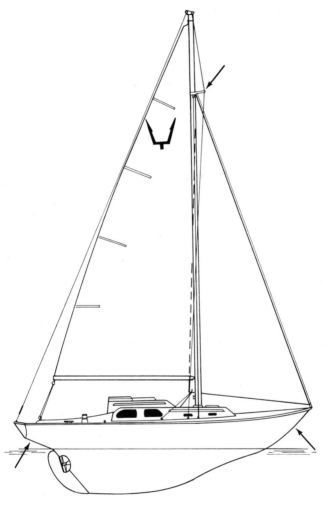

Triton

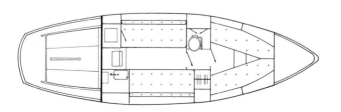

Alberg 29

Length: 29 ft. 3 in. LOA;
22 ft. 3 in. LWL
Beam: 9 ft. 1½ in.
Draft: 4 ft. 6 in.
Displacement: 9000 lbs.
Sail area: Main, 196 sq. ft.; jib,
160 sq. ft.; genoa, 326 sq. ft.
(150%), 208 sq. ft. (110%)
Hull: FRP

Spars: Aluminum
Berths: 6
Engine: 2-cylinder 15 HP
Fuel: Diesel, 15 gals.
Head: Standard
Galley: 2-burner propane
Water: 30 gals.
Rating: None
Designer: Carl Alberg

Counter. Spoon bow. Two-level cabin roof. Three-and-two porthole arrangement.

While the Alberg 29 has a full keel, it is not long. The bow and counter combine to give a short, 22-ft., 3-in. waterline. The bow is fine, the keel cut away. Bilges are firm and the wide beam gives stability. Like other full-keel boats, she tracks well. The rig is high aspect and there is a large foretriangle for windward performance.

Below, a quarter berth and navigation station are to port, with a galley to starboard. There is an insulated ice box. The main cabin has a double berth to port, a permanently mounted table, and a single berth to starboard. The head is to port with the counter and sink to starboard. The optional shower would be located amidships. Forward is the chainlocker and two vee berths. Trim is teak; the sole is teak and holly. There are six opening ports, a forward plexiglass hatch, and four fixed portholes.

On deck, the T-shaped cockpit has wheel steering. There are jib and genoa tracks and winches. Pulpit, rail stanchions, and sternrail are stainless. Cleats and chocks are bronze.

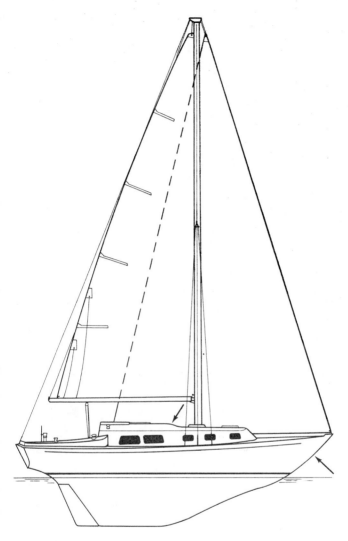

Alberg 29

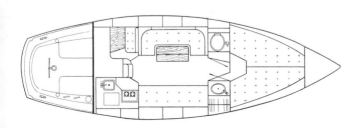

Annie

Length: 29 ft. 5 in. LOA;
24 ft. 6 in. LWL
Beam: 9 ft. 6 in.
Draft: 4 ft. 6 in.
Displacement: 11,027 lbs.
Sail area: Main, 186 sq. ft.; jib,
100% foretriangle, 279 sq. ft.;
genoa, storm, working jibs.
Hull: FRP
Spars: Aluminum

Berths: 4
Engine: Westerbeke 2 cylinder
Fuel: Diesel, 18 gals.
Head: Standard
Galley: 2-burner kerosene and
oven
Water: 37 gals.
Rating: None
Designer: C. W. Paine

Strong sheer. Cutter. High aspect ratio to main. Transom-mounted rudder. Cabin vertical fore and aft.

Annie is a heavy-displacement boat, but she has a very tall rig and much greater sail area in the jib than older boats. In addition, freeboard is low, the bow is sharp, and the keel is quite narrow. The forefoot is cut away. With the long keel and the heavy displacement, Annie should track well. The tall rig will assist in light air.

Two options are available for the cabin, both providing berths for four. As shown, the head is forward, but it can also be aft in the location of the chart table. Both configurations have a wet locker draining into the bilge. A curtain separates the two cabins. If the head is aft, the forecabin has a dresser. A stove is optional. Main cabin berths are fitted with lee boards. Installation of a shower is optional; it involves modification of the fresh-water engine cooling to obtain hot water. Cabin trim is teak. There are nine opening ports.

There are the necessary winches, a genoa track, traveler, and jiffy reefing with winch. Sails and electronics are extra.

Annie

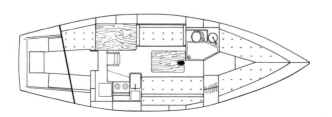

Leigh 30

Length: 29 ft. 7 in. LOA;
  23 ft. 4 in. LWL
Beam: 9 ft. 7 in.
Draft: 4 ft. 7 in.
Displacement: 9100 lbs.
Sail area: Main, 195 sq. ft.;
  100% foretriangle, 225 sq. ft.
Hull: FRP
Spars: Anodized aluminum

Berths: 4 or 5
Engine: Westerbeke 13 HP
Fuel: Diesel, 18 gals.
Head: Standard
Galley: 2-burner kerosene
Water: 37 gals.
Rating: PHRF 192
Designer: C. W. Paine

Double-ended. Curves of bow and transom remarkably similar. Cutter. Long waterline, moderate beam.

The Leigh is moderate displacement, but the ballast/displacement ratio is 48 percent and she is stiff. The high freeboard is extended by bulwarks, making for a dry boat. The keel is moderately long, the forefoot cut away, and the sail plan balanced, so she should steer easily.

The accommodation plan shown can be varied, with the most noticeable differences a balanced settee-berth arrangement in the main cabin, a smaller head, and the sink and ice box moved aft of the stove. As shown, there are berths for four and a very short berth on the port settee. Surprisingly, the starboard main-cabin berth is a pilot and the settee does not convert. The galley has a top-loading ice chest and manual water. Kerosene, relatively inflammable, is used for fuel. Opposite the head is a large hanging locker. The cabin interior is finished in mahogany, pine, and painted wood. There are lots of lockers and bins. Nine bronze ports open and there is a hatch over both the main cabin and the forecabin.

The deck plan shows a small cockpit sole surrounded by seats. There is a locker and tiller steering, with a wheel optional. Two primary winches are in the cockpit and there is a halyard winch and a sheeting winch on the cabin roof. The side decks have inboard tracks. In the bow there is a roller for the CQR anchor. Teak is used for the companionway hatch, rails, cap rails, and coamings. Pulpits and lifelines are standard.

Leigh 30

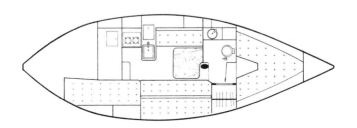

Bahama 30

Length: 29 ft. 11 in. LOA;
  24 ft. 7 in. LWL
Beam: 10 ft.
Draft: 5 ft. (standard)
  4 ft. (shoal)
Displacement: 8230 lbs.
  (standard); or 8322 lbs. (shoal)
Sail area: Main, 194 sq. ft.;
  100% foretriangle, 255 sq. ft.;
  genoa, 383 sq. ft.

Hull: FRP
Spars: Painted aluminum
Berths: 5
Engine: Volvo 13 HP
Fuel: Diesel, 20 gals.
Head: Standard, with shower
Galley: 2-burner alcohol
Water: 25 gals.
Rating: None
Designer: Bob Finch

Unusual main-boom sheeting. Clipper bow. Aspect ratio about 3 to 1. Very slight reverse transom.

This Bahama model is available in shoal draft, when to maintain stiffness it is slightly heavier. In either case the keel is quite short and the rudder is mounted well aft.

Below-decks layout is quite typical. There is a large quarter berth to starboard; the galley, with insulated ice box, is to port. The ice box can be loaded from the cockpit. Forward, the settee to starboard converts into a double berth. The head is placed across the boat and has a midships shower. There are two hanging lockers and a double berth forward. Ventilation is by four opening ports and a forward translucent hatch. The bulkheads are teak, the sole holly and teak, and the headliner vinyl.

Storage above deck is in a forepeak locker and in two under-seat lockers and a lazarette locker. Toe-rails are aluminum. The genoa track is inboard and is recessed. Main sheeting is to a traveler. There are winches for the main and jib, and two winches for the jib sheets. Slab reefing is provided. Halyards are internal and there is a topping lift.

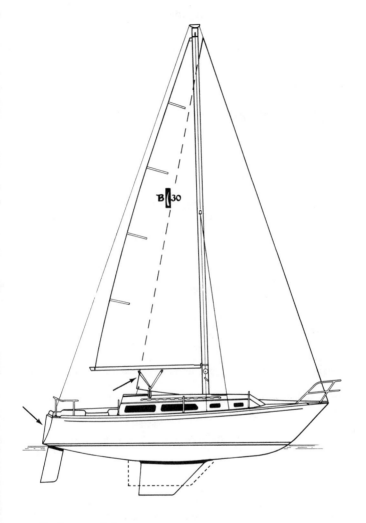

Bahama 30

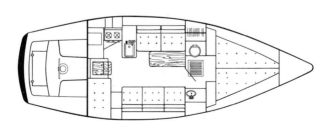

Bristol 29.9

Length: 29 ft. 11 in. LOA;
24 ft. LWL
Beam: 10 ft. 2 in.
Draft: 4 ft. 4 in.
Displacement: 8650 lbs.
Sail area: Main, 180 sq. ft.; jib,
138 sq. ft.; 150% genoa, 311
sq. ft.
Hull: FRP
Spars: Anodized aluminum

Berths: 6
Engine: Yanmar 15 HP
Fuel: 19 gals.
Head: Standard
Galley: 2-burner
Water: 63 gals.
Rating: PHRF 193 average;
D–PN 85.5 suspect
Designer: Halsey C. Herreshoff

Spoon bow. Slight reverse transom. Ventilator just forward of mast. Skylight.

The Bristol 29.9 was designed for racing under the MORC and IOR rules. The waterline is long compared to overall length. The hull is balanced, the rudder and its skeg are well aft, and the short keel has a centerboard. Beam is quite wide.

There are two cabin plans available, with the main difference lying in galley arrangement. To port of the ladder is a navigation station with a quarter berth behind. Immediately forward is a seat convertible to a double berth. The galley and another seat/berth lie to starboard. A bulkhead and door isolate the forward cabin, vee berth, head, and hanging locker. Above the central table is an operating skylight-hatch, and there is a second hatch above the forecabin. Trim is mahogany and the sole is teak.

The cockpit has wheel steering and a locker under the starboard seat. There is forepeak stowage. A traveler for the mainsheet is on the cabin roof immediately forward of the companionway hatch. There are genoa tracks and jiffy reefing. Four winches are standard.

Bristol 29.9

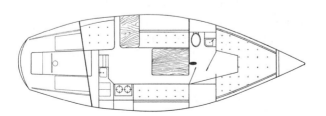

O'Day 30

Length: 29 ft. 11 in. LOA;
  25 ft. 5 in. LWL
Beam: 10 ft. 9 in.
Draft: 4 ft. 11 in. (keel); or 7 ft.
  2 in. (keel/centerboard)
Displacement: 10,150 lbs. (keel);
  or 10,600 lbs. (keel/
  centerboard)
Sail area: Main, 173 sq. ft.;
  100% foretriangle 268.3 sq. ft.
Hull: FRP

Spars: Painted aluminum
Berths: 6
Engine: Universal 16 HP
Fuel: Diesel, 26 gals.
Galley: 2-burner alcohol, oven
Water: 25 gals.
Rating: PHRF 178 average (keel);
  PHRF 177 average (keel/
  centerboard)
Designer: C. Raymond Hunt
  Associates

Maximum beam well aft. Split backstay. Straight bow. Sheeting to cockpit.

The 30 is not designed solely as a racer, but she has modern lines. The skeg-mounted rudder is high aspect. Either a fixed keel or a combination keel/centerboard is available. Beam is widest aft, just at the center of activity. With the wide beam and a ballast/displacement ratio of 39 percent she should be stiff.

The galley extends under the cockpit floor, with the counter crossing under the ladder. Fresh water is manual, but hot and cold pressure water is optional throughout the boat. To starboard there are a quarter berth and a chart table. The saloon seats five around the octagonal table, which drops for conversion into a double berth. A straight settee-berth is opposite. Forward is the head with molded sink and hand-held shower. The hanging locker is to port and has louvered doors. With a filler, the vee berths become a double. All berths have storage bins beneath.

There are two halyard winches on the mast. Two more are on the cockpit coaming for genoa sheets, and two more will be required for the spinnaker. The main is sheeted to a traveler on the bridge deck and a vang is available. Teak is used for the cap and handrails. There are two fixed portlights for the vee berth and four fixed and four opening ones elsewhere.

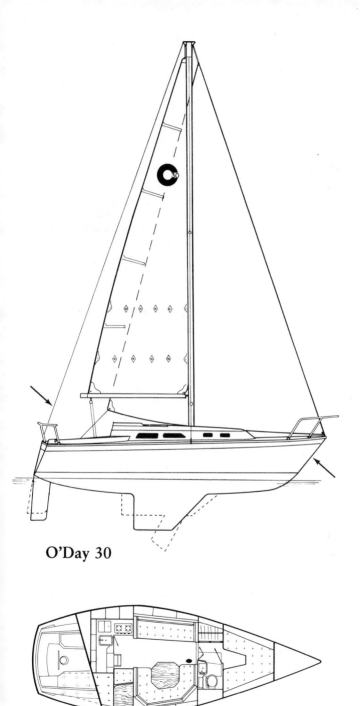

O'Day 30

S2 9.2C

Length: 29 ft. 11 in. LOA;
  25 ft. LWL
Beam: 10 ft. 3 in.
Draft: 3 ft. 11 in. (shoal);
  or 4 ft. 11 in. (deep keel)
Displacement: 9800 lbs.
Sail area: Total, 468 sq. ft.
Hull: FRP, balsa core
Spars: Hard-coated aluminum

Berths: 5
Engine: Yanmar 15 HP
Fuel: Diesel, 18 gals.
Head: Standard, shower, tub
Galley: 2-burner alcohol
Water: 37 gals.
Rating: PHRF 187 average
Designer: Arthur Edmunds

*Center cockpit. Aft-cabin port. Aspect ratio almost 3 to 1.
Straight bow.*

The raised deck indicates that this S2 is intended primarily for cruising. For a boat of this size, there is a lot of space below. The ballast/displacement ratio of 41 percent indicates that she will be stiff and, with her center cockpit, dry.

The 9.2C sleeps five, and there is a short settee which can be used for a child's berth. A passageway aft leads from the companionway to the master cabin, where there is a double berth, a vanity, and a hanging locker. A hatch above and four opening ports provide light and ventilation. In the passageway are three hanging lockers and the navigation station. The chart table lifts to provide access to the engine. The galley has pressure water. To starboard is the head with a shower and a small tub. There is pressure water here as well. In the main cabin the table folds. The bulkhead separating the main and forward cabins is partial, and there is no door. A second hatch is above the vee berths. In addition to the aft-cabin ports, four opening ports are in the forward part of the main cabin and ports from the cockpit serve the chart table area and the head. The large ports indicated on the drawing are fixed.

The center cockpit has pedestal wheel steering, and all running rigging is accessible. There are two halyard and two sheeting winches. Halyards, the 4:1 outhaul, and the reef system are internal. The Cunningham is 2:1 and leads to the cockpit. Forward is an anchor locker. The topping lift is fixed, and the 4:1 main sheet system leads to the roof of the aft cabin. Trim above and below is teak. Jibs sheet to a full-length toe-rail.

S2 9.2C

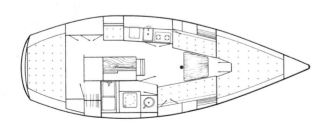

Santana 30/30

Length: 29 ft. 11 in. LOA;
  25 ft. 5 in. LWL
Beam: 10 ft. 3 in.
Draft: 5 ft. 6 in.
Displacement: 6500 lbs.
Sail area: Main and 170%
  foretriangle, 637 sq. ft.
Hull: FRP
Spars: Epoxy on aluminum
Berths: 6

Engine: Volvo 13 HP
Fuel: Diesel, 20 gals.
Head: Standard
Galley: 2-burner alcohol, oven
Water: 20 gals.
Rating: PHRF 141 average; IOR
  26.2; MORC 26.9
Designers: Bruce Nelson and
  Bruce Marek

*Tall masthead rig. Straight bow. Moderate transom overhang.
Long smooth curve of cabin roof. Two spreaders.*

This Santana was designed to the MORC rule. Displacement is
moderate. The bow is fine and the transom broad. The overhanging transom will reduce length and wetted surface in light
air, increasing waterline as heeled. She is a performance cruiser,
with the emphasis on performance.

Interior design is intended to keep weight amidships and the
ends light. To preserve the settees for use, the quarter berths
are large and can be used for doubles. Another racing consideration is the location of large bins for the crew's gear and safety
equipment outboard of the settees. The galley is split and the
ice-box cover doubles as a navigation station. The head has a
hanging locker. In the forward compartment the large acrylic
hatch facilitates sail handling.

On deck, controls lead to the cockpit. The traveler is amidships. Halyards are internal and lead to the coach roof, where
there are four winches. The 3:1 Cunningham and a 2:1 foreguy
are also led aft. The vang is 12:1. The boom has an internal
topping lift and combination outhaul and two flattening reefs.
The toe-rail and the genoa tracks are aluminum. There is tiller
steering.

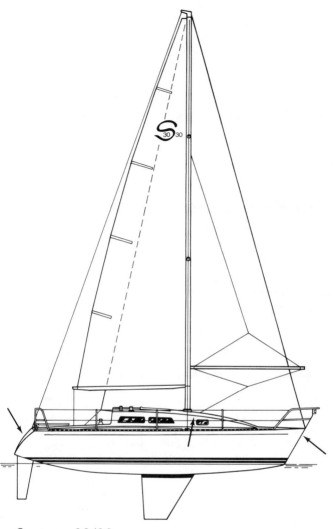

Santana 30/30

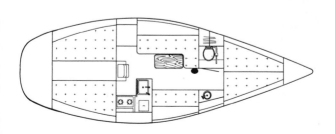

Cal 9.2

Length: 29 ft. 11½ in. LOA;
  25 ft. 5 in. LWL
Beam: 10 ft. 4 in.
Draft: 5 ft. 7 in. or 4 ft. 7 in.
Displacement: 7000 lbs.
Sail area: Main, 162.5 sq. ft.;
  100% foretriangle, 225.6 sq. ft.
Hull: FRP
Spars: Painted aluminum

Berths: 6
Engine: Universal 11 HP
Fuel: Diesel, 11 gals.
Head: Standard
Galley: 2-burner alcohol
Water: 21 gals.
Rating: None
Designer: Ron Holland

Straight bow, curved reverse transom. Very long fixed portlight. Transom triangular from aft.

No ratings appear for the 9.2 yet, but they undoubtedly will, as she is designed for racing. After the many Cals designed by William Lapworth, this Cal is one of a new type called "Cal Meter Editions." The series is intended to be high performance. The hull is a descendent of the Holland Half Tonner. The boat is made with two keels—"deep and deeper."

The two cabins are separated by a door, and a curtain further separates the forecabin from the head. A hanging locker is behind the WC. The seating is directly opposed, with a dropleaf table between. The mast is mounted on the cabin roof, but an interior stainless steel support is forward of the table. The galley and the chart table are at the foot of the companionway ladder. Seating for the latter is on the starboard quarter berth. Racing, the forecabin would be used for sail storage.

Definite signs of the racing intent are above deck. There are four internal halyards, all of which lead to the cockpit. The outhaul and two reefs are also internal, and there is a topping lift. The backstay is adjustable and there are a vang and a Cunningham. Genoa sheeting is to a track or to the toe-rail and from there to either of two winches. The halyard winches are mounted on the cabin. One translucent hatch is over the forecabin and one over the main cabin. A ventilator is over the head. There are an anchor locker, a cockpit locker, and coaming stowage.

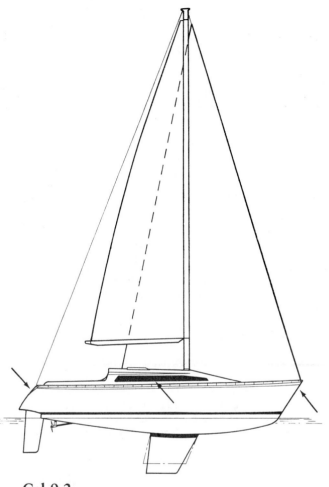

Cal 9.2

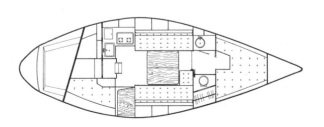

Seafarer 30

Length: 29 ft. 11½ in. LOA;
   25 ft. 7 in. LWL
Beam: 10 ft.
Draft: 4 ft. 9 in. (keel); or 3 ft. 6
   in. (centerboard up)
Displacement: 8600 lbs.
Sail area: Main, 155 sq. ft.;
   100% foretriangle, 234 sq. ft.
Hull: FRP

Spars: Aluminum
Berths: 7
Engine: Yanmar or Westerbeke
Fuel: Diesel, 20 gals.
Head: Standard
Galley: 3-burner alcohol
Water: 43 gals.
Rating: PHRF 181 average
Designer: McCurdy and Rhodes

*High bow. Aspect ratio 3.25 to 1. Cabin forward of mast high
and long. Three-and-two port arrangement.*

The Seafarer is available in a standard rig or in a racing design
with 521 sq. ft. of sail. Two hulls are available, one with keel
and one with centerboard; the keel version is shown.

Berths, and especially the quarter berths, appear large. Both
main-cabin settees convert to double berths, so that conceivably
the boat can sleep eight. At the ladder the galley is to port with
the 2 × 3-ft. chart table across. Just forward of the galley is a
hinged drop-leaf that provides additional counter space and a
service table for the main dinette table. The latter folds against
the bulkhead forward. The head spans the hull and has two
doors for privacy. There are two hanging lockers. Forward, the
vee berth converts to a double. Wood is teak. There are fixed
ports for light and eight opening ports. There are hatches
above both the forward and the main cabin. In addition, there
are two Dorade cowl ventilators.

Two sheet winches are on the coaming, and the internal halyards lead to two more on the cabin roof. The traveler is on
the bridge deck. There are a boom lift, jiffy-reefing gear, and
outhaul. Storage on deck is in two seat lockers and an aft
cockpit locker. Coaming lockers are optional.

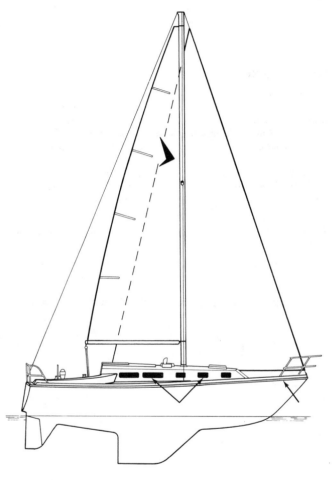

Seafarer 30

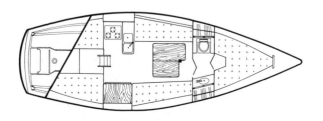

Island Packet

Length: 30 ft. LOA;
  24 ft. 1 in. LWL
Beam: 10 ft. 6 in.
Draft: 3 ft. 8 in. (keel); or 6 ft.
  (centerboard)
Displacement: 8000 lbs.
Sail area: Main, 200 sq. ft.; jib,
  220 sq. ft.; genoa, 300 sq. ft.
Hull: FRP
Spars: Anodized aluminum

Berths: 5
Engine: Yanmar 15 HP
Fuel: Diesel, 18 gals.
Head: Standard
Galley: 2-burner alcohol
Water: 31 gals.
Rating: None
Designers: Robert Johnson,
  Walter Scott

Broad beam. Cutter. Bowsprit. Aspect ratio deceptive, is about 2.4 to 1. End-boom sheeting.

The keel model is standard, the centerboard version available at additional cost. The Packet is a cruiser, not intended for racing. The broad beam gives an unusually spacious interior.

Forward, the vee berth is full width. The head is just aft, on the starboard side. Pressure water system is available. In the main cabin there is a settee to port, forward of the galley. It may be used as a berth. The starboard settee converts to a double. The folding table in between stores against the WC bulkhead. There are six opening ports and a foredeck hatch. Wood is teak; the sole, teak and holly.

The cockpit will seat eight adults. The ice box is located in the cockpit, which also has two seat lockers. There is wheel steering. The traveler is on the taffrail. Two winches are provided for the halyards and two for the jib sheets. The bowsprit has an anchor roller.

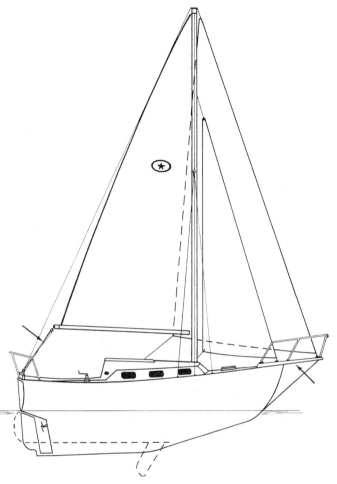

Island Packet

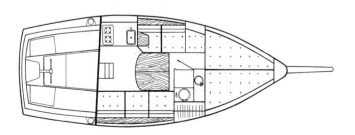

Pearson 303

Length: 30 ft. 3½ in. LOA;
25 ft. 4 in. LWL
Beam: 10 ft. 11 in.
Draft: 4 ft. 4 in.
Displacement: 10,400 lbs.
Sail area: Main, 187 sq. ft.;
100% foretriangle, 269 sq. ft.
Hull: FRP, balsa core
Spars: Painted aluminum

Berths: 6
Engine: Yanmar 13 HP
Fuel: Diesel, 22 gals.
Head: Standard
Galley: 2-burner alcohol
Water: 38 gals.
Rating: None
Designer: William Shaw

Straight bow. Vertical transom. High freeboard. Ports almost identical size.

Almost all Pearsons are rated, but the 303 is new. Design intent was for a spacious cruising boat that would sail at low angles of heel, have a shallow draft, and perform well. Design was not to any rule.

Pearson claims that the quarter berth is an honest double. With that the case, there are berths for six, with two more in the main cabin and two in the forecabin. The latter has an insert for conversion to a double, and is isolated from the main cabin by a folding door. There is also a bureau. Just aft is a hanging locker with a shelf top, and the head to starboard. Optional hot and pressure water may be installed. Both settees convert to berths and have stowage behind. The folding table is over a teak and holly sole. In the galley the five-foot ice box has urethane insulation. Pressure water and an oven are optional.

Above deck there is stowage in the anchor well and in cockpit seats, with the locker to port especially large. Steering is wheel, and there is an emergency tiller. Eight ports open, as do the translucent hatches over the main cabin and forecabin. The main sheets to a traveler on the bridge deck, and the genoa has tracks. Shrouds are inboard. Companionway and other trim is wood. There are two genoa winches and two for halyards. Jiffy reefing is internal.

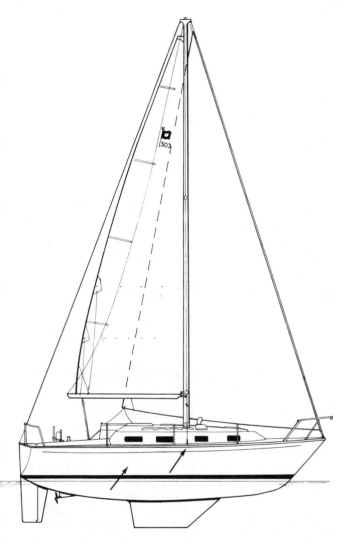

Pearson 303

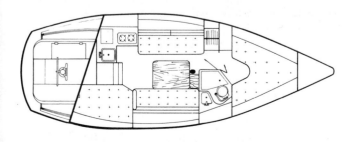

Nonsuch 30

Length: 30 ft. 4 in. LOA;
 28 ft. 9 in. LWL
Beam: 11 ft. 10 in.
Draft: 4 ft. 11½ in. or
 3 ft. 11½ in.
Displacement: 11,500 lbs.
Sail area: 540 sq. ft.
Hull: FRP, balsa core
Spars: Aluminum

Berths: 5
Engine: Westerbeke 29 HP
Fuel: Diesel, 30 gals.
Head: Standard, shower
Galley: 2-burner propane, oven
Water: 80 gals.
Rating: PHRF 175 average
Designer: Mark Ellis

Cat. Cambered cabin roof. Strong sheer, plumb bow. Wishbone boom.

The Nonsuch is typical of this type of boat. Although recently popular, there is nothing really new about either the cat rig or the wishbone boom. The mast is unstayed. The wishbone eliminates the need for vangs or travelers, and imparts a draft to the sail. The sail can be raised, lowered, sheeted, and reefed from the cockpit. The catboat hull has been modified. Maximum beam is farther aft, entry is finer, aft lines are flat, there is a spade rudder, and the fin keel is available with two depths.

With no mast in the cabin and with wide beam, the cabin is roomy. Aft are three bunks, with the double quarter berth to starboard. The galley and the head are opposite. The head has cold pressure water. The galley has ample storage and manual water. The saloon is normal, with two settees, a drop-leaf table, and a hatch above. Forward are a bureau and two hanging lockers with louvered doors. There is access to the forepeak and the mast structure. Dorades are located over the head and galley, and there are nine opening ports.

In the cockpit are seat hatches and wheel steering. As below, trim is teak. There are four winches. Two are for reefing, one is for the mainsheet, and the last is for the halyard. A cradle of light lines is between two booms, and dropping the sail into the cradle reefs the sail.

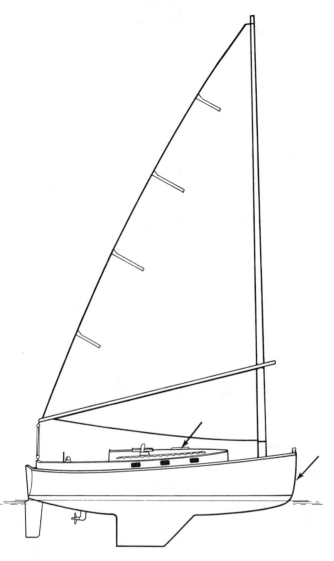

Nonsuch 30

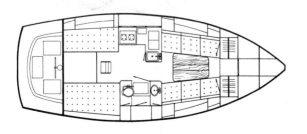

Southern Cross 28

Length: 30 ft. 5 in. LOA;
  20 ft. 2 in. LWL
Beam: 8 ft. 6 in.
Draft: 4 ft. 8 in.
Displacement: 8500 lbs.
Sail area: Main, 164.5 sq. ft.;
  100% foretriangle, 198 sq. ft.
Hull: FRP and Airex core
Spars: Aluminum

Berths: 5
Engine: Universal 11 HP
Fuel: 15 gals.
Head: Standard, manual shower
Galley: 2-burner alcohol
Water: 47 gals.
Rating: PHRF 230 average
Designer: Tom Gillmer

Bowsprit. Double-ended. Inner forestay runs almost to bow. Coach roof continues past curved coaming.

The keel is modified full, and the rudder skeg is substantial. Forward, the hull flares. Displacement is moderate. With a self-tending staysail, singlehanding is simple. As with all cutters, the amount of sail carried can be varied significantly. As the manufacturer says, the Southern Cross "looks like a sailboat."

The forecabin is standard, with vee berths and shelves. The head is split across the boat and isolated from the main cabin, and includes storage and a hanging locker. The starboard settee pulls out to form a double berth, and the port berth extends under the lavatory in the head. The galley is quite large. Sink and burners are to port, as is food storage. The ice box, to starboard, serves as a large navigation table. Interior trim is teak. There are a forward hatch, Dorade boxes, three cowl ventilators, and six opening ports. A midships opening hatch is optional.

All deck hardware is either epoxy or hard-coated. Companionway, weather boards, seahood, Dorade boxes, and bowsprit are teak. Two winches are included for the halyards, and there are two genoa winches. The boom has jiffy reefing and a topping lift. In the cockpit are two seat lockers and tiller steering. Options include roller-furling gear, vang, spinnaker gear, and genoa tracks.

Southern Cross 28

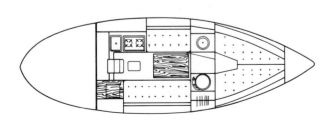

Allmand 31

Length: 30 ft. 9 in. LOA;
    27 ft. 11 in. LWL
Beam: 11 ft. 4 in.
Draft: 4 ft.
Displacement: 12,850 lbs.
Sail area: Main and 100%
    foretriangle, 461 sq. ft.
Hull: FRP
Spars: Aluminum

Berths: 7
Engine: Universal 20 HP
Fuel: Diesel, 40 gals.
Head: Standard
Galley: Type not stated
Water: 50 gals.
Rating: PHRF 180 average
Designers: Walter Scott and
    T. R. Allmand

Three-and-two port arrangement. Note bow. Long curve to coaming. Long waterline.

The Allmand is claimed to have a tacking angle of 84 degrees. Because beam on deck is 11 ft. 4 in. and 8 ft. 6 in. at the water, after initially heeling she picks up a large amount of buoyancy and is stiff. The long waterline allows for additional internal volume.

There is a private cabin aft with a double berth, fold-down chart table, overhead hatch, and hanging locker. The galley is at the bottom of the ladder, has pressure water, and has a top-loading eight-cubic-foot ice box. In the saloon the dinette will seat seven. The settee to port converts to a double, with storage below. There is a settee-berth across. The head is forward to port and also has pressure water. Two hanging lockers are opposite, and the forward cabin, with vee berths, has a door for privacy.

Shrouds are inboard, but sheeting is to the toe-rail. The main sheets to a traveler forward of the hatch, and has a winch. There are also winches for the jib and main halyard, with the latter mounted on the mast. A sail locker and a lazarette may be reached from the cockpit. In addition to the aft-cabin hatch there are hatches over the main cabin and forecabin, and seven opening ports. The large ports shown are fixed. Steering is wheel.

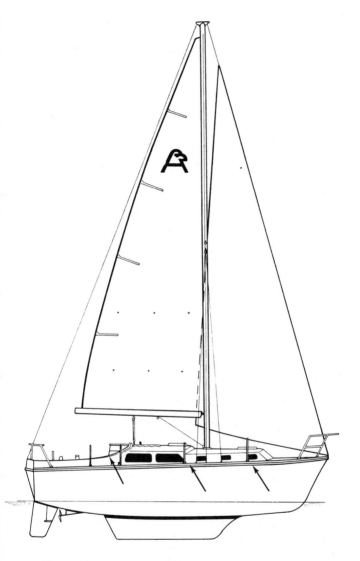

Allmand 31

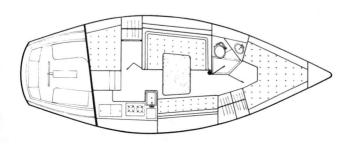

Herreshoff 31

Length: 31 ft. LOA;
   27 ft. 6 in. LWL
Beam: 10 ft. 4 in.
Draft: 4 ft.
Displacement: 8640 lbs.
Sail area: Main and mizzen,
   393 sq. ft. total
Hull: FRP, polyurethane over
   wood

Spars: Not stated
Berths: 6
Engine: Outboard
Head: Standard, shower
Galley: 2-burner
Water: Not stated
Rating: None
Designer: Halsey C. Herreshoff

Cat-ketch. Wishbone booms. Main larger than mizzen. Curved tiller.

The recent popularity of cat-ketches is due to the ease with which they can be sailed. Masts are usually unstayed and running rigging is simple. Tacking does not have to involve sail handling. Many of these boats have a fairly high ballast/displacement ratio, are good (though not excellent) sailers on all points, and have a lot of room below.

The Herreshoff 31 looks bigger below than it is. There is no bulkhead between the forecabin and main cabin; instead, the two are separated by a hanging locker and a bureau. The spaces merge visually. The forecabin has widely separated vee berths, ports, and shelves. Except for upholstery, the cabin is finished in wood. The main cabin has two berths, one convertible to a double, and a central stowable table. There are drawers under the berths. At the companionway the head is located to port and the galley to starboard.

The rig is designed for simplicity. There are no stays. The only running rigging consists of outhauls, halyards, downhauls, and sheets. Either sail may be reefed, or the boat sailed on one alone. The masts are designed to flex automatically for various wind loads. Sails are loose-footed. Sheets may be adjusted by hand, and there are no winches. A mizzen staysail is common.

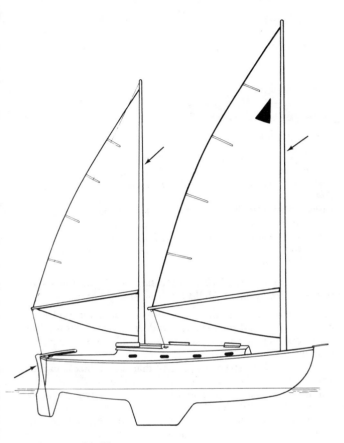

Herreshoff 31

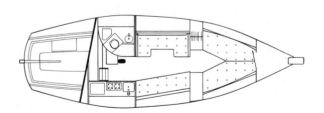

Niagara 31

Length: 31 ft. 3 in. LOA;
  24 ft. 3 in. LWL
Beam: 10 ft. 3½ in.
Draft: 5 ft.
Displacement: 8500 lbs.
Sail area: Main, 225 sq. ft.;
  100% foretriangle, 267 sq. ft.
Hull: FRP
Spars: Aluminum

Berths: 5
Engine: Westerbeke 21 HP
Fuel: Diesel, 22 gals.
Head: Standard, shower
Galley: 2-burner propane
Water: 40 gals.
Rating: PHRF 162 average
Designer: German Frers

Aspect ratio 3 to 1. End-boom sheeting to cockpit. One-and-two port arrangement. Slight transom, straight bow.

Beam is moderate and the hull is V-form. Design is modern, with a fin keel and semibalanced rudder. While this is a tall rig, the foretriangle is not excessively large, and sail handling of foresails is reduced.

The galley is to starboard, except that the ice box is in the after portion of the navigation station, across. In the nav station the chart table lifts up and the seat swings away. Space is provided for electronics. The double berth is to port and makes up when the dinette table is lowered. A settee-berth is across. Both have storage under and above. A folding door isolates the head and a second the forward cabin. The head has a fresh water footpump and a teak grating over the shower sump. Opposite are a hanging locker and a bureau. In the forward cabin is a double vee berth with filler panel. There is a translucent hatch above, as in the main cabin. Two of the ports open and four are fixed. Teak is used in the main cabin and there is varnished pine trim.

The bulwark has sheeting tracks. In the cockpit are wheel steering, seat lockers port and starboard, a separate compartment for propane, and a traveler with four-part mainsheet. Two winches are provided for sheets on the coaming and one for the main halyard on the aft cabin roof. There are also two winches for outboard reef lines, Cunningham, and outhaul. There is a topping lift and a four-part boom vang. Trim topsides is teak.

Niagara 31

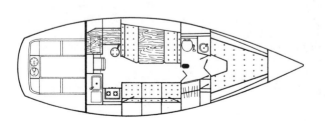

Contest 32 CS

Length: 31 ft. 10 in. LOA;
  24 ft. 7 in. LWL
Beam: 10 ft. 11 in.
Draft: 4 ft. 3 in. (shoal); or
  5 ft. 3 in. (deep)
Displacement: 14,300 lbs.
  (shoal); or 13,860 lbs. (deep)
Sail area: main, 225 sq. ft.; jib,
  250 sq. ft.; genoa, 404 sq. ft.;
  spinnaker, 918 sq. ft.

Hull: FRP
Spars: Aluminum
Berths: 6 or 7
Engine: Volvo 25 HP
Fuel: Diesel, 62 gals.
Head: Standard
Galley: 3-burner LPG
Water: 92.5 gals.
Rating: None
Designer: Dick Zaul

Sloop or center-cockpit ketch. Standard sheer. Curved transom.

The Contest is built in Holland to Lloyds rules, and was designed to the IOR rules. The boat is available either ketch or sloop rigged, and with either a shallow or deep keel. Teak or mahogany is available for the interior.

The aft cabin, reached from a starboard passageway, is unusual with its double and single berth. There is also a hanging locker just aft of the door, and a sink. In the passageway is the galley and additional storage. A partial-height bulkhead separates the galley from the main cabin. The head is to port and has a shower. Hot and pressure water are available options. In the main cabin are a drop-leaf table and two settees. A navigation table is aft of and above the port berth. Forward the vee berth is full width. Storage bins are below, and a hatch above. There are also hatches in the main and aft cabins.

The cockpit has wood seats and wheel steering. A second, small wheel can be located on the forward port bulkhead; and with a dodger, the Contest becomes a motor sailer. Gas for cooking is kept in a lazarette hatch, and there is an anchor well. The boom has slab reefing. Two winches are provided for sheets and a mast winch for halyards. Some of the many options include vang, additional winches, refrigeration, and hot-air heating.

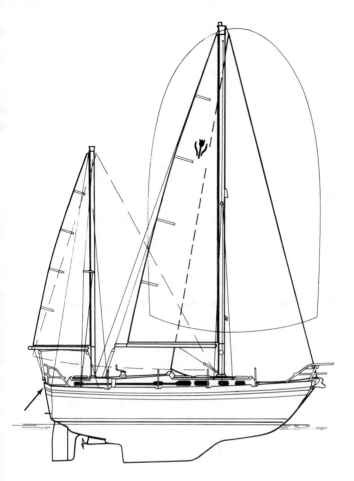

Contest 32 CS

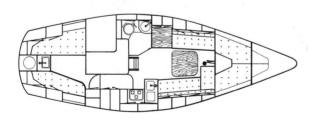

Morgan 32

Length: 31 ft. 11 in. LOA;
25 ft. LWL
Beam: 11 ft. 6 in.
Draft: 4 ft. (shoal); or 5 ft. 4 in.
(deep)
Displacement: 11,000 lbs.
approx.
Sail area: Main, 207 sq. ft.;
foretriangle, 277 sq. ft.
Hull: FRP

Spars: Aluminum
Berths: 6
Engine: Yanmar 22.5 HP
Fuel: Diesel, 27 gals.
Head: Standard
Galley: 2-burner alcohol, oven
Water: 35 gals.
Rating: PHRF 175 average
Designers: Ted Brewer and Jack
Corey

Masthead rig. Aspect ratio about 3 to 1. Straight bow. Main sheets to bridge deck.

This Morgan is offered in either a shoal or a deep-keel model. The drawing shows the shoal version. She will sleep six, but as with most boats this size, five is better and four is best. The design is scaled down from the Morgan 38. An updated model, the 323, is available.

Cabin layout is normal. The galley is to port and has a seven-cubic-foot ice box and single sink with foot-operated pump. The quarter berth opposite serves as the seat for the chart table. There are Dorade vents above both. The lounge area seats convert to berths, with the double to starboard. Here there are six opening ports. The ceiling has ash strips, with other trim teak. There is a full head with manual water, one opening port light, and a hanging locker to port. The forward cabin has a door. Storage is in drawers, in lockers, and under berths. A louvered door gives access to the chain locker, and there is an overhead hatch.

Sheeting is mid-boom with a 6:1 purchase to the bridge-deck traveler. In the cockpit are two seat lockers, teak-covered seats, and a wheel steering pedestal. There is a genoa track which may be mounted inboard. There are two winches for sheets and two for halyards. Options include jiffy reefing, a bow roller chock, and pressure water.

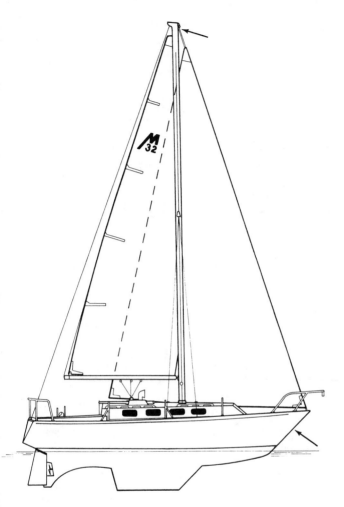

Morgan 32

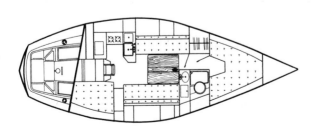

Bayfield 32

Length: 32 ft. LOA;
   23 ft. 3 in. LWL
Beam: 10 ft. 6 in.
Draft: 3 ft. 9 in.
Displacement: 9600 lbs.
Sail area: 525 sq. ft.
Hull: FRP
Spars: Aluminum

Berths: 5
Engine: Yanmar 15 HP
Fuel: Diesel, 20 gals.
Head: Standard
Galley: 2-burner alcohol, oven
Water: 20 gals.
Rating: None
Designer: H. Ted Gozzard

Very unusual bow. Cutter. Model C has four-foot-taller mast, longer bowsprit. Masthead rig.

This Bayfield is a cruiser. The long, full keel and the clipper bow, which has inlaid ornamentation, are traditional. Maximum beam occurs amidships.

Forward there is a vee berth with filler. The door will isolate either the head, to starboard, or the entire forward section. There is a hanging locker here. The shower grating is teak. Head ventilation is by porthole and Dorade ventilator. In the main cabin there are three berths, with the pull-out double to starboard. Beside the ladder, the chart table stows flush in the ceiling panel. Converted, there is a quarter berth. The galley is to starboard. It has pressure water, a four-foot ice box with teak ice grate, and a stainless steel sink.

The bow and stern pulpits are stainless, also. There is a forward translucent hatch, five fixed ports, and the opening in the head. Staysail tracks are inboard; the genoa tracks are mounted on the bulwarks. Steering is wheel. There are two primary two-speed and two secondary one-speed winches in the cockpit. Three halyard winches and cleats are on the aft coach roof. The main sheet is on a traveler which has a car.

Bayfield 32

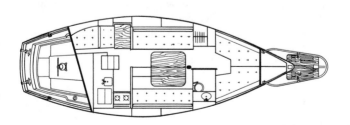

Aloha 32

Length: 32 ft. 5 in. LOA;
  25 ft. LWL
Beam: 10 ft. 10 in.
Draft: 4 ft. 9 in.
Displacement: 9800 lbs.
Sail area: Main, 213 sq. ft.;
  genoa, 305 sq. ft.
Hull: FRP
Spars: Aluminum

Berths: 5
Engine: Atomic 16 HP
Fuel: Diesel
Head: Standard, shower
Galley: 2-burner kerosene
Water: Tank provided
Rating: None
Designer: Mark Ellis

Short counter. Straight bow. Bowsprit, bobstay. Very high apparent aspect ratio.

The Aloha is light and should accelerate well. It is primarily a cruiser.

The starboard quarter berth is a double. Amidships are the galley and the head. The former has footpumps, while the latter is pressurized. There is a single sink and a two-burner stove with oven. In the saloon are two settee-berths, table, and six lockers. Forward are two hanging lockers and further storage in the bow. The main-cabin ceiling has teak battens. The sole is teak and holly and lockers have cane doors. Trim is teak. Two large and two small translucent hatches and six opening ports with screens provide ventilation.

The Aloha comes with sails. An Ulmer main, no. 3 genoa, and no. 1 genoa are provided. The main has a cover. Two halyards are internal, as are the reefing and outhaul. There is an anchor roller and locker. On-deck rails and coaming caps are teak and there is wheel steering.

Aloha 32

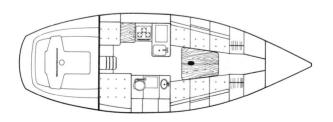

Watkins 32

Length: 32 ft. 6 in. LOA;
   26 ft. 7 in. LWL
Beam: 10 ft. 2 in.
Draft: 4 ft.
Displacement: 10,800 lbs.
Sail area: Main and lapper,
   470 sq. ft.
Hull: FRP
Spars: Aluminum

Berths: 6
Engine: 15 or 22 HP
Fuel: Diesel, 30 gals.
Head: Standard, shower
Galley: 2-burner, alcohol, oven
Water: 40 gals.
Rating: None
Designer: Watkins Yachts

High freeboard. Medium aspect ratio, masthead rig. Portholes evenly spaced. Slight angle to transom, rudder partially visible.

While the freeboard is high, the cabin is kept low to reduce windage. Both the keel and the rudder are medium in depth, and with a draft of four feet, the Watkins can be used for gunk-holing.

The forepeak has vee berths and access to the anchor locker; a hatch overhead is standard. (The hatch in the main cabin is optional.) Just aft, there are two hanging lockers opposite the full head. Main-cabin arrangement is normal, and the U-shaped settee converts to a double. The galley is to starboard and can be modified with a propane stove and refrigeration. A combination nav station and quarter berth are to port. Internal doors are louvered teak.

On deck all halyards and the outhaul are internal. There is a topping lift and internal jiffy reefing. Two sheet winches are supplied, with the halyard winches optional. Six ports open. There is a perforated toe-rail and an anchor locker on the foredeck.

Watkins 32

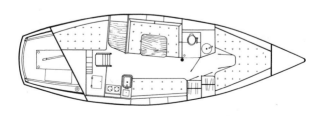

Hans Christian 33

Length: 32 ft. 9 in. LOA;
29 ft. 2 in. LWL
Beam: 11 ft. 8 in.
Draft: 5 ft. 6 in.
Displacement: 18,500 lbs.
Sail area: Main, 258 sq. ft.; jib,
181 sq. ft.; staysail, 159 sq. ft.
Hull: FRP
Spars: Aluminum

Berths: 5
Engine: 30–35 HP
Fuel: Diesel, 80 gals.
Head: Standard, shower
Galley: 3-burner, oven
Water: 120 gals.
Rating: None
Designer: Harwood S. Ives

*Cutter. High bow, bowsprit. Double-ended. Three high vents.
Strong conventional sheer. Note taffrail.*

This is a small ocean cruiser which evolved from the Hans
Christian 38 and 42. The design emphasizes appearance and
cruising accommodations. The rudder is very large and, for a
full-keel boat, far aft. Allowance has been made in the design
for a generator and air conditioning.

Below, the two double berths present a strikingly different
appearance. They are both well elevated and semimasked from
the cabin by a partial bulkhead with curved cut-outs. The galley at the bottom of the ladder is almost a part of the main
cabin. The settee-table to port does not convert, but the settee
across becomes a single. Forward of the main cabin there is a
large hanging locker to starboard and an elevated double berth
to port, with storage drawers under. The forward part of the
boat has a head and more storage.

The cockpit, decks, and cabin roof are teak. In addition to
the three pairs of vents, there is a forward hatch and a second
over the main cabin. Four bronze ports on each side open, as
do two into the cockpit. Steering is wheel. Winches are
mounted on the mast and the cockpit coaming. The bowsprit
shown is optional.

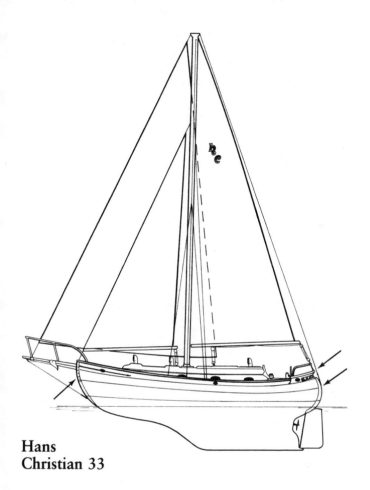

**Hans
Christian 33**

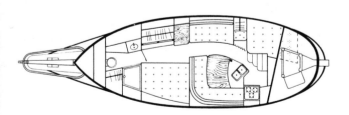

BB 10 Meter

Length: 32 ft. 10 in. LOA;
    23 ft. 11 in. LWL
Beam: 7 ft. 6 in.
Draft: 4 ft. 10 in.
Displacement: 4956 lbs.
Sail area: Main, 216 sq. ft.; jib,
    136 sq. ft.; genoa, 211 sq. ft.
    (155%); spinnaker, 545 sq. ft.
Hull: FRP, foam core

Spars: Aluminum
Berths: 4
Engine: Optional, or outboard
Fuel: Diesel, 10 gals.
Head: None
Galley: 2-burner alcohol
Water: No tank provided
Rating: PHRF 120
Designer: Borge Borressen

Long deck aft of cockpit. Very long bow. Smooth curve from coach roof to coaming. Very narrow beam.

The BB is a boat for racing, not cruising. Its very narrow beam sacrifices interior volume for speed. The narrow beam and light displacement also are penalized by the IOR. However, BB is claimed to beat at 6 knots in 6 knots of wind, reach at 8, and semiplane at 13 in 18 knots of wind.

There are two sea berths doubling as settees and a forward vee berth. The galley slides out from beside the companionway. Finish is wood. There is no standing headroom.

Rigging is stainless rod. The cockpit is big and deep. The deck is wood and toe-rails are aluminum. There is a hatch just forward of the forestay. There are two lazarette lockers. Steering is by tiller. There is a table for the cockpit. All lines lead to the cockpit, including spinnaker-boom control. There is a translucent hatch just forward of the mast. Four deck winches handle the spinnaker and genoa.

BB 10 Meter

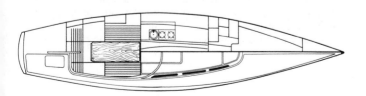

Hobie 33

Length: 33 ft. LOA; 31 ft. LWL
Beam: 8 ft.
Draft: 5 ft. 6 in.
Displacement: 3800 lbs.
Sail area: Main, 219 sq. ft.; jib, 210 sq. ft.; 155% genoa, 325 sq. ft.; spinnaker, 838 sq. ft.
Hull: FRP, foam core

Spars: Aluminum
Berths: 5
Engine: Outboard 9 HP
Head: Chemical, portable
Galley: Alcohol, optional
Water: 5 gallons
Rating: PHRF 91 average
Designer: Hobie Alter

Narrow beam. Low profile. Ports combine to form long triangle. Boom is low. Straight sheer, long straight runs.

This boat is Hobie Alter's first venture into monohulls and offshore boats. She is ultra-light-displacement and designed for one-design racing, but will sleep two couples. The 33 tends to sail well heeled. The narrow beam is required so the boat can be trailered, at which time the keel is lifted. When sailing, the keel is bolted down.

Below, accommodations are for four or five. There are two quarter berths, a double vee berth, and a settee to starboard. The central table folds down. The other settee converts to a galley when the back is folded down. There is a dish locker and space for a stove. The portable ice chest goes beneath the ladder. There is a vanity with sink and water pump, and room for a portable toilet. The six windows are fixed, but there is a large forward hatch with an acrylic panel.

There is tiller steering and two sheet winches in the cockpit. All halyards lead aft and serve the main, genoa, and spinnaker. The ⅞ rig has a headfoil and four internal halyards. The mast step is hinged. There are a concealed backstay adjuster, 4:1 mainsheet purchase, 4:1 vang purchase, topping lift, and internal boom outhaul. The outboard well is designed so that the motor can be tilted up and a plug inserted to close the opening. Accessories available include a marine head, spinnaker and gear, and a bridle to use with the spinnaker pole raising the mast.

Hobie 33

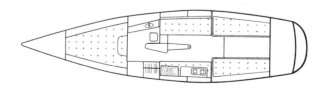

San Juan 33

Length: 33 ft. LOA;
27 ft. 9 in. LWL
Beam: 7 ft. 11 in.
Draft: 5 ft. 11 in.
Displacement: 6000 lbs.
Sail area: Main, 263 sq. ft.;
100% foretriangle, 201 sq. ft.
Hull: FRP
Spars: Aluminum

Berths: 4
Engine: Optional
Head: Optional (portable
or marine)
Galley: Optional 2-burner
Water: 9 gals.
Rating: PHRF 118 average
Designer: David Pedrick

Rudder may be visible. Reverse transom. Aspect ratio over 3 to 1. Jumper stay. Almost flush deck.

This San Juan is designed for racing, and accommodations are somewhat austere. She is ultra light. The fractional rig allows for a larger-than-normal mainsail; the smaller foresails are easier to handle. The unusually narrow beam means that initial stability is limited, but the ballast/displacement ratio of 60 percent is very high. The designer claims that the only need for a genoa to replace the self-tending jib will be in very light airs.

There are four berths below, stowage for sails, and space for the optional head, galley, and engine.

Halyards lead to the cockpit, which has two primary, two secondary, and two spinnaker winches. There are also winches for the jib and the main. The main has jiffy reefing and a flattening reef. There is a vang and an internal outhaul. The main sheets to a traveler. Because the boat is so narrow, sheeting the jib to the toe-rail provides a narrow angle. Rigging is rod, and a headfoil is optional. The split backstay allows adjustment of the very flexible mast.

San Juan 33

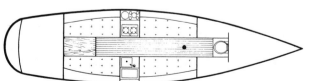

Cape Dory 33

Length: 33 ft. ½ in. LOA;
    24 ft. 6 in. LWL
Beam: 10 ft. 3 in.
Draft: 4 ft. 10 in.
Displacement: 13,300 lbs.
Sail area: Main, 259 sq. ft.;
    100% foretriangle, 280 sq. ft.
Hull: FRP
Spars: Aluminum

Berths: 6
Engine: Volvo 23 HP
Fuel: 21 gals.
Head: Standard, shower
Galley: 3-burner alcohol, oven
Water: 84 gals.
Rating: PHRF 186 average
Designer: Carl Alberg

Long spoon bow. Significant counter. Wide beam. Wood coamings, with winch islands outboard.

Like all Cape Dory boats, the 33 is designed by Carl Alberg, has a full keel, and has a medium-aspect rig. Ballast is 42 percent of displacement. Beam is wide and is extended well aft.

There is no vee berth forward; instead, there is a single to port, a seat, and a bureau. The berth will extend, converting to a double. A hatch is overhead. In the main cabin the settee converts to a double and there is a third berth to starboard. There are hanging lockers ahead to starboard and the head has a grate. The sole is teak and holly. Aft there is a hanging locker beside the ladder, a quarter berth, and the chart table. The galley is opposite.

The deck is balsa-cored, and teak is used for the taffrail, coamings, and grab rails. There are two sail lockers, a lazarette, and wheel steering. The traveler is mounted on the bridge deck. Five winches serve the main halyard, the genoa halyard, the jiffy reefing, and the genoa sheets. Hatches are above the forward and main cabins, and 10 bronze ports open. There are Dorade ventilators.

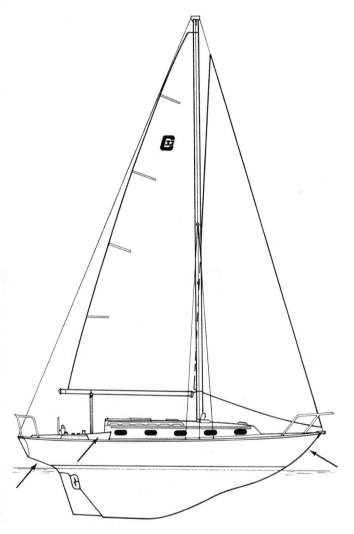

Cape Dory 33

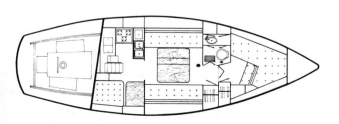

Tartan Ten

Length: 33 ft. 1¾ in. LOA;
27 ft. LWL
Beam: 9 ft. 3 in.
Draft: 5 ft. 10½ in.
Displacement: 6700 lbs.
Sail area: With 100%
foretriangle, 486.72 sq. ft.
Hull: FRP
Spars: Aluminum
Berths: 6

Engine: Farymann 9 HP
Fuel: Diesel
Head: Standard
Galley: Sink
Water: 19 gals.
Rating: D–PN 80.1 suspect;
PHRF 126 average
Designer: Sparkman and
Stephens

Flush deck. Bow and stern parallel. Narrow beam. Seven-eighths rig. Spreaders swept back.

While the Tartan Ten was not designed to any rule, she was designed primarily for racing. The flush deck leaves little room in the cabin; and while there are six berths, the general cabin appointments are for weekends and overnights, not extended cruising. The Ten is a one-design and is delivered complete. No hull or rig alterations are allowed.

There are two quarter berths aft. Forward to port and centered in the boat is the galley, with sink and manual water. The ice chest is portable. A counter to starboard doubles as a galley surface and chart table. Forward are two berths with the head under. There is a privacy curtain.

Above, the mast can be bent by both shroud and backstay adjustment. The latter has a 4:1 purchase. All halyards and the reef lines are internal. The outhaul, also internal, has a 4:1 ratio. There are two cockpit winches for sheets and two halyard winches mounted on the cabin top. The boom vang is 4:1 and leads either to the mast base or, when used as a preventer, to the rail. On the foredeck is a large hatch for both sail handling and ventilation. The perforated toe-rail is full length and a genoa track is optional.

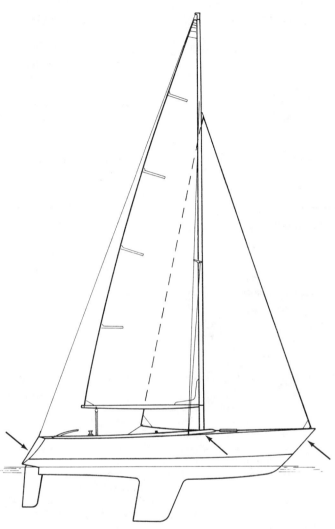

Tartan Ten

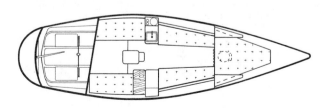

db

Length: 33 ft. 2 in. LOA;
26 ft. 7 in. LWL
Beam: 11 ft. 2 in.
Draft: 6 ft. 2 in.
Displacement: 7275 lbs.
Sail area: Main, 341 sq. ft.;
genoa, 328 to 156 sq. ft.;
spinnaker, 716 sq. ft.
Hull: Aluminum frame, Kevlar
and FRP skin

Spars: Anodized aluminum
Berths: 6
Engine: 30 HP
Fuel: Diesel, 11.9 gals.
Head: Standard
Galley: 2-burner
Water: 19.8 gals.
Rating: PHRF 129
Designer: E. G. Van de Stadt

Curved reverse transom. Continuous port covering. Note running backstays.

The db is claimed to be the fastest one-design production ¾-tonner in the world, and has won at Cowes, at Kiel, and in the Southern Ocean Racing Circuit. The emphasis is on racing rather than cruising.

Below, the forecabin has only a head. There is no vee berth, and the space is available for storage. Brighton (the manufacturer) lists 11 different sails, so space will be needed. In the main cabin there are two settee-berths, two pilot berths, and two quarter berths. The chart table is to starboard and has storage. Teak is used extensively. There is a galley, but no ice box is shown or mentioned.

Above decks there is lots of gear. All running rigging leads to the cockpit, which has a tiller and under-sole and transom storage. There are standing and running backstays. There are winches for the running backstays and two halyard and two genoa winches. The traveler mounts across the cockpit. Halyards are internal, as are the outhaul and reefing lines. Both the jib and the genoa have barber haulers mounted on tracks. The boom vang is tubular and there is a Cunningham. Options are primarily safety equipment and instrumentation.

db

Tanzer 10.5

Length: 34 ft. 5 in. LOA;
27 ft. 6 in. LWL
Beam: 11 ft. 6 in.
Draft: 6 ft. 6 in.
Displacement: 13,000 lbs.
Sail area: Main, 245 sq. ft.; jib,
270 sq. ft.; 150% genoa, 481
sq. ft.; spinnaker, 1300 sq. ft.
Hull: FRP

Spars: Painted aluminum
Berths: 6
Engine: Yanmar 30 HP
Fuel: Diesel, 35 gals.
Head: Standard, shower
Galley: 3-burner propane, oven
Water: 70 gals.
Rating: None
Designer: Dick Carter

Pilot house with wraparound window. Straight bow. Rudder mounted on both transom and skeg.

With its lifting keel fully up and fully housed, the 10.5 draws 2 ft. 1 in. The lifting mechanism is hydraulic. The housing for the keel is in both the pilot house and the main cabin. In the main cabin it impinges very slightly on the settee. In the pilot house it is beside the galley sink.

From the deck, access to the pilot house is down a short ladder. A steering position is to starboard with the chart table outboard. Just aft is the head, and across is the galley. Two more steps descend to the aft cabin and its double berth. There are a long seat on the port side, a hanging locker, and a vanity. The coach roof extends over the main cabin area, and the result is that the helmsman and the cook, while two steps above the main cabin, are not isolated from it. Note that the helmsman's position is partially in the main cabin. Here the dinette seats eight and converts to a double berth. To starboard are a seat and a hanging locker. Up forward is a vee berth. The head of the starboard berth is above, and crosses over the berth to port.

The deck steering position has a wheel. A locker for propane is aft and there is a seat locker for sails. There is a total of seven deck hatches and there are also three opening ports. Two winches are mounted on the coaming. There are a traveler, topping lift, outhaul, and two reef lines. All are internal. The boom vang is four-part. The jib sail area noted is for a self-tending jib, but a 110 percent lapper is available. The spinnaker is for cruising and is poleless.

Tanzer 10.5

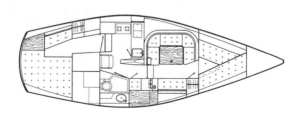

Cal 35

Length: 35 ft. LOA;
   28 ft. 9 in. LWL
Beam: 11 ft. 3 in.
Draft: 6 ft.
Displacement: 13,000 lbs.
Sail area: Main, 247 sq. ft.;
   100% foretriangle, 360 sq. ft.
Hull: FRP sandwich
Spars: Aluminum

Berths: 5
Engine: Universal 32 HP
Fuel: 37 gals.
Head: Marine, shower
Galley: 3-burner alcohol, oven
Water: 84 gals.
Rating: PHRF 136
Designer: William Lapworth

Straight bow, reverse transom. Long waterline.

In order, Cal designs have been the 40, 36, 39, and the 35. All are moderately light displacement and have fin keels, long waterlines, and high-efficiency rudders. The hulls are balanced.

Cabin layouts may be varied. A design not shown has a distinct separation between living and working areas, with dining and berths forward, and the galley, large head, and navigation station aft. The layout shown is quite normal, with the galley aft to port and navigation area to starboard. Here they are part of the main cabin, which has a double and a single berth. The head is large, and there are two hanging lockers. The vee berth forward is full width. There are four opening ports in the main saloon, two opening ports in the forward cabin, four fixed ports in the cabin house, and a Dorade ventilator over the head.

In the cockpit there is pedestal steering. Flush deck deadlights are mounted over the galley and forward berths. The mainsheet has a cabin-mounted traveler and there are genoa tracks mounted on deck. There are two-speed sheet winches, a winch for the mainsheet, and two halyard winches. The boom has a topping lift, double internal reef, internal outhaul, and a 4:1 boom vang.

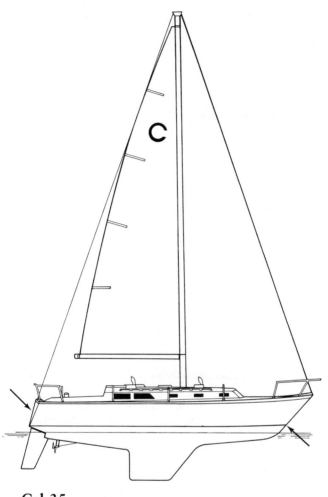

Cal 35

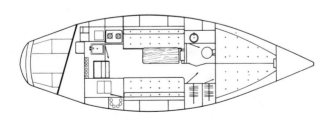

Niagara 35

Length: 35 ft. 1 in. LOA;	*Berths:* 5
26 ft. 8 in. LWL	*Engine:* Westerbeke 29 HP
Beam: 11 ft. 5 in.	*Fuel:* Diesel, 20 gals.
Draft: 5 ft. 2 in.	*Head:* Standard, shower
Displacement: 15,000 lbs.	*Galley:* 3-burner propane, oven
Sail area: Main, 238 sq. ft.;	*Water:* 80 gals.
100% foretriangle, 360 sq. ft.	*Rating:* PHRF 144 average
Hull: FRP, balsa core	*Designer:* Mark Ellis
Spars: Aluminum	

Tall, with aspect ratio over 3 to 1. Masthead rig. High free-board. Straight bow cuts away at forefoot.

This Ellis sloop was designed for cruising, but the forward cabin arrangement is planned to facilitate sail handling. The entire cabin layout is unusual.

The companionway does not lead to the saloon but aft to the master cabin, which sleeps three in a single to starboard and a double to port. There is a hanging locker and the chart table. There are two passageways forward to the saloon: to port through the galley and to starboard through the head. The galley has the stove and ice box outboard, the sink inboard. The head is reached from either the aft or the main cabin and has a teak grating over the shower sump. Because of the companionway location, both head and galley would be dark if it were not for the hatch provided above each. The standard saloon layout has the double berth to starboard and there are two hanging lockers and other storage. The folding table has a sky-light above it. The forward cabin is designed for sail handling and does not have a vee berth. There are bins, a workbench, and a large hatch above. The bench and its seats serve as the ladder to the foredeck. There is a single folding berth stored overhead to port.

The bulwark has sheeting tacks and a toe-rail cap. There are also sheeting leads inboard. Trim is teak. The four-part main halyard has its own winch on the mast. Two more winches are on the cabin roof and two on the coaming. There are four-part vang, slab-reefing control lines, a topping lift, and an internal clew outhaul. In addition to the hatches, there are four fixed windows and six opening ports, two of which are between the cockpit and the aft cabin.

Niagara 35

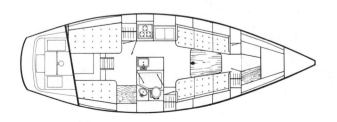

Southern Cross 35

Length: 35 ft. 3 in. LOA;
   28 ft. LWL
Beam: 11 ft. 5 in.
Draft: 4 ft. 11 in.
Displacement: 14,461 lbs.
Sail area: Main, 245 sq. ft.;
   150% genoa, 587 sq. ft.;
   staysail, 171 sq. ft.; spinnaker,
   1371 sq. ft.
Hull: FRP sandwich hull and
   deck

Spars: Anodized aluminum
Berths: 5 or 6
Engine: Yanmar 30 HP
Fuel: Diesel, 35 gals.
Head: Standard, shower
Galley: 3-burner propane
Water: 90 gals.
Rating: None
Designer: Tom Gillmer

Masthead cutter. Fine bow. Curved coaming. Cockpit way aft. Canoe stern.

The Southern Cross 35 is a new boat and the specifications given are preliminary. They should not change very much. The forefoot is cut away and entrance is fine. The keel is raked. Many other sails are available, including other genoas, storm sails, jibs, and jib-topsails. The optional sixth berth is a quarter berth. Construction is sandwich, with an Airex core for the hull and balsa used for the deck.

The forecabin has vee berths with a filler. There is a seat in front of the hanging locker and a hatch above. The galley has pressure water, an opening hatch, and an opening port. The fiberglass shower pan has a teak grate. In the main cabin are a bureau and hanging locker. The settee to port converts to a double berth. The drop-leaf table mounts on the mast. There is a grate in the sole, which is teak planked. The galley has three burners and an oven, a footpump for the fresh water, and four inches of insulation for the ice box. There is a wet locker at the navigation area opposite. The main cabin also has a hatch, and there are eight opening ports.

Above, the cockpit has two seat lockers. A traveler crosses just in front of the pedestal wheel steering. Hardware is epoxy-coated or hard-anodized. Halyard winches are mounted on the coach roof, and there are two genoa winches. The genoa track allows for close sheeting, and there are jiffy reefing and a topping lift. The staysail is normally self-tending. On the foredeck is a well for the anchor and a locker for the rode.

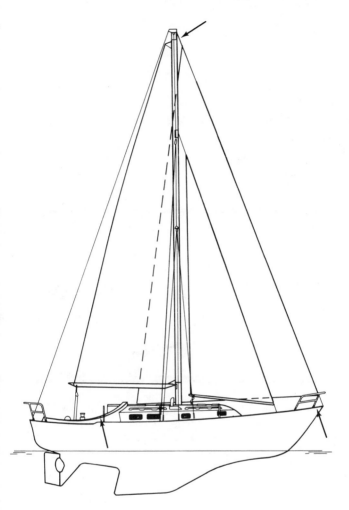

Southern Cross 35

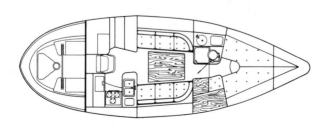

Ericson 36

Length: 35 ft. 7 in. LOA;
29 ft. LWL
Beam: 11 ft. 10 in.
Draft: 6 ft. 3 in.
Displacement: 11,600 lbs.
Sail area: Main, 252 sq. ft.;
100% foretriangle, 346 sq. ft.
Hull: FRP
Spars: Coated aluminum

Berths: 7
Engine: 24 HP
Fuel: Diesel, 50 gals.
Head: Standard, shower
Galley: 2-burner alcohol, oven
Water: 70 gals.
Rating: PHRF 108 average
Designer: Ron Holland

Straight bow. Curved reverse transom. Sheer at deck quite straight. Note angles in portlights. Aspect ratio 3.6 to 1.

This Ericson is a racing boat, but the construction technique minimizes weight, allowing for a full cruising interior. Ballast constitutes 45 percent of the total displacement, so she should be stiff.

The forward cabin has a double berth with removable insert, storage under, shelves, and an access door to the anchor locker. Just aft, there are storage for an outboard and a hanging locker to port, and the full head, with pressure water, to starboard. In the main cabin, the port berth is a double, and there is a pilot berth across. The folding table is teak, and the sole is teak and holly. The galley has pressure water and also foot-pumped fresh and salt water. A wet locker is adjacent to the companionway, and a double quarter berth and the navigation station are to starboard.

In the cockpit, pedestal steering is optional and seats are teak with storage under the port seat. The traveler is mounted on the bridge deck. Genoa tracks are located both inboard and outboard. Two primary, two secondary, and four cabin-roof winches are shown. The optional staysail stay is fixed to an adjustable track. There are hatches over both the main and forward cabins.

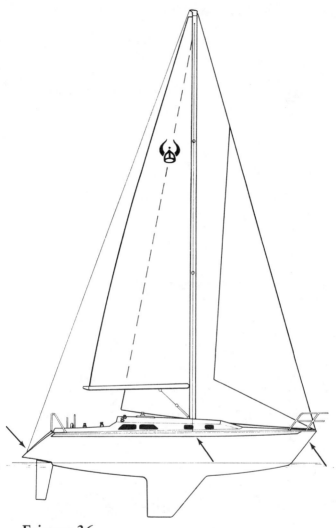

Ericson 36

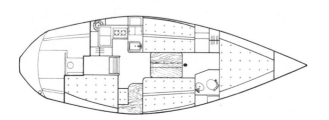

Goderich 35

Length: 35 ft. 7½ in. LOA;
28 ft. 4 in. LWL
Beam: 11 ft. 5½ in.
Draft: 4 ft. 9 in.
Displacement: 16,900 lbs.
Sail area: Main, 314 sq. ft.; jib,
219 sq. ft.; staysail, 126 sq. ft.;
genoa, 515 sq. ft.
Hull: Steel
Spars: Aluminum

Berths: 6
Engine: Volvo 24 HP
Fuel: Diesel, 80 gals.
Head: Standard, shower
Galley: 3-burner
Water: 80 gals.
Rating: None
Designer: Brewer, Walstrom and
Assoc., Inc.

*Wide beam. Cutter, no bowsprit. Steel hull. High bow,
standard sheer. Club-foot staysail, if used.*

This steel cutter is built in Canada. Stiffness comes from the
beam, as the ballast is moderate. The ballast/displacement ratio
is 37 percent. To minimize sweating, the hull is insulated with
urethane foam.

Cabin layout is standard, but there are interesting details. At
the ladder the area under the cockpit is put to use. A galley
locker is located aft of the 14-cubic-foot ice box. There is a
shelf inboard of the quarter berth. Seating for the navigation
station is on the quarter berth, and there is chart storage under.
A locker for oilskins is just forward of the table. In the main
cabin the table folds. Settee-berths are on both sides, and a
pilot berth is to port. The head may be reached from either the
forecabin or the main cabin. Opposite, there is a large hanging
locker in the main cabin and a second in the forward cabin.
This cabin also has a seat, a bureau, another locker, and a
hatch overhead.

Deck storage includes a locker in the forepeak, a cockpit sail
bin, and three smaller bins. The hull finish is urethane paint
and the decks are nonskid. Steering is by tiller. There are five
opening portlights and four opening ports.

Goderich 35

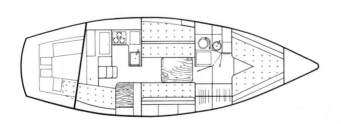

S2 11.0

Length: 36 ft. LOA;
  28 ft. 3 in. LWL
Beam: 11 ft. 11 in.
Draft: 4 ft. 8 in.
Displacement: 15,000 lbs.
Sail area: Main and 100%
  working jib, 625 sq. ft.
Hull: FRP
Spars: Aluminum

Berths: 6
Engine: Pathfinder 42 HP
Fuel: Diesel, 70 gals.
Head: Standard, shower-bathtub
Galley: 2-burner alcohol, oven
Water: 80 gals.
Rating: None
Designer: Arthur Edmunds

Center cockpit. Shrouds inboard. Long straight bow. Counter, transom.

This is the 11.0 C model, and has the same underwater lines as the 11.0 A. There is substantial weight and a broad beam for stability. The deep keel and rudder help track off the wind. The center cockpit has become very popular for cruisers, and the 11.0 has a big one.

Because of the center cockpit there is a private cabin aft reached by a passageway to port. Outboard are the galley, a hanging locker, and a drawer unit. Inboard is access to the engine. In the cabin are another hanging locker, a double bunk, a drawer unit, and storage cabinets. Behind the companionway to starboard is a large head with a shower and tub. Head and galley both have pressure water. In the main cabin is the remainder of the galley, to port, with the navigation station opposite. In order to obtain the maximum working space, there is no fixed seat. Instead, the seat swings away to stow over the starboard settee-berth. The large cabin table hinges down. Sliding louvered doors isolate the full-width vee berths forward. Cabin light and ventilation are via 2 large windows, 2 Dorade vents, 10 opening ports, and 2 acrylic hatches faced with teak strips.

There are two aft-deck lockers and a self-draining anchor locker. The traveler is mounted just aft of the cockpit. Two primary winches are on the cockpit coamings, and there are two halyard winches on the coach roof forward. The genoa track is mounted on the rail. The boom has a 5:1 outhaul and internal double reef. The rig is masthead, and has a moderate aspect ratio.

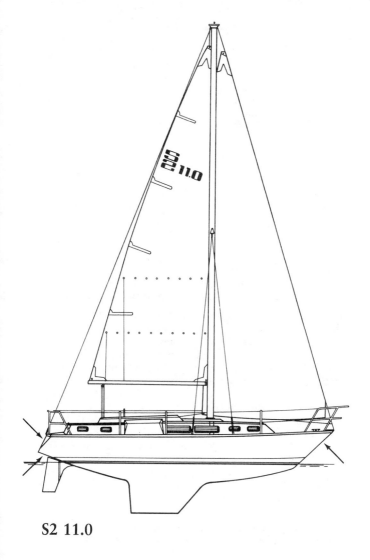

S2 11.0

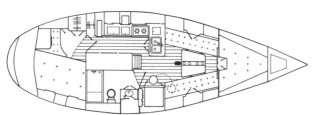

Vancouver 36

Length: 36 ft. LOA;
   27 ft. 11 in. LWL
Beam: 11 ft.
Draft: 5 ft.
Displacement: 18,000 lbs.
Sail area: Total 700 sq. ft.
Hull: FRP
Spars: Aluminum

Berths: 4
Engine: Volvo 35 HP
Fuel: Diesel, 65 gals.
Head: Standard, shower
Galley: 3-burner
Water: 140 gals.
Rating: None
Designer: Robert Harris

Cutter, double-ended, rudder inboard. Aft ports higher than those forward. Upper jumper faces forward.

Robert Harris also designed the Vancouver 27, 32, and 42, but the first two are produced in England and the latter in Taiwan. The 36 has an unusual cabin layout. With a large space but only four bunks, she is designed for long-range cruising. Entry is fine, bilges are hard, and the maximum beam is well aft. Ballast/displacement ratio is 42 percent.

Cabin plans may vary. One particularly interesting design is shown. Behind the ladder to port are a locker for oilskins and a very large locker for sails. Entrance to the engine is through the latter. The navigation station is unusually large, as is the galley, which has a 12-cubic-foot ice box. There are two steps down into the main cabin, which gives it very high headroom. Layout here is more normal, with a berth to port and a pilot berth to starboard. Note, however, that there is a fireplace. The large forward cabin is again unusual. Across from the large double berth is a workbench with storage both below and above. The head is also large, with cabinets and lockers. Another large sail locker is located forward, but aft of the chain locker.

Some of the space below came out of the cockpit. It is small, seating four, which in view of the boat's purpose is adequate. There are two cockpit lockers. Deck plans indicate four deck hatches and two cowl vents. The traveler is on the coach roof. Shrouds are inboard, while the genoa sheets to the toe-rail.

Vancouver 36

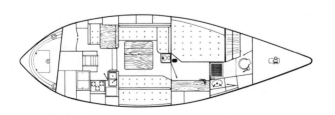

F3

Length: 36 ft. 3 in. LOA; 29 ft. 6 in. LWL	*Berths:* 6
Beam: 11 ft. 10 in.	*Engine:* Westerbeke 29 HP
Draft: 6 ft. 9 in.	*Fuel:* Diesel, 25 gals.
Displacement: 10,900 lbs.	*Head:* Standard
Sail area: Main, 280 sq. ft.; jib, 350 sq. ft.; genoa, 525 sq. ft.; spinnaker, 650 sq. ft.	*Galley:* 3-burner propane
	Water: 40 gals.
	Rating: IOR 28.5 estimated; PHRF 96 average
Hull: FRP, balsa core	*Designer:* German Frers
Spars: Aluminum	

Running backstays. Long, sloping coach roof. Aspect ratio over 3 to 1. Sharply reversed transom. Masthead rig.

This boat has been designed for both racing and cruising. The hull and rig give a lot of consideration to the IOR without completely succumbing to it. Neither is radical. While the boat is suited for cruising, the interior has certain features which are meant for racing. Balance, in particular, has been emphasized.

Actually, there are berths for eight. When the boat is raced the forepeak is used for sail storage. The berths for racing are the two quarter berths, two pilot berths, and the converted settee. For cruising, or in port, the pilot berths can be augmented by the forward vee berth. The intent is quite deliberate. The vee berths will fold up out of the way or can be removed. If there are two watches of four people each, the pilot and quarter berths may still be used leaving the settees available. The galley can be equipped with refrigeration. Water is from a foot-operated pump. To port there is a navigation station with its own seat. The head, opposite two hanging lockers, has pressure water and a teak grating over the shower pan. Ventilation is from a forecabin hatch, a port in the head, and opening ports for the quarter berths.

There are long, inboard genoa tracks which allow for very close (8 degree) sheeting. The cockpit is T-shaped and has a wheel. All halyards and reefing controls are led to the cockpit. The toe-rail is slotted its full length. There are four winches on the coach roof for halyards and spinnaker topping lift, and two primary and two secondary winches. The traveler is recessed into the deck just forward of the cockpit. There are two cockpit lockers and a special locker for propane stowage.

F3

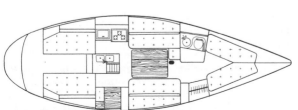

Swan 371

Length: 36.84 ft. LOA;
  29 ft. 9 in. LWL
Beam: 11.32 ft.
Draft: 6.8 ft.
Displacement: 15,400 lbs.
Sail area: Main, 246 sq. ft.;
  100% foretriangle, 351 sq. ft.
Hull: FRP
Spars: Aluminum

Berths: 7–9
Engine: BUKH 20 HP
Fuel: Diesel, 37 gals.
Head: Standard, shower
Galley: 3-burner propane, oven
Water: 66 gals.
Rating: PHRF 112 average
Designer: Ron Holland

Reverse transom. Running backstays. Very flush deck. Straight bow, high freeboard.

Swans are built by Nautor in Finland; and as might be expected, wood is featured both in the cabin and on deck. A basic design intention was for a racing boat with a large master cabin. The racing intent may be seen in the running backstays, which are not strictly required for mast support but give a steadying effect in rough water and may be used to shape the mainsail.

Also indicating an intention for serious racing is the forward-cabin layout. It is designed for sail stowage but has two pipe berths. There is a hatch overhead and doors lead to the forepeak. Aft to port are drawers and a hanging locker. The head has a hand-held shower over a fiberglass shower pan. The drop-leaf table in the main cabin is removable. There are two transom berths and either one or two pilot berths. In the galley, refrigeration for the ice chest is optional. The chart table is opposite and has space for charts under the table top. There is a partial bulkhead, with cutouts, between the galley and navigation area and the main cabin. Going aft, a door provides privacy to the master cabin. There are a double and a single quarter berth, stowage, and access to the steering gear and the batteries. For light and air there are the foredeck hatch, two openable ports in the main cabin, a light prism over the head, and an openable port from the cockpit to the aft cabin.

Halyards lead to two winches on the coach roof. On the coaming are two genoa-sheet winches and two more for the spinnaker. The main sheets to a winch on the bridge deck, and there is a traveler. Genoa tracks and shrouds are inboard. An eye for a staysail is provided on the foredeck. There is stowage for a liferaft and for a propane bottle. The decks, trim, and cabin woodwork are teak.

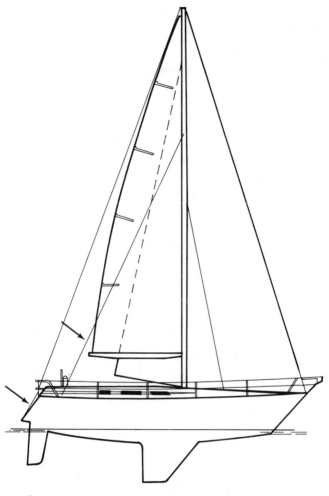

Swan 371

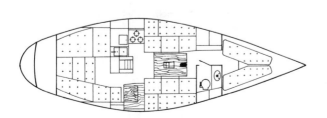

Seidelmann 37

Length: 36 ft, 10 in. LOA;
29 ft. 6 in. LWL
Beam: 12 ft.
Draft: 5 ft. 11 in. (deep); or
4 ft. 11 in. (intermediate)
Displacement: 13,500 lbs. (deep);
or 13,900 lbs. (intermediate)
Sail area: Main and jib,
643 sq. ft. total
Hull: FRP

Spars: Aluminum
Berths: 6
Engine: 24 HP
Fuel: Diesel, 18 gals.
Head: Standard, shower
Galley: 2-burner alcohol, oven
Water: 70 gals.
Rating: PHRF 120 (deep keel)
Designer: Bob Seidelmann

*Aspect ratio almost 4 to 1. Slight reverse transom. Sheer
sweeps down toward stern. Slight roach. Straight bow.*

Like many Seidelmanns, this one has a very tall rig. The beam,
however, is wide in relation to length. The result is a spacious
interior.

There is a total of six berths, with a seventh pilot berth possible above the double berth-settee. Two berths are forward,
two in the main cabin, and there is a quarter berth with stowage under. In the galley there are two sinks, two burners, and a
top-loading ice box. The navigation station is opposite. Sections show the table at an angle, but it can be made level for
additional counter space. The dinette table folds away against
the forward bulkhead. Storage is under all berths, in four
drawers near the head, in two hanging lockers, in three lockers
in the forward compartment, and elsewhere. Many of the
locker doors are louvered. Also louvered are the head door and
the door to the forecabin. Wood is teak. There is pressure
water. Light and ventilation are from two Dorade vents, forecabin and main-cabin hatches, and four opening ports.

A traveler is mounted on the bridge deck forward of the
T-shaped cockpit. Halyards, the topping lift, and the reef line
are internal. Two halyard winches are mounted on the mast
and there are two cockpit winches. Genoa tracks are inboard.
Deck stowage includes two cockpit lockers and an anchor well.
Handrails and the companionway are teak.

Seidelmann 37

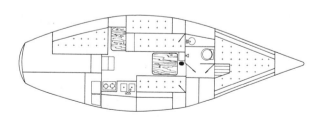

Crealock 37

Length: 36 ft. 11 in. LOA;
27 ft. 9 in. LWL
Beam: 10 ft. 10 in.
Draft: 5 ft. 4 in.
Displacement: 16,000 lbs.
Sail area: Main, 272 sq. ft.;
100% foretriangle, 347 sq. ft.
Hull: FRP
Spars: Aluminum

Berths: 7
Engine: 32 HP
Fuel: Diesel, 47 gals.
Head: Standard
Galley: 3-burner, oven
Water: Not stated
Rating: PHRF 174
Designer: Wib Crealock

Sloop, cutter, or yawl, so hull is important. Distinctive stern. Long spoon bow with chin. Two-and-three porthole layout.

Underwater lines show a very normal fin keel, but the canoe stern is unusual. The cutter rig shown does not indicate staysails. Maximum beam is aft.

Below, the main saloon appears spacious. A double berth is to starboard, a single to port. There is unusual storage in the fo'c'sle, with five drawers, a hanging locker, and a vanity to port, and three drawers under the double berth. The head has a grating over the shower drain. Aft is a navigation station, seat, and double quarter berth. The galley is to starboard and has three burners, a double sink, top-loaded refrigerator, and oven.

The cockpit has three seat lockers, and there is a transom locker. Two skylights are over the forecabin and the saloon. A short jib track, a traveler, and three winches are mounted on the coach roof. A genoa track is mounted on deck inboard, with leads to two primary cockpit winches. There is pedestal wheel steering.

Crealock 37

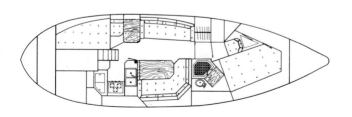

Alajuela 33

Length: 37 ft. LOA;
27 ft. 6 in. LWL
Beam: 10 ft. 8 in.
Draft: 4 ft. 9 in.
Displacement: 13,500 lbs.
Sail area: Main, 241 sq. ft.;
genoa, 135%, 450 sq. ft.;
staysail, 132 sq. ft.; genoas,
Yankee, trysails, spinnaker
Hull: FRP

Spars: Aluminum
Berths: 6
Engine: Pisces 27 HP
Fuel: Diesel, 50 gals.
Head: Standard
Galley: 3-burner propane, oven
Water: 75 gals.
Rating: None
Designer: Ray Richards

Double-ended. Bowsprit. Cutter. Four oval ports. Dorade ventilators.

There is a long keel for tracking, and the forefoot is cut away for turning. With significant sheer, this boat has a traditional look. The keel is quite thick, as it contains ballast, water, fuel, and the holding tank.

The head is located in an unusual position, amidships on the port side. This tends to separate the cabin into distinct areas, with a small space at the base of the companionway ladder. A hanging locker for wet gear and the navigator's station are located here. The cabin is finished in teak with a vinyl headliner. Ventilation is handled by two Dorade ventilators, three hatches, and eight bronze opening ports.

The decks are wide and the cockpit has 7½-foot-long seats, with two storage lockers and a lazarette for propane bottles. Steering is by wheel or tiller. There are optional running backstays, and the staysail stay can be removed. There are spinnaker, genoa, and staysail tracks. The 4:1 mainsheet has a traveler, and the main has a 2:1 internal outhaul.

Alajuela 33

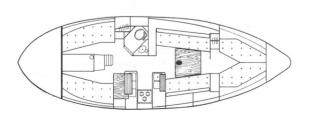

Baltic 37

Length: 37 ft. LOA;
    28 ft. 10½ in. LWL
Beam: 12 ft.
Draft: 5.76 ft.
Displacement: 13,600 lbs.
Sail area: Not given. I, 49 ft.;
    J, 15.56 ft.; P, 43.5 ft.;
    E, 11.75 ft.
Hull: FRP, balsa core
Spars: Anodized aluminum

Berths: 8
Engine: Volvo 23 HP
Fuel: 21 gals.
Head: Standard
Galley: 3-burner propane
Water: 34.3 gals.
Rating: IOR 27.5;
    PHRF 113
Designer: C & C Design Group

Sharp clipper bow. Sharp reverse transom, some counter. Low cabin. Tall rig for size.

Baltic has a fin keel with high-aspect spade rudder. With a narrow beam at the waterline she would be initially tender but gain stiffness as she started to heel. Aft sections are full to increase sailing length when heeled. C & C wants to maintain speed off the wind without a strong weather helm.

Companionway stairs land amidships. To port is the head; access to the aft cabin is to starboard. The aft cabin has a double berth, seat, stowage, and a hanging locker. Amidships is an L-shaped galley and the navigation area. The former has a stainless steel ice box. Foot-operated pumps deliver fresh water and seawater. There is a hanging locker aft of the navigator's seat, and stowage under the stairs. Settees in the main cabin convert to berths, and there are two pilot berths. Forward are berths to port and starboard with stowage under. There are two hanging lockers and shelves. The interior is faced with teak. There are two tinted-glass hatches. The aft cabin and the head have opening portholes; other windows are fixed.

Topside, rigging, except the midstay, is stainless steel. There are winches for the main halyard and sheet; two for reefing, the Cunningham, the spinnaker pole, and the topping lift; two for the genoa and spinnaker halyards; and two each for the genoa and spinnaker sheets. Equipment is unusually complete and includes such items as turning blocks, bosun's chair, anchor, fenders, etc. The cockpit is T-shaped and has wheel steering. Teak is optional for the deck.

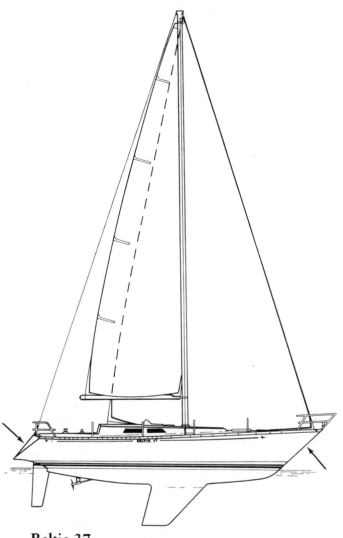

Baltic 37

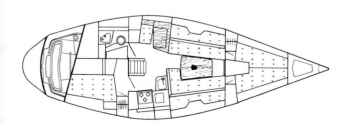

Dickerson 37

Length: 37 ft. LOA;
　28 ft. 10 in. LWL
Beam: 11 ft. 6 in.
Draft: 4 ft. 6 in.
Displacement: 15,950 lbs.
Sail area: Main, jib, and mizzen,
　675 sq. ft. total
Hull: FRP, deck balsa core
Spars: Aluminum

Berths: 6
Engine: Perkins 37 HP
Fuel: Diesel, 45 gal.
Head: Standard, shower
Galley: 3-burner alcohol
Water: 90 gals.
Rating: None
Designer: George Hazen

Center-cockpit ketch. Masthead rig. High aspect ratio. Pulpit/platform.

The overhangs and sheer have been deliberately designed for a traditional appearance, but the center cockpit and aft cabin are modern. The Dickerson 37 is designed as a cruiser for two or three couples. Dickerson has specialized in cruising ketches for many years.

The aft cabin may be reached from its own companionway, or through a passage below. There are berths for two and storage. In the passageway to the main cabin are lockers and access to the engine. The galley to starboard has a pressure water system, as does the large head. In the main cabin the L-shaped dinette converts to a double berth. There is an opening hatch above, and all ports operate. The sole is teak and holly, with access panels to the bilge. Forward, the isolated cabin has vee berths, a hanging locker, and a bureau. A second hatch is above.

On deck, handrails and cap rails are teak, as are coamings and the bow platform. There is wheel steering in the center cockpit. The mizzen has a traveler and the main a vang. There are three halyard winches, genoa tracks and cleats, and two genoa winches. Both the main and the mizzen have jiffy reefing.

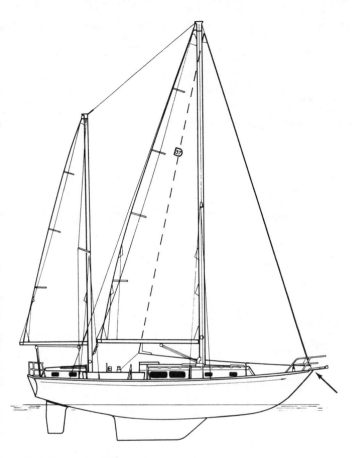

Dickerson 37

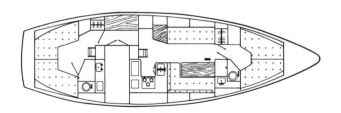

Dockrell 37

Length: 37 ft. LOA; 30 ft. LWL
Beam: 10 ft. 2 in.
Draft: 8 ft. 4 in.
Displacement: 11,500 lbs.
Sail area: Main, 220 sq. ft.;
  jib, 224 sq. ft.; no. 1 staysail,
  131 sq. ft.; genoa, 395 sq. ft.
Hull: FRP
Spars: Aluminum

Berths: 7
Engine: Yanmar 30 HP
Fuel: Diesel, 20 gals.
Head: Standard
Galley: 2-burner propane, oven
Water: 40 gals.
Rating: None
Designer: Dockerell Yachts

Cutter. Distinctive rudder shape. Masthead rig. Reverse transom.

This boat, built to Lloyd's specifications, has the beam restricted to 10 feet for use in European canals or for overland transportation. She is light displacement, has a low wetted surface, and combines a fixed with a swing keel. Lines from the keel through the rudder skeg are unusual.

The quarter berth is a double. Its isolation from the main cabin is an unusual feature. This layout indicates the galley backed up to port of the companionway, but other drawings show a plan with the galley parallel to the hull. In either design there is electric refrigeration and a double sink. The main cabin is finished in teak and mahogany. With its standard layout, three are accommodated for sleeping. Forward is the head and stowage, and the forecabin with vee berths for two. Hatches are over the saloon and aft cabin, and there is a forward opening port in the forecabin.

The cockpit is small and self-draining. The waterline is relatively long, while overhangs are moderate. The bow has very little flare.

Dockrell 37

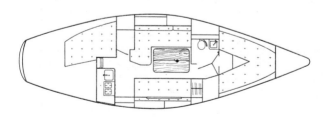

Alberg 37

Length: 37 ft. 2 in. LOA; 26 ft. 6 in. LWL	*Engine:* Volvo MD11C
Beam: 10 ft. 2 in.	*Fuel:* Diesel, 35 gals.
Draft: 5 ft. 6 in.	*Head:* Standard, shower
Displacement: 16,800 lbs.	*Galley:* 3-burner alcohol, oven
Sail area: Total, 686 sq. ft.	*Water:* 60 gals.
Hull: FRP	*Rating:* PHRF 162
Spars: Aluminum	*Designer:* Not stated; manufactured by Whitby Boat Works
Berths: 7	

Yawl. Mainmast backstay split. Mizzen sheets to stern pulpit.

This yawl was derived from the Albert 37 sloop and is available in that rig. Lines are classic, with a long counter, full keel, and spoon bow. Beam is moderate and the hull quite symmetrical.

The companionway ladder interferes with work at the galley sink, but large counters are to the side and out of the way. One ladder step will fold out of the way when the sink is used. A quarter berth and the navigation station are to port, and there is a wet locker directly below the ladder. In the main cabin the table folds against the forward bulkhead for storage. The port settee makes up into a double berth, and there are an extension berth and a pilot berth opposite. The head has pressure water and a grating over the sump. A sliding door closes it off. Across is a large hanging locker. The forward cabin has a door for privacy, lockers, a hanging locker, the vee berths, and storage under.

Teak is used for the inlaid cockpit seats and for the fixed main-cabin skylight. A forward skylight over the forecabin opens. There are winches for both main and jib halyards, one for the mainsheet, and two for the genoa. Genoa tracks have cars and blocks. There is a vented anchor locker in the forepeak.

Alberg 37

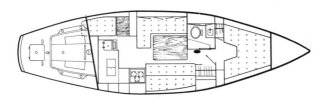

Endeavour 37

Length: 37 ft. 5 in. LOA;
  30 ft. LWL
Beam: 11 ft. 7 in.
Draft: 4 ft. 6 in.
Displacement: 21,000 lbs.
Sail area: Main, 312 sq. ft.;
  100% foretriangle, 414 sq. ft.
Hull: FRP
Spars: Aluminum

Berths: 6
Engine: Perkins 50 HP
Fuel: Diesel, 55 gals.
Head: Standard, shower
Galley: 3-burner alcohol, oven
Water: 101 gals.
Rating: PHRF 186
Designer: Endeavour-Yacht Corp.

Cutter. Bowsprit. Curved coaming. Possible ketch rig. High bow. Vertical transom. Aspect ratio 2.4 to 1.

With a private stateroom aft and with a total of six bunks, the Endeavour qualifies as a live-aboard boat with a lot of storage space. With two or four aboard there is no need to use the settees for berths. The keel is long and the displacement hull is heavy. Draft is shallow. When the boat is rigged as a ketch, the mizzen goes through the cockpit just forward of the binnacle. A more conventional cabin arrangement is available.

The aft cabin is to port and has a double berth, seat, and hanging locker. There is direct access to the head. On the other side of the boat there is a double quarter berth and the nav station. The bulkhead between this area and the galley is only partial height, so there is no isolation. The galley is U-shaped and has pressure water. There is also a footpump. The ice chest is 10 cubic feet. The main cabin entrance to the head is opposite. The forward area of the cabin is devoted to the dinette and to storage. The central table folds. No bulkhead separates these areas, which contributes to a feeling of spaciousness. Wood is teak and the sole is teak parquet. Ten ports and three hatches open.

On deck, teak is used for the coaming and rail caps as well as for handrails. Main sheeting is to the bridge deck. A winch for the main halyard and one for the genoa are mast-mounted. Two primary sheeting winches are on the coaming. Jibs lead to a track on the rail.

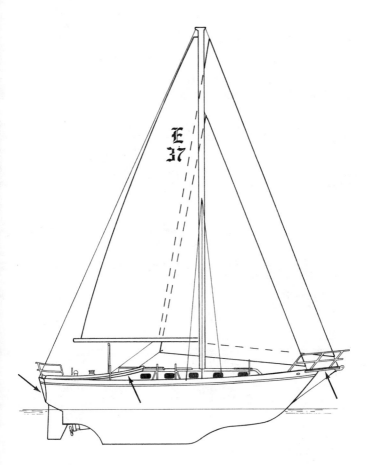

Endeavour 37

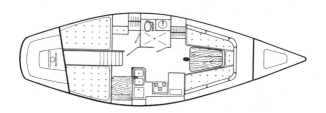

Shannon 38

Length: 37 ft. 9 in. LOA;
    30 ft. 10 in. LWL
Beam: 11 ft. 6 in.
Draft: 5 ft.
Displacement: 18,500 lbs.
Sail area: (Ketch): mizen, 169.4
    sq. ft.; main, 285.9 sq. ft.;
    total, 751 sq. ft.
Hull: FRP

Spars: Aluminum
Berths: Custom
Engine: Perkins 40 HP
Fuel: Diesel, 70 gals.
Head: Standard, shower
Galley: 3-burner propane, oven
Water: 120 gals.
Rating: PHRF 181.5 average
Designer: Schultz and Stadel

Motor sailer or standard. Ketch and cutter have double fore-sails. Staysail self-tending. Bowsprit.

This Shannon has been designed for long-range offshore cruising. The keel is long and full. Basic options include either a cutter or a ketch rig and either a standard·or a pilot house design. Cabin layout is semicustom and will depend upon the choices above.

As shown, the design is for a standard deck arrangement. The companionway leads directly to the navigation station and the galley. Pressure water is standard in the latter, and there is a nine-cubic-foot ice box located just aft of the stove. A quarter berth serves as the seat for the chart table, which is located just aft of a wet locker. In the layout shown both settees extend, and there is a pilot berth above the port settee. The central table is drop-leaf. Forward is the head, with pressure water and an independent pump for the shower sump; a hanging locker; and other storage. The forward cabin is somewhat unusual, with a double berth to starboard and a workbench and sail bin across. Interior surfaces are teak. There are four Dorade vents, hatches over the main and forward cabins, and 12 bronze opening ports.

On deck, the trim, including the coaming and the bowsprit, is teak. There are eight winches, including primary, staysail sheet, mainsheet, genoa, main, staysail halyards, and reefing. Both the main and the staysail have travelers. The propane locker is vapor-proof and has an overboard vent.

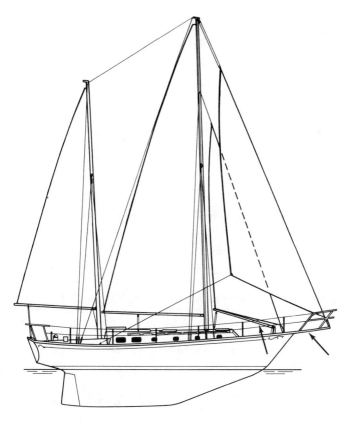

Shannon 38

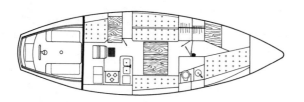

Sabre 38

Length: 37 ft. 10 in. LOA;
   31 ft. 2 in. LWL
Beam: 11 ft. 6 in.
Draft: 6 ft. 6 in. (keel); or 8 ft.
   (keel/centerboard)
Displacement: 15,200 lbs. (keel);
   or 15,600 lbs. (keel/
   centerboard)
Sail area: Main, 168 sq. ft.;
   100% jib, 234 sq. ft.; 150%
   genoa, 351 sq. ft.

Hull: FRP
Spars: Aluminum
Berths: 6
Engine: Westerbeke 33 HP
Fuel: Diesel, 10 gals.
Head: Standard, shower
Galley: 3-burner alcohol, oven
Water: 94 gals.
Rating: PHRF 111
   (manufacturer)
Designer: Sabre Design Team

*Aspect ratio over 3 to 1. Masthead. Sheer almost straight.
Straight bow. Long cabin.*

The hull and rig are designed for speed, while the cabin arrangement is comfortable for cruising. Fuel and water are adequate for offshore sailing. The keel model is standard, the keel/centerboard is optional. Other Sabres are the 28, 30, and 34.

Both the galley and the head appear quite spacious. Note how the ice box is partially under the cockpit. Refrigeration is available. Water here and in the head is pressure. In the forward cabin are vee berths, drawers, lockers, and storage compartments. Opposite the head are wet and dry hanging lockers. In the main cabin the port settee converts to a double. The table folds forward against a magazine rack. Aft to starboard is the nav station with its separate seat and a large quarter berth. There are hatches over both forward and main cabins.

The traveler is mounted on the coach roof just forward of the companionway hatch. The cockpit is T-shaped and has cockpit lockers and wheel steering. Primary winches are self-tailing, and there are winches for the main and genoa halyards, the mainsheet, and reefing. Eight ports open. A boom vang and spinnaker gear, including winches, are optional.

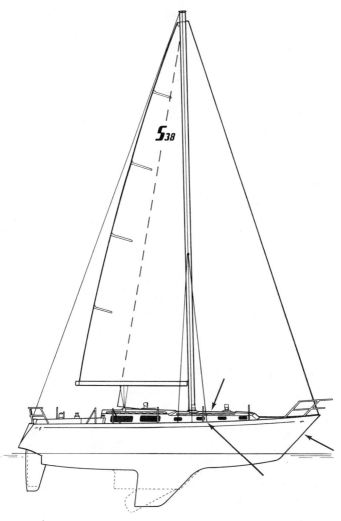

Sabre 38

Alajuela 38

Length: 38 ft. LOA;
   32 ft. 7 in. LWL
Beam: 11 ft. 6 in.
Draft: 5 ft. 7 in.
Displacement: 27,000 lbs.
Sail area: Main, 366 sq. ft.; jib,
   344 sq. ft.; staysail, 178 sq. ft.
Hull: FRP
Spars: Aluminum

Berths: 5
Engine: Pisces 40 HP
Fuel: Diesel, 85 gals.
Head: Standard
Galley: 2-burner propane, oven
Water: 100 gals.
Rating: None
Designer: Terry Wells

Cutter. Bowsprit. Cruiser bow. Two backstays, one to each quarter. Double-ended. Square lines to cabin.

This is a passage or cruising boat, not a racer. Long keel gives directional stability, but Alajuela will not turn on a dime. Double-enders offer less area to pooping seas, and are intended for cruising. Alajuela has a fast-draining, relatively small cockpit for insurance.

The main cabin is located forward and has a double berth, small settee, vanity, hanging locker, and the head to starboard. There is access to the chain locker. There are two berths and a pilot berth in the main cabin, as well as the U-shaped galley and a chart table. The ice box is top loading. Between the engine room and the galley is a wet locker. The interior is teak with contrasting planked ceiling. The sole is teak and holly.

There are three two-speed halyard winches and five two-speed sheet winches. The tiller may be replaced by a wheel. The nonskid surface is ground walnut shell. Side decks are 22 in. wide, and the pulpit has a teak footwalk. A teak skylight is optional. There are genoa and staysail tracks, a 6:1 mainsheet with traveler, and a 2:1 internal outhaul. There are four teak ventilators, teak coaming, a Samson post, and a lazarette for propane storage.

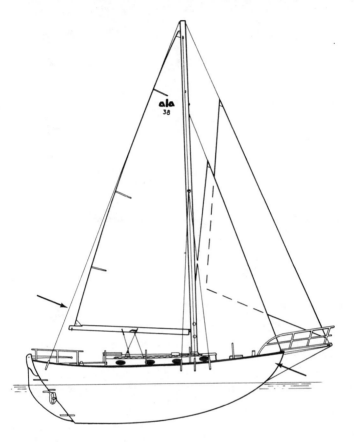

Alajuela 38

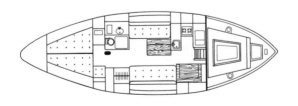

Catalina 38

Length: 38 ft. 2 in. LOA;
30 ft. 3 in. LWL
Beam: 11 ft. 10 in.
Draft: 6 ft. 9 in. (standard); or
4 ft. 11 in. (shoal)
Displacement: 15,900 lbs.
(standard); or 16,700 lbs.
(shoal)
Sail area: Main, 253 sq. ft.;
100% foretriangle, 386 sq. ft.
Hull: FRP

Spars: Aluminum
Berths: 5
Engine: Atomic 30 HP
Fuel: Diesel, 36 gals.
Head: Standard
Galley: 2-burner
Water: 41 gals.
Rating: D–PN 80.1 suspect;
PHRF 116 average, keel
Designer: Frank Butler

Distinctive counter and transom. Boom appears very short, aspect ratio high. Long smooth sheer. Balanced hull.

The Catalina is available with either a standard or a shoal-draft keel. Entry is fine and rig tall, which should assist in going to weather. Maximum beam is amidships.

Photographs show a quarter berth on the starboard, which would increase berths to six. The cabin finish is oiled teak. There is a skylight over the main cabin and a hatch forward. The galley is U-shaped and has double sinks and an ice box. Pressure water is standard. To starboard is the navigation station. The dinette is U-shaped and has a settee opposite. Just forward of the partial bulkhead there are drawers and lockers to starboard and the head, with teak shower grating, to port. Vee berths are forward.

The cockpit has pedestal wheel steering and lockers. An anchor locker is in the forepeak. Two halyard winches are on the coach roof, as is a traveler for the mainsheet. There are primary winches indicated for the genoa. Tracks are on the bulwarks.

Catalina 38

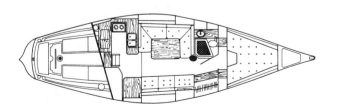

Farr 38

Length: 38 ft. 3 in. LOA;
  31 ft. 2 in. LWL
Beam: 12 ft.
Draft: 6 ft. 4 in.
Displacement: 10,600 lbs.
Sail area: Main, 397 sq. ft.;
  100% foretriangle, 286 sq. ft.
Hull: Epoxy and polyurethane
  over wood structure

Spars: Aluminum
Berths: 8
Engine: Pathfinder 40 HP
Fuel: Diesel, 26 gals.
Head: Standard
Galley: 2-burner LPG, oven
Water: 75 gals.
Rating: PHRF 83 average
Designer: Bruce Farr

Reverse counter. Continuous port covering. Long, sloping coach roof. Spreaders swept back.

Cold-molded wood, unusual in a boat of this size, is used for construction. The hull framing is cedar and the skins, spruce. Planking is thin strips adhesive-bonded in diagonal and longitudinal laminations. The result is a high-performance cruiser that has been successfully raced.

Below decks the layout is fairly standard except for the number of berths. There are two quarter berths, one double and the other single. In the main cabin are a double and a single settee. Vee berths are in the peak. The head with shower is forward to port with hanging lockers opposite. At the bottom of the ladder are the navigation station and the galley.

Above is lots of sail control. There are four halyard, two primary, two secondary, and one general-purpose winch. Halyards are internal, as is the outhaul and the quick reef for the main. The boom vang is four-part and the backstay is adjustable. Spars are painted with polyurethane. There are a traveler, genoa track, and lead blocks. Options include pressure water, refrigeration, wheel steering, and anodized spars. A cedar deck may also be chosen.

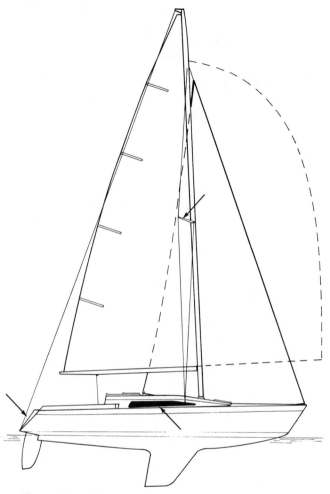

Farr 38

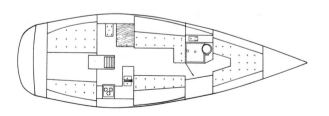

Clark 31

Length: 38 ft. 7 in. LOA;
26 ft. 3 in. LWL
Beam: 9 ft. 3 in.
Draft: 5 ft.
Displacement: 11,800 lbs.
Sail area: Main, jib, and foresail,
579 sq. ft.
Hull: FRP
Spars: Spruce or aluminum

Engine: Volvo 25 HP
Fuel: Diesel, 50 gals.
Head: Standard
Galley: Standard
Water: 45 gals.
Rating: None
Designer: Modified from
L. Francis Herreshoff

Classic clipper bow. Bowsprit. Spars possibly wood. Boomkin for backstay.

When L. Francis Herreshoff designed the H–28 in 1939 it may have been his most popular boat. This modification has a counter transom, a taller and more powerful rig, and a higher ballast ratio; and it is deeper and is wider on deck. However, the hull lines, bowsprit, boomkin, and round ports are classic, as is the rectangular coach roof.

Clark calls the cabin layout "sensible," but it is also somewhat unusual forward. The forecabin, instead of having the standard vee berths, has a berth to port and a work counter starboard. Aft, the head is opposite a hanging locker. The starboard berth converts to a double. Farther aft is a navigation table with the quarter berth serving as the seat. The galley is to port. The counter beside the seat folds down for storage, and the four-cubic-foot ice box can be loaded from the cockpit.

The prototype of the Clark was rigged as a yawl. Bronze hardware such as a boom bail, outhaul, and gooseneck were developed for this boat. Most other hardware and the eight opening ports are also bronze. Hatches are teak, as is the skylight. The bulwarks are mahogany with a teak cap.

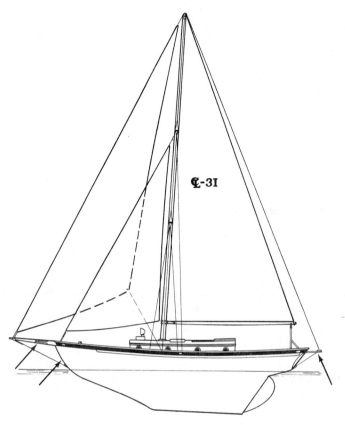

C-31

Clark 31

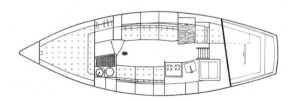

Corbin 39

Length: 38 ft. 9 in. LOA;
31 ft. 11 in. LWL
Beam: 12 ft. 2 in.
Draft: 5 ft. 6 in.
Displacement: 21,500 lbs.
Sail area: Main, 367 sq. ft.; jib,
455 sq. ft.; genoa, 709 sq. ft.;
spinnaker, 1593 sq. ft.
Hull: FRP sandwich
Spars: Aluminum

Berths: 7
Engine: BMW D–35
Fuel: Diesel, 104 gals.
Head: One with shower; aft
wash basin
Galley: 3-burner, oven
Water: 128 gals.
Rating: None
Designer: Dufour Yacht Design

Rounded stern. Straight bow, pulpit. May be center-cockpit or pilot-house, cutter or ketch. Running backstays on cutter.

The Corbin may be purchased in various stages of completion. Rig may be ketch or cutter, and the cockpit may be aft or amidships for either, although the mizzen will go through the aft cockpit of a ketch. Corbin is pleased that their boat has been termed "overbuilt," as they intend it for cruising. Data is for the tall rig, but a shorter rig may be purchased.

The companionway leads to an aft cabin that has its own wash basin. The main cabin is forward of a bulkhead and has a navigation station to starboard and the galley against the bulkhead and to port. Two hatches are above the galley, with another two over the dinette area. A hanging locker and the head are aft of the forecabin bulkhead. The berths in the forecabin are to starboard, with a settee to port. A hatch is above. Water systems are pressurized. Additional ventilation is through six Dorade boxes.

On deck, trim is teak. Storage includes two foredeck sail lockers, one cockpit locker, coaming lockers, and a locker for the anchor chain. There are two mast winches, two primary winches, a genoa track with a traveler, and a mainsheet traveler. Running backstays are used.

Corbin 39

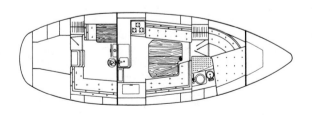

Cal 39

Length: 39 ft. LOA;
   32 ft. 1 in. LWL
Beam: 12 ft.
Draft: 6 ft. 8 in. or 5 ft. 6 in.
Displacement: 19,000 lbs.
Sail area: Standard rig: main,
   303 sq. ft.; 100% foretriangle,
   417 sq. ft. Tall rig: main,
   326.6 sq. ft.; 100%
   foretriangle, 450 sq. ft.
Hull: FRP

Spars: Painted aluminum
Berths: 6
Engine: Universal 44 HP
Fuel: Diesel, 45 gals.
Head: Two
Galley: 3-burner alcohol, oven
Water: 152 gals.
Rating: D–PN 79.4 suspect;
   standard, PHRF 114
Designer: William Lapworth

*Sloop or cutter, optional tall rig. Either is high aspect. Straight
bow. Note reverse transom and line of rudder.*

A Lapworth design, this Cal has a long waterline, aft-extending
rudder, and a substantial sailplan. In addition to the two rigs
offered, a shoal-draft keel is available. The fastest boat incorporates the tall rig and the deep keel and has a PHRF of about
106.

The Cal 39 provides privacy for three couples. There is an
aft cabin with a double berth entered from portside beside the
companionway. In addition to the sink/hanging locker plan
shown, an optional full head is available. If selected, it occupies
the space shown for the navigation station. The galley is a large
one, with double sinks, three burners and an oven, and an
eight-cubic-foot ice box. Forward of the galley is the saloon
with two settee-berths and a folding table. A second head is
forward and also has pressure hot and cold water. A teak door
gives privacy to the forward cabin with its double berth and
hanging locker. Light and ventilation are through two translucent hatches, one over the foredeck and one over the main
cabin. There are four fixed and eight opening ports, deadlights
over the head and the passageway, and a Dorade ventilator
over the galley.

The cockpit is T-shaped and has pedestal wheel steering.
Winches include one for the mainsheet, two for halyards, and
two for genoa sheets. Halyards are internal, as is the outhaul.
The mainsheet is on a traveler and has a 5:1 mechanical advantage. There are tracks for the jib sheets. Stowage includes
an anchor locker, a lazarette, and two lockable seat lockers.

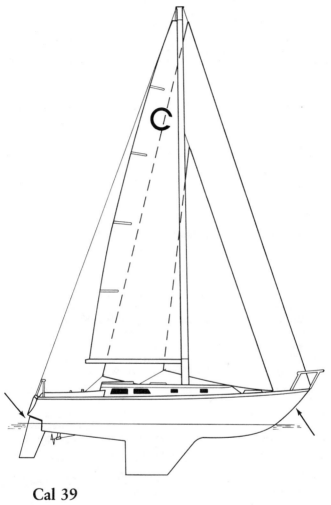

Cal 39

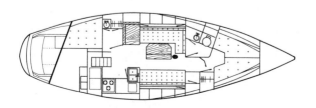

Freedom 39

Length: 39 ft. LOA; 31 ft. LWL
Beam: 12 ft. 10 in.
Draft: 5 ft. 6 in.
Displacement: 18,500 lbs.
Sail area: Main, 456 sq. ft.;
  foresail, 288 sq. ft.
Hull: FRP, balsa core
Spars: Carbon fiber
Berths: 6

Engine: Perkins 50 HP
Fuel: Diesel, 100 gals.
Head: Standard, shower
Galley: 3-burner propane, oven
Water: 160 gals.
Rating: None
Designers: Ron Holland and
  Garry Hoyt

*Pilot-house schooner. Unstayed. Two vangs. Modern hull lines.
Forward port long and low, rear port large.*

This cruiser was designed to offer the advantages of a schooner
but with improved windward sailing characteristics. Since there
is no forestay it cannot sag, and upwind performance is improved. The pilot house is very low and does not block vision
from the cockpit.

There is a private cabin aft reached from the pilot house. It
has a private head, hanging lockers, shelves, and a double
berth. The pilot house has a settee–double berth to port. Opposite is the below-deck steering position with a captain's
chair, the instrumentation, and a navigation station. The galley
is large and U-shaped. Opposite is a second head with molded
fiberglass shower stall. In the forecabin are a double berth,
hanging lockers, and a seat. Ventilation is through four hatches
and two opening ports. The former are over the forecabin, forward head, galley, and main cabin. The ports are in the aft
cabin.

Boat control, as in most Hoyt designs, is intended to be from
the cockpit. Two winches and sheet stoppers are centrally located for the main and mizzen sheets, halyards, reef lines, and
vangs. There is a full-length toe-rail. Both steering positions use
wheels.

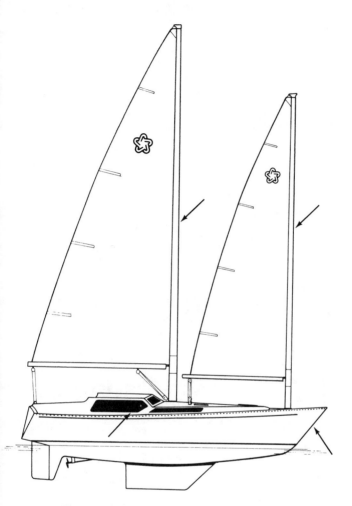

Freedom 39

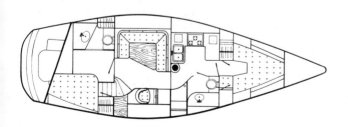

Nautical 39

Length: 39 ft. LOA; 32 ft. 6 in.
LWL
Beam: 12 ft.
Draft: 5 ft. 4 in.
Displacement: 22,500 lbs.
Sail area: Sloop: main,
314 sq. ft., 100% foretriangle,
363 sq. ft.
Hull: FRP
Spars: Aluminum

Berths: 8
Engine: 50 HP
Fuel: Diesel, 60 gals.
Head: Two, standard, shower
Galley: 3-burner, oven
Water: 200 gals.
Rating: None
Designers: Charles Morgan,
Roger Warren

*Sloop or ketch. Center cockpit. Aft cabin has raised deck.
Transom portlights. Waterline long in relation to LOA.*

The Nautical 39 is the smallest of the line, with other boats at
56 and 60 feet. With three cabins, two full heads, lots of water
and fuel, and a center cockpit, she is designed for cruising. A
ketch is also available.

In the forecabin the vee berths can convert to a double with
a filler. There are a hanging locker and an overhead hatch. Access to the full head is private. Just aft is a second door to the
head and stowage. In the main cabin the dinette is fixed, but
the port settee converts to a double. All ports open, and there
are hatches both here and in the aft cabin. The galley has a 12-
cubic-foot ice box, and refrigeration is available. Outboard the
passageway is a very large chart table/workbench. A door allows access to the engine room. The aft cabin has a private
head and shower, dressing table, hanging locker, and shelves.

In the cockpit, winch bases are molded in and two can be
accommodated on each side. There are genoa tracks and a
three-point traveler. Two sheet winches are provided, as is a
winch for the mainsheet and two mast-mounted halyard
winches. Handrails, toe-rails, and other exterior trim are teak.
There is a roller in the bow for the anchor. Steering is pedestal
wheel.

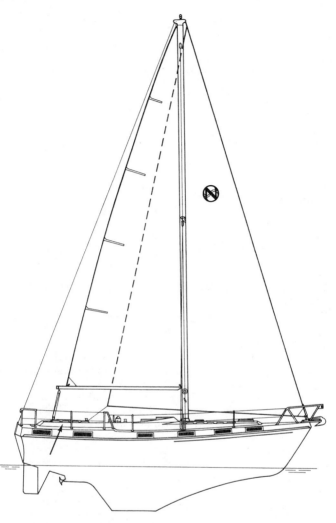

Nautical 39

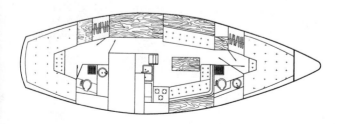

Islander 40

Length: 39 ft. 6½ in. LOA;
30 ft. 10 in. LWL
Beam: 11 ft. 10 in.
Draft: 7 ft. 2 in.; or 5 ft. 1 in.
(shoal)
Displacement: 17,000 lbs.
Sail area: Main, 297 sq. ft.;
100% foretriangle, 437 sq. ft.
Hull: FRP

Spars: Aluminum
Berths: 6
Engine: Pathfinder 42 HP
Fuel: Diesel, 38 gals.
Head: Standard, shower
Galley: 3-burner propane, oven
Water: 48 gals.
Rating: PHRF 82 average
Designer: Doug Peterson

Rudder partially exposed. Reverse transom. Note main sheeting. Straight bow.

The Islander 40 is available with either deep keel or shoal draft. The latter has a 297 sq. ft. main and a 100 percent foretriangle with a 421 sq. ft. area.

The forecabin is private and has its own access to the head. There are two berths, which may be converted to sail storage; and drawers; and a hanging locker. Aft to starboard is a hanging locker with sliding door. The head has hot and cold pressure water and a hand-held shower with teak grating over the sump. In the main cabin is a settee-berth to starboard and a second to port with a pilot berth over. The navigation area is large and has space for electronics. Both pressure water and a footpump serve the galley. To starboard is a large quarter berth. Six ports open and there are both forward and mid-cabin hatches. Wood is oiled teak.

On deck, stowage includes an anchor well, two seat lockers, and two lazarettes. The main has a traveler on the coach roof. All sheets and halyards lead to the cockpit or to the cabin roof aft of the mast. There are two jib winches, one for the main and one for the jib halyards, and secondary winches are optional. There are a topping lift, internal outhaul, and internal reefing. The vang bale is designed for hydraulics. A baby stay package with track, car, and other necessary gear is included.

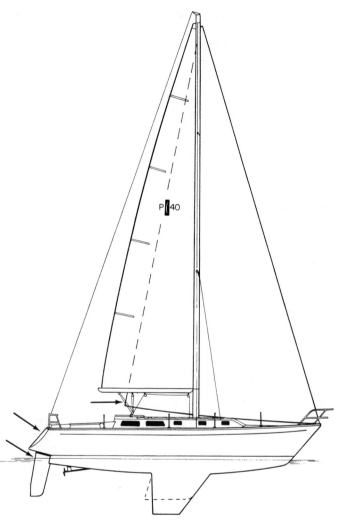

Islander 40

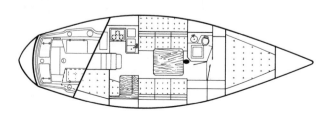

C & C 40

Length: 39 ft. 7 in. LOA;
   31 ft. 4 in. LWL
Beam: 12 ft. 8 in.
Draft: 7 ft. (keel)
Displacement: 17,100 lbs.
Sail area: Main and 100%
   foretriangle, 742 sq. ft.
Hull: FRP, balsa core
Spars: Aluminum

Berths: 7
Engine: Standard
Head: Standard, shower
Galley: 3-burner propane, oven
Water: 60 gals.
Rating: Wide variation depending
   upon keel and rig height;
   PHRF from 84 to 102.
Designer: C & C Design Group

Very sharp bow. Maximum beam amidships. Very short counter. Reverse transom. Low cabin profile.

The model shown is aft cabin. Previous C & C 40s had the head forward. The designers obtained space by moving the companionway forward. This necessitated moving the traveler from the cabin roof to the bridge deck. As noted in rating data above, various models are available. Only one mast height is shown, but note the shallow keel, deep keel, and swing keel. In any case, entry is fine and the forefoot is deep. The V forward becomes a U further aft. The spade rudder is high aspect.

The aft cabin has a double berth to port. There is a hanging locker and a seat. There are two doors for the head, so it may be entered either from the aft cabin or from the main cabin. The galley is to port and the large navigation station is opposite. A hanging locker is behind the navigator's seat. In the main cabin the double berth is to port. The midships table folds. Pilot berths are available. Forward are a double berth, a bureau, and hanging lockers. The forward cabin has a door for privacy. The number of opening ports will vary by model, but the minimum is two. Hatches are above the head, the aft cabin, the main cabin (three), and the forward cabin.

The cockpit is T-shaped and has pedestal wheel steering. Genoa tracks are inboard but there is also a slotted toe-rail. The deck plan shows six winches just aft of the mast, two secondary at the cockpit. Some photographs show variations. There is a locker for the anchor.

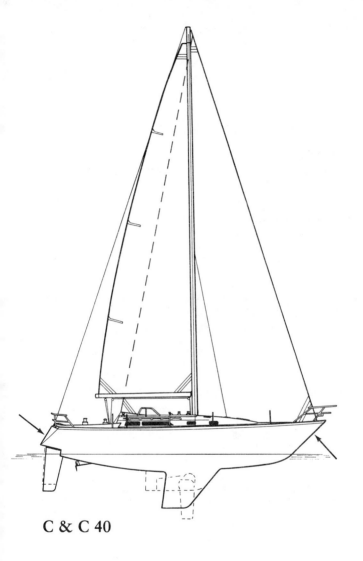

C & C 40

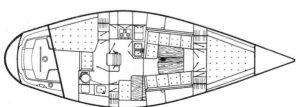

Nordic 40

Length: 39 ft. 8½ in. LOA;
32 ft. 6 in. LWL
Beam: 12 ft. 5 in.
Draft: 6 ft. 4 in. (deep); or
5 ft. 6 in. (shoal)
Displacement: 18,000 lbs.
Sail area: Main, 336 sq. ft.;
100% foretriangle, 420 sq. ft.
Hull: FRP

Spars: Painted aluminum
Berths: 6
Engine: Universal 32 HP
Fuel: Diesel, 55 gals.
Head: Standard
Galley: 3-burner propane, oven
Water: 130 gals.
Rating: PHRF 105
Designer: Robert H. Perry

Straight bow parallel to reverse transom. Note portlight arrangement. Running backstays.

The Nordic shows many of the hull features that have become popular since the late sixties. The hull is fine forward, has a short underwater length, and flattens aft toward the skeg and the spade rudder. The keel is short, thin, and quite deep. Overhangs are short.

In the forecabin are vee berths and a hanging locker, with a skylight-hatch above. The head is large and has a molded fiberglass shower stall with seat. Opposite are lockers and a shelf. In the saloon the L-shaped settee and folding table are to port with another settee to starboard. Aft is a small private cabin with a double quarter berth, hanging locker, and a chart table with swing-away seat. The U-shaped galley across is also large. There is a nine-cubic-foot ice box. Propane for the stove is kept aft in the lazarette well. Provisions for light and air include three hatches at the companionway, main cabin, and forecabin; four Dorade boxes with cowls; two fixed windows; and six opening portlights.

Control lines are internal and include five halyards, a topping lift, a spinnaker-pole topping lift, and three reef lines. Seven winches are standard. There are two primary, one for the genoa halyard, one for the main halyard, one for the main sheet, and one for reefing and for the outhaul. The toe-rail is slotted and there is an inboard sheeting track. Shrouds are inboard. The traveler is mounted on the cabin roof. Backstay adjustment can be added.

Nordic 40

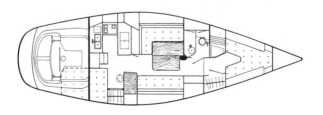

Concordia Yawl

Length: 39 ft. 10 in. LOA;
28 ft. 6 in. LWL
Beam: 10 ft. 3 in.
Draft: 5 ft. 8 in.
Displacement: 18,000 lbs.
Sail area: Total, 650 sq. ft.
Hull: Mahogany
Spars: Wood

Berths: 4
Engine: Gray 30 HP
Fuel: Gasoline, 20 gals.
Head: Standard, shower
Galley: Alcohol
Water: 60 gals.
Rating: PHRF 168 approx.
Designer: C. Raymond Hunt

Wood hull and spars. Mizzen sheets to transom. Long counter. Jumper stays on both masts.

The Concordia was first built in 1938, but the majority of the boats were built after World War II. On most boats many of the items listed, such as the gasoline engine and wood spars, have certainly changed. While this classic yawl is no longer built, most of the boats are still sailing. "Malay" and "Babe" both won the Bermuda race.

Most hulls were built by Abeking and Rasmussen in Germany and finished in the United States. The cabin plan shown is typical, and has two folding berths in the forward cabin with seats under. A sail bin with slatted floor is in the forepeak. There is a door for privacy. Just aft to port is the head, and there are five lockers opposite. In the main cabin the berths fold to form backrests and the central table folds. The galley lies across the boat, with ice box and sink to port and the stove to starboard.

Decks are canvas-covered. All plank fastenings and hardware are bronze, as are the winches. Two skylights, one over the main cabin and one over the forecabin, provide light. Dinghy chocks are on the cabin roof.

Concordia Yawl

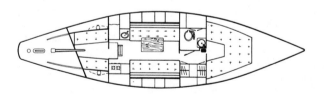

Endeavour 40

Length: 40 ft. LOA; 32 ft. LWL
Beam: 13 ft.
Draft: 5 ft.
Displacement: 25,000 lbs.
Sail area: Sloop: main, 338 sq. ft.; 100% foretriangle, 405 sq. ft.
Hull: FRP
Spars: Aluminum

Berths: 6
Engine: Perkins 50 HP
Fuel: Diesel, 75 gals.
Head: Two, standard, shower
Galley: 3-burner alcohol, oven
Water: 135 gals.
Rating: PHRF 126
Designer: Endeavour Yachts

Sometimes a ketch. Center cockpit fairly far aft. Four forward ports rectangular, aft ports more oval. Sweeping sheer, with offset upwards amidships.

Endeavour is a big, comfortable cruiser intended for extended trips. Note that both fuel and water capacity are high. Ballast/ displacement ratio is 36 percent. The cockpit, like most center cockpits, is high and therefore dry.

The galley is set beside the companionway and does not obstruct traffic. It is still close enough to the main seating area to allow the cook to communicate. There is hot and cold pressure water, a fresh-water pump, and refrigeration. The navigation station is also aft of the ladder. Here, the table folds down out of the way allowing access to the seat. Going aft there is a step down to the passageway. The central engine room may be entered, and a workbench, hanging locker, and stowage are outboard. The aft cabin is one step up. There are a double berth, a chest of drawers, and a private head. The main cabin has a central folding table and two settees. Lockers are suspended and have paneled doors. The head forward has two doors so that it may be entered either from the forecabin or from aft. Water is pressure and there is a shower. Opposite are hanging lockers and drawers.

Storage on deck includes two lazarette bins, an anchor well, and an insulated locker in the cockpit. There are a traveler, slab reefing, and a topping lift. Two winches are for the main and jib halyards, one is for the mainsheet, and there are two for genoa sheets. There are 16 opening ports and 4 cabin-top hatches. Teak is used on deck and below.

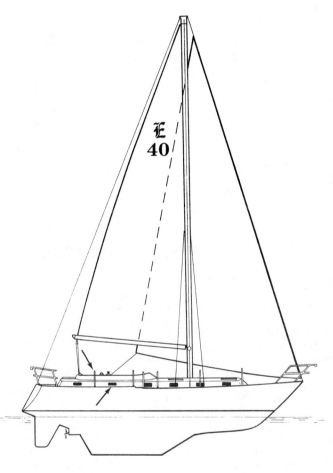

Endeavour 40

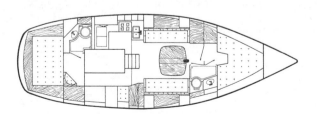

Bristol 40

Length: 40 ft. 2 in. LOA;
27 ft. 6½ in. LWL
Beam: 10 ft. 9 in.
Draft: 5 ft. 4½ in.
Displacement: 17,580 lbs.
Sail area: Main, 317 sq. ft.; jib,
265 sq. ft.; no. 1 genoa, 495
sq. ft.; spinnaker, 1189 sq. ft.
Hull: FRP

Spars: Aluminum
Berths: 6
Engine: Westerbeke
Fuel: Diesel, 31 gals.
Head: Standard
Galley: 3-burner alcohol, oven
Water: 130 gals.
Rating: PHRF 166 average
Designer: Ted Hood

*Classic lines. Full keel. Long bow. Foredeck ventilators. May
be rigged as yawl.*

The Bristol 40 is designed as a racer-cruiser. Many options, including a yawl rig, and several interior layouts are available for
the owner who favors cruising. This boat, with its long bow
and counter and full keel, is not for round-the-marker sailing,
but it will do well on longer races.

The layout shown is quite traditional, with the galley aft to
port with an opposing navigator's station. Some photographs
show this arrangement flipped, and the nav station coupled
with a quarter berth. A dinette, used as a double berth, is
shown to port. The starboard berth and a pipe berth above are
standard. The portside head has a draining floor for the
shower. There is a lot of storage, with 10 drawers and 2 shelf
compartments. The head may be entered from either the forecabin or the main saloon. Note the cross bulkhead at the mast.
The forecabin has vee berths and a hanging locker. A hatch
above this cabin is double-hinged, and will open fore or aft.

There is an Edson wheel. The bow pulpit, stern rail, genoa
tracks, and anchor roller on the stem are provided. Two primary, two secondary, and a jib-halyard winch come with the
boat. There is jiffy reefing.

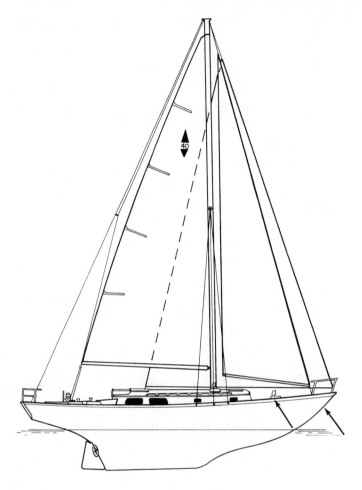

Bristol 40

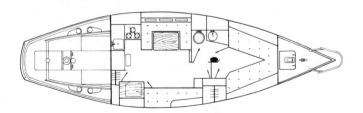

Bermuda 40

Length: 40 ft. 9 in. LOA;
27 ft. 10 in. LWL
Beam: 11 ft. 9 in.
Draft: 4 ft. 3 in. (board up); or
8 ft. 9 in. (board down)
Displacement: 20,000 lbs.
Sail area: Main, 260 sq. ft.;
mizzen, 96 sq. ft.; 100%
foretriangle, 427 sq. ft.
Hull: FRP

Spars: Coated aluminum
Berths: 6
Engine: Westerbeke 40 HP
Fuel: Diesel, 48 gals.
Head: Standard, shower
Galley: 3-burner propane, oven
Water: 110 gals.
Rating: PHRF 163 average
Designer: William H. Tripp, Jr.

Also a sloop. Note long curved counter leading to short vertical transom. Mizzen sheets to stern pulpit. Cruiser bow.

The centerboard on this cruiser is bronze and is operated by a worm gear. There is an override for grounding. Cabin layout may be modified, and there is a sloop model available.

The galley–navigation area crosses the boat at the foot of the companionway ladder. The stove and sink are to port. On the opposite side the ice-box top serves as the chart table, and there is space allocated for electronics and chart stowage. Refrigeration is available. The main-cabin layout shown has two extension berths with pilot berths over and stowage under. The center table is drop-leaf. Other storage space includes a bridge deck and a wet locker aft, shelves, bookcases, and a hanging locker forward to starboard. The head is opposite and has a teak grate over the shower pan. A bulkhead and a door give privacy to the forward cabin, which has vee berths with a seat between, a hanging locker, and stowage under the berths.

The cockpit has wheel steering, sail bins under the seats, and a lazarette. There are two secondary and two primary winches, and winches for the main and jib halyards, the mizzen halyard and sheet, and the mainsheet. Jiffy reefing on the main boom allows for two reef points. Coamings and trim are varnished teak.

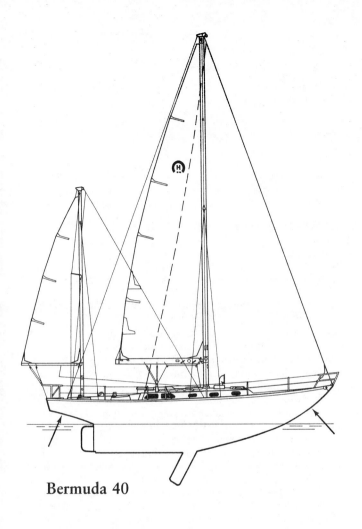

Bermuda 40

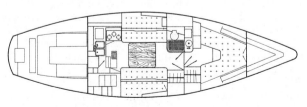

Dickerson 41

Length: 41 ft. LOA;
  31 ft. 6 in. LWL
Beam: 12 ft. 6 in.
Draft: 4 ft. 6 in.
Displacement: 24,500 lbs.
Sail area: Main, mizzen, and jib,
  791 sq. ft.
Hull: FRP
Spars: Aluminum, epoxy finish

Engine: Westerbeke 50 HP
Fuel: Diesel, 100 gals.
Head: One standard; second
  depending on cabin plan
  selected
Galley: 3-burner alcohol
Water: Tank provided
Rating: None
Designer: Ernest Tucker

Aft deck house. Clipper bow, bowsprit. Identical ports uniformly spaced. May be rigged as a cutter or a ketch.

The 41 is the intermediate Dickerson. There are also a 37 and a 50. All are based on Dickerson's long experience with cruising ketches. The 41 has a number of rig options, such as a cutter or ketch rig, a self-tacking forestaysail, twin headsails, and a roller-furling genoa.

There are also many optional cabin plans. The aft cabin shown has a private head/shower, but a navigation station may be substituted. The two berths may be converted to a double. In place of the workbench shown, storage may be located across from the engine-room doors. In the main cabin the dinette converts to a double. In this view, the navigation station is shown aft of a settee, but there may be two chairs with a table. Pilot berths are available. There is a hanging locker just aft of the forecabin door. The cabin itself has a private head, vee berths convertible to a double, and storage. Both heads have pressure water, as does the galley. Trim is teak; the sole is teak and holly. There are 2 port lights, 3 opening ports, and 3 acrylic hatches.

Teak is used above deck for handrails, toe-rails, hatch covers, and coamings. There are lockers in the coaming and an anchor locker in the bow. The aluminum spars are epoxy-painted. Standard equipment includes three halyard winches, genoa tracks and blocks, and two two-speed genoa winches. The main and mizzen have jiffy reefing.

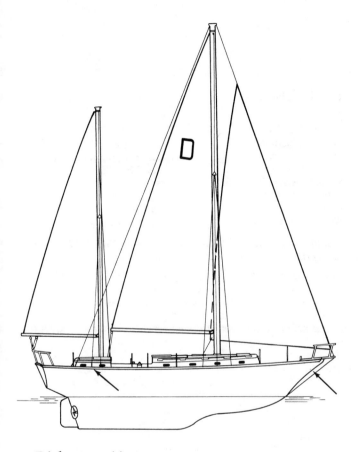

Dickerson 41

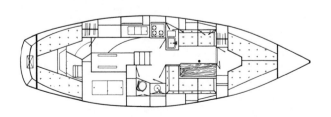

Lord Nelson 41

Length: 41 ft. LOA;
  36 ft. 2 in. LWL
Beam: 12 ft. 10 in.
Draft: 5 ft. 8 in.
Displacement: 30,500 lbs.
Sail area: Main, 395 sq. ft.;
  100% foretriangle, 661 sq. ft.
Hull: FRP
Spars: Painted aluminum

Berths: 5–8
Engine: BMW 50 HP
Fuel: 120 gals.
Head: Standard, shower
Galley: Three-burner propane,
  oven
Water: 200 gallons
Rating: None
Designer: Loren Hart

Double-ender. Deep sheer with high bow and stern. Pulpit on bowsprit. Boom gallows. Pronounced rub-rail.

The designer must be a navigator, as he has his own berth at the navigation station. This is a big cutter intended for cruising. Hull design is traditional, as are the finishing touches, such as actual belaying pins and a Samson post.

The galley, at the foot of the ladder, has a double sink. Hot and cold water is pressure, as is the case at the head and shower. The settee just forward is large and U-shaped. It converts to a double berth. The navigation station and its berth are opposite. Forward is a private cabin with side-entering double berth, curved settee, and hanging locker. It has its own entrance to the head. A second private cabin is aft. Here there are a double berth, seat, hanging locker, and sink. There are louvered doors on lockers and bookcases in each cabin. Three opening hatches and 14 opening portlights are bronze.

The cockpit is large and could be used for sleeping. Two winches are for halyards, one for the main sheet, two for staysail sheets and the halyards, and two for primary sheets. The main sheets to a traveler bridge. Of the two lazarette hatches, one is insulated for use as an ice box.

Lord Nelson 41

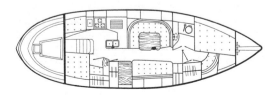

Newport 41

Length: 41 ft. LOA;
  32 ft. 3 in. LWL
Beam: 11 ft. 3 in.
Draft: 6 ft. 3 in.
Displacement: 18,000 lbs.
Sail area: Main and jib,
  750 sq. ft.
Hull: FRP
Spars: Anodized aluminum

Berths: 7
Engine: Standard
Fuel: Diesel, 35 gals.
Head: Optional
Galley: 3-burner alcohol, oven
Water: 75 gals.
Rating: PHRF 114;
  D–PN 80.2 suspect
Designer: C & C Design Group

Spoon bow. Counter, reverse transom. Tall masthead rig. Mid-boom sheeting to cabin roof. One-and-two port arrangement.

Perhaps the most unusual aspect of the Newport 41 is the cluster of winches around the mast, all located on the cabin roof. There are five winches which almost complete a circle. These are all for halyards and vangs. All sheeting leads to the cockpit. There are two winches on the coach roof and two primary and two secondary winches at normal locations in the cockpit.

Cabin layout is quite normal. In the main cabin are a quarter berth, nav station, and settee to starboard. The latter converts to a bunk, and a pilot berth over is optional. The galley to port is U-shaped with sink, ice box, stove, storage, and counter space. A trash bin is accessible from the cockpit. Forward is an L-shaped settee and fold-down table. The settee converts to a double berth. The head is forward to port and has a molded fiberglass shower pan. Water here and in the galley is manual, with pressure optional. The head has an opening port. Across from the head are two hanging lockers. The forward cabin is closed off with a curtain; there are drawers, a double berth, and a hanging locker. The chain locker may be reached from below. Ventilation is through two translucent hatches and two opening ports. There are also four fixed windows.

The traveler is mounted on the coach roof. The hard-anodized toe-rail accepts blocks, and an inside sheet track is optional. Above and below, trim is teak. The cockpit has wheel steering and two lockers. Some options are an internal outhaul, vang, head, salt-water pump in the galley, and spinnaker gear.

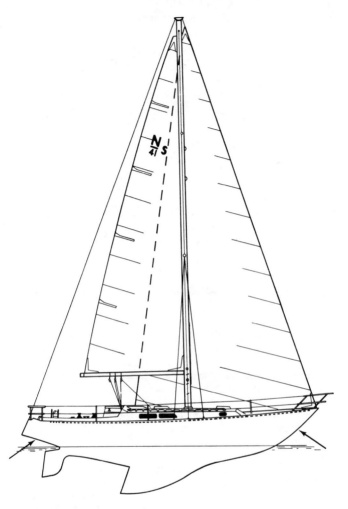

Newport 41

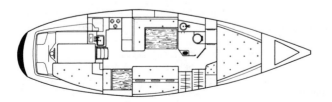

Morgan Out Island 41

Length: 41 ft. 3 in. LOA;
34 ft. LWL
Beam: 13 ft. 10 in.
Draft: 4 ft. 2 in.
Displacement: 27,000 lbs.
Sail area: Main, 312 sq. ft.;
100% foretriangle, 413 sq. ft.;
mizzen, 153 sq. ft.
Hull: FRP

Spars: Aluminum
Berths: 7
Engine: Perkins 62 HP
Fuel: Diesel, 90 gals.
Head: Two, marine; showers
Galley: 2-burner alcohol, oven
Water: 200 gals.
Rating: D–PN 75.9; PHRF 192
Designer: Morgan Yacht Inc.

Ketch. Center cockpit. Semiclipper bow. Only visible ports are aft. Curved coaming.

The Morgan Out Island 41 may be the world's most popular cruising boat. Over 800 have been built, and the boat is used extensively in the charter industry. There is often roller furling for the jib. There are two double cabins that are really private; a main cabin with a double and a single; and in desperate cases, the nav station and workbench could be used for one person.

The aft cabin can be entered by a passageway or through its own companionway. There are a double berth, hanging lockers, a private head, and a seat. Going through the passageway, a workbench is to port and the double-door access to the engine room to starboard. In the main cabin is the chart table, which has a 7-cubic-foot ice box below. The galley is at the foot of the main ladder and has a second ice box with 10-cubic-foot capacity, double sink, and pressure water. The saloon table is mounted on the bulkhead, and stores. A door isolates the forward cabin with its vee berth, hanging locker, and separate head and shower. Wood is teak. Air and ventilation is through 14 opening ports, 2 transom opening ports, the companionways, aft and galley hatches, and a forecabin hatch. A prism in the cockpit sole admits light to the engine room.

On deck, there are full-length toe-rails for jib sheeting. Winches include two two-speed sheet winches, two halyard winches on the main mast, and one on the mizzen. Both main and mizzen have topping lifts and there is a roller for the anchor. The cockpit has wheel steering and a seat locker. Teak is used for trim above and below.

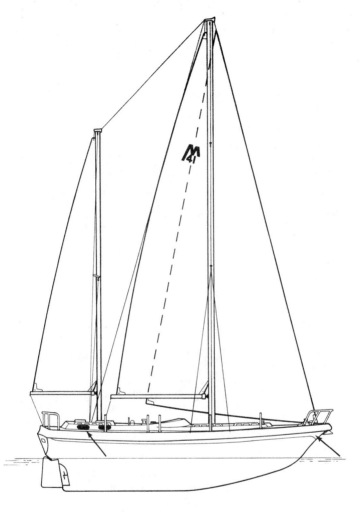

Morgan Out Island 41

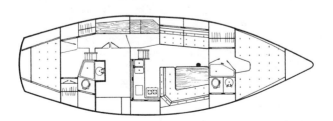

Albin Nimbus

Length: 41 ft. 6 in. LOA;
 34 ft. 2 in. LWL
Beam: 12 ft. 6 in.
Draft: 5 ft. 10 in.
Displacement: 21,500 lbs.
Sail area: Main, 368 sq. ft.; jib,
 486 sq. ft. (100%); various
 genoas and spinnakers
Hull: FRP
Spars: Polyurethane-coated
 aluminum

Berths: 8
Engine: Pathfinder 50 HP
Fuel: Diesel, 60 gals.
Head: Two
Galley: 3-burner propane, oven
Water: 120 gals.
Rating: PHRF 90–99
Designer: Kaufman and Ladd

High-aspect masthead rig. Backstay, running backstays. Cutter or sloop. Low, long ports.

Nimbus is a big auxiliary with three cabins, but with a tall, high-aspect rig for racing. Shrouds are inboard for good windward sheeting angles. The keel is relatively short and the rudder is well aft.

There is an aft master stateroom that will sleep three and has its own settee, vanity, hanging locker, and head with shower. The galley is to port midships and has two sinks and a large ice box. Opposite is the chart table, with chart stowage. Under the companionway stairs is a wet locker. The dinette converts to a double, and to starboard is a settee-berth. Forward are a second head with shower, a vee berth, and a hanging locker. In all there are more than forty drawers and lockers. The cabin and sole are finished in teak and holly. Ventilation is through six translucent opening hatches, two Dorade vents, and four deck cowls. There are also four deck prisms for lighting.

Above, the decks are teak. There are six internal halyards, with one for the main, two for genoas, two for the spinnaker, and one for the staysail. They lead to four halyard winches and four two-speed self-tailing winches. Both spinnaker pole and boom have topping lifts. The genoa and the spinnaker pole have tracks and cars. There is a foredeck anchor storage locker and two aft lazarettes.

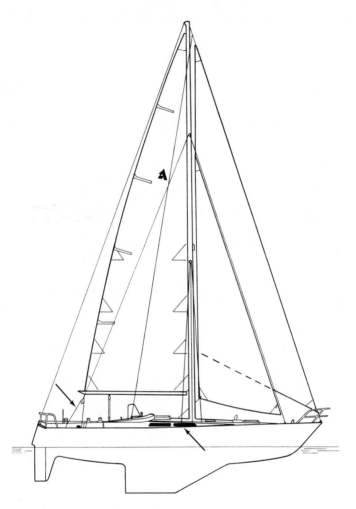

Albin Nimbus

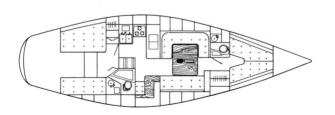

Irwin 41

Length: 41 ft. 8 in. LOA;
  33 ft. 4 in. LWL
Beam: 13 ft. 4 in.
Draft: 4 ft. 6 in. (shoal)
Displacement: 25,000 lbs.
  approx.
Sail area: Total, 959.8 sq. ft.
Hull: FRP
Spars: Coated aluminum

Berths: 7
Engine: Perkins 62 HP
Fuel: Diesel, 150 gals.
Head: Two separate with showers
Galley: 3-burner propane, oven
Water: 150 gals. approx.
Rating: None
Designer: Ted Irwin

Ketch. Dinghy may be on davits. Bowsprit with pulpit, two foresails. Main has double backstay.

The Irwin 41 was designed as a blue-water cruiser. The hull is moderate displacement, the keel is long, and the ballast/displacement ratio is 32 percent. Optional hulls are a centerboard/keel and a deep keel. The sail plan is balanced and designed to be handled by two people.

The passageway to the aft cabin passes an optional entertainment center with wet bar, stereo, and television. It continues past the chart table. The cabin itself has hanging lockers, a double berth, and a private head with shower. Forward at the companionway the galley is tucked away to starboard. At this location the sole is tile. The main saloon has a berth to starboard and the port settee makes into a double when the table is dropped. Forward there is storage to starboard and a second full head to port, reached from either the forward or the main cabin. The bow cabin has a vee berth.

The main sheets to the aft coaming, has a winch, and is four-part purchase. There are winches for the main halyard, the genoa sheets, the jib and mizzen halyards, and the mizzen sheets. Both the main and the mizzen have vangs and topping lifts. The main has slab reefing on the boom; both booms have internal outhauls. Handrails, toe-rails, and coaming boards are teak. The bowsprit is aluminum and the pulpits are stainless steel. Seven cabin hatches open.

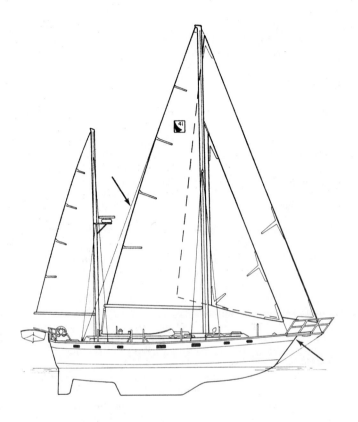

Irwin 41

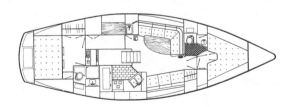

Landfall 43

Length: 42 ft. 1 in. LOA;
  34 ft. 5 in. LWL
Beam: 12 ft. 7½ in.
Draft: 5 ft. 6 in.
Displacement: 24,600 lbs.
Sail area: Total with 100%
  foretriangle, 796 sq. ft.
Hull: FRP
Spars: Aluminum

Berths: 7
Engine: Westerbeke
Fuel: 60 gals.
Head: Two
Galley: 3-burner propane, oven
Water: 130 gals.
Rating: None
Designer: C & C Design Group

Ketch or sloop. Center cockpit. Stanchions at hatches forward and aft of the mast.

The Landfall 43 evolved from her sister ships, the 48 and the 35. Draft is moderate and the fin keel is fairly long. The rudder is semibalanced. The designers claim particular success controlling helm characteristics when the boat is heeled, thus allowing for more sail area in light air.

As might be expected in a boat this large, systems are sophisticated. Refrigeration and hot and cold pressure water are standard; there is optional air conditioning and heating; and space designed to accept a diesel generator is under the workbench. The aft cabin is large and has a hanging locker and a private head. The passageway forward has a workbench outboard and engine access inboard. Entering the main cabin, the large galley is to port and the navigation station just ahead. In the main cabin is a U-shaped dinette which converts to a double and a settee across. There are six lockers behind the berths. Forward is a head, accessible from either the main cabin or the forecabin. The forward cabin berth is a double, and there are lockers, hanging lockers, and other storage.

Sheeting is to a traveler on the aft-cabin roof. Winches are provided for the mainsheet, the genoa and main halyards, the outhaul and reefing system, and the primary foresail sheets. There are hatches over the aft, forward, and main cabins. Steering is pedestal wheel. A ketch rig is optional, as is roller furling.

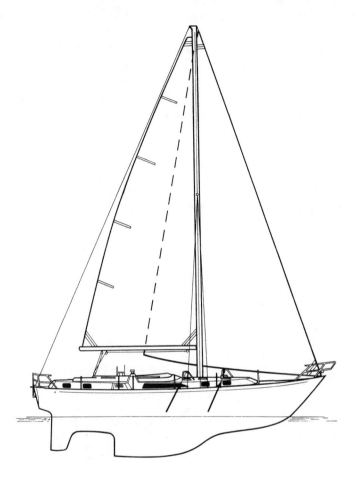

Landfall 43

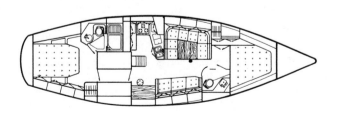

Tayana 37

Length: 42 ft. 2 in. LOA;
 30 ft. 10 in. LWL
Beam: 11 ft. 6 in.
Draft: 5 ft. 8 in.
Displacement: 22,500 lbs.
Sail area: Main, 342 sq. ft.; jib,
 292 sq. ft.; staysail, 230 sq. ft.
Hull: FRP
Spars: Spruce

Berths: 7
Engine: Yanmar 33 HP
Fuel: 90 gals.
Head: Standard
Galley: 3-burner propane, oven
Water: 100 gals.
Rating: PHRF 126
Designer: Robert Perry

Cutter or ketch. Double-ended. Boom gallows. Pilot house or trunk cabin. Bowsprit with pulpit.

When the Tayana is built with a pilot house, the quarter berth and chart table are replaced by the interior helm, a seat, and a wet locker. The galley is rearranged to provide another seat to port. Tayana is in many respects—perhaps excepting the double-ended design—typical of the many high-performance designs built today that retain a traditional appearance.

In the trunk-cabin version the U-shaped galley, with refrigerator, is to port at the foot of the companionway. The quarter berth opposite serves as the seat for the navigation station. The large settee converts to a double and the seat opposite is also a berth. There is a pilot berth above the latter. Cabin trim is teak. The head, forward to port, has hot and cold pressure waters and a teak grating over the shower sump. To starboard is a large storage area with drawers, shelves, and two hanging lockers. There are shelves in the forward cabin and storage under the vee berths. Two doors give access to the forepeak. There are a teak forward hatch, a teak skylight, and 11 bronze opening ports.

Decks are teak, as are the coaming top and the cockpit seats. There are two travelers, with the main traveler located just forward of the companionway hatch. Two winches are provided for jib sheets, one for the mainsheet, one for the staysail, and three for halyards. Tracks for the genoa are on the toe-rail, and shrouds are outboard.

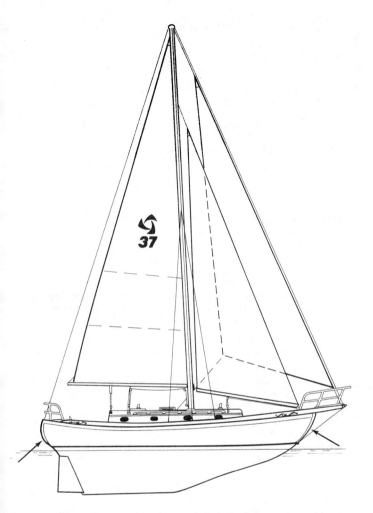

Tayana 37

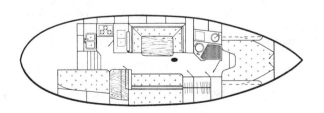

Nauticat 44

Length: 43 ft. 7 in. LOA;
  38 ft. 8 in. LWL
Beam: 12 ft. 1 in.
Draft: 6 ft.
Displacement: 39,700 lbs.
Sail area: Main, 306 sq. ft.;
  staysail, 118 sq. ft.; jib, 296 sq.
  ft.; forestaysail, 96 sq. ft.
Hull: FRP

Spars: Aluminum
Berths: 6 or 7
Engine: Ford 120 HP
Fuel: Diesel, 285 gals.
Head: Two standard
Galley: 2-burner gas, oven
Water: 200 gals.
Rating: None
Designer: Nauticat Inc.

Motor sailer rigged as ketch, sloop, or schooner. Slight clipper bow, bowsprit. Stern ports. If ketch, main mounts over third port aft and mizzen over aft deck.

This big motor sailer is shown primarily because of its schooner rig. It is also included because of the wheelhouse and the cabin plan peculiar to a motor sailer. The large quantities of water and fuel give a cruising range under power of 900 nautical miles.

Typical of the breed, there are helms both inside and outside the wheelhouse. Various options are possible in the master cabin. A center berth is shown. In addition to the private head there is a hanging locker, and there are lots of drawers and cabinets. Ports open, and there is a skylight hatch. Passage to the main cabin is up and through the wheelhouse. Here there are an L-shaped settee, a navigation table, the helm, and the helmsman's seat. There is a sliding hatch above, and two sliding doors give access to the side decks. Forward and below is the main cabin. To port is a large U-shaped settee which will seat eight, and which converts to double berth. Another settee is to starboard. The galley is forward and has two stainless sinks and a refrigerator. A second head is across. Two berths, storage, a hanging locker, and an overhead hatch are in the forecabin.

Decks are teak plank, as is the rub strake. An anchor roller and genoa furling gear are forward. There are two halyard winches on each mast and four for the sheets.

Nauticat 44

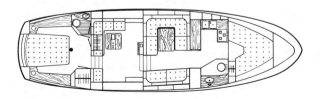

Worldcruiser 44

Length: 43 ft. 11 in. LOA;
33 ft. 4 in. LWL
Beam: 11 ft.
Draft: 6 ft. 2 in.
Displacement: 23,000 lbs.
Sail area: Main, 280 sq. ft.;
100% foretriangle, 356 sq. ft.;
foresail, 136 sq. ft.; fisherman,
230 sq. ft.
Hull: FRP

Spars: Painted aluminum
Berths: 5
Engine: varies; 25–50 HP
Fuel: Diesel, 60 gals.
Head: Standard, shower
Galley: 3-burner, oven
Water: 100 gals.
Rating: None
Designer: Bud Taplin

Traditional schooner. Might have a genoa and a gollywobbler. Long overhangs. Bowsprit and boomkin.

Worldcruiser feels that the sails on a boat over 40 feet should be small enough to handle without a large crew and that two-masted rigs are the answer. In light weather, flying a genoa instead of the headsails and with a gollywobbler in place of the foresail and fisherman, the boat has a total sail area of over 2000 sq. ft.

Cabin layout is unusual. Aft of the ladder is a double berth to port. In the center, free-standing, is the engine box. To starboard are two desks, a bookcase, storage for charts, and a large hanging locker. Forward, the galley is across from the dinette, which can convert to a single. In the galley, water is pressure. A second work area is just forward and has the electrics behind and a bookcase, coffee table, and desk. A second double berth is to starboard, and a very large hanging locker and drawers ahead to port. The head is very large and crosses the boat. There are a hamper, linen storage, and general stowage. In the forepeak are separate sail and chain lockers. Trim is ash and teak. Four hatches are shown and all opening portlights are bronze.

The staysails have self-tending booms leading to travelers. The deckhouse may be extended forward of the mast, providing more headroom, or held between the masts. The deck aft of the main mast is flush, except for the distinct scuttle over the aft cabin.

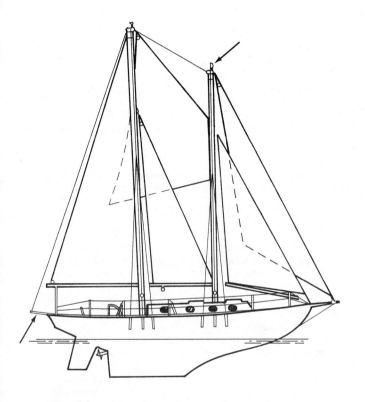

Worldcruiser 44

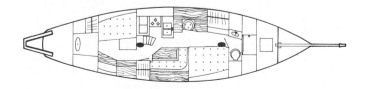

Alden 44

Length: 44 ft. 2 in. LOA;
34 ft. 1 in. LWL
Beam: 12 ft. 6 in.
Draft: 8 ft. 9 in.
Displacement: 24,500 lbs.
Sail area: Rated for IOR with
150% genoa, 1085.7 sq. ft.
Hull: FRP, balsa core
Spars: Aluminum

Berths: 7
Engine: Perkins 4–108
Fuel: Diesel, 80 gals.
Head: Standard, shower
Galley: Propane oven and stove
Water: 160 gals.
Rating: D–PN 79.4 suspect;
PHRF 99
Designer: John G. Alden

Straight bow. Note porthole arrangement, ventilator arrangement. Cutter rig. Counter and reverse transom.

The Alden is designed for IOR competition but has many cruising amenities. The hull is moderate displacement. She is claimed to be fast, dry, stiff, and close-winded.

There are two companionways and the owner's stateroom is entered aft. Layouts can vary. The one shown indicates two berths and the chart table, lockers, and a bureau. There is a hatch to port. The head, to port, and the galley, to starboard, are slightly behind the main companionway. The galley has hot and cold water, six drawers, and two lockers. There is a six-cubic-foot refrigerator and a four-foot freezer. The head is large and has access from both the aft stateroom and the main cabin. The main cabin has berths for two or, with a pilot berth, three. The table is drop-leaf. Storage includes a hanging locker, bookshelves, and two storage lockers. Like the other ceilings, the main cabin ceiling is detailed with ash battens. The forward cabin has two berths, a hanging locker, and a chest of drawers. Ventilation includes seven opening ports and five translucent hatches.

Most winches are self-tailing. There are two for the main halyard, two for the genoa, two for the spinnaker, one for the Cunningham, one for the outhaul, two for the staysail halyard, two primary, two secondary, two for the mainsheet, two for the genoa sheets, and two for spinnaker sheets. There is a topping lift. A club-footed staysail is available. For racing, the staysail stay is removed.

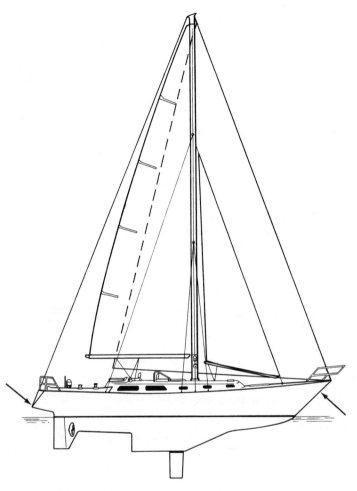

Alden 44

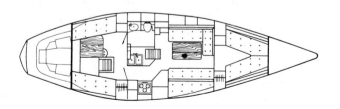

Bayfield 40

Length: 45 ft. 6 in. LOA;
  30 ft. 6 in. LWL
Beam: 12 ft.
Draft: 4 ft. 11 in.
Displacement: 21,000 lbs.
Sail area: Topsail, staysail, main,
  and mizzen: 1109 sq. ft. total
Hull: FRP
Spars: Aluminum

Berths: 6
Engine: Westerbeke 52 HP
Fuel: Not stated
Head: Standard
Galley: 2-burner propane
Water: 100 gals.
Rating: None
Designer: Ted Gozzard

Ketch. Note counter. Clipper bow and bowsprit. Double head-sails.

The lines of the hull are traditional. The foresail rig is unusual in a big ketch. Cabin layout, with a midships galley and no vee berths, is distinctly different.

The companionway lands at two aft berths, which may be converted to small staterooms. Both are identical, with top hatch, opening port, drawers, and a hanging locker. Both have double berths. Privacy is afforded by bulkhead panels which may be raised, and by sliding doors. Forward to starboard is a large dining area which converts to a double berth. The table has swing-out seats midships. To port is a full navigation station. There is a swivel chair, and the table will take a full-sized chart. The galley has electric refrigeration and two opening ports. A large hanging locker is opposite. Forward, the shower is separate from the rest of the head. Two hatches and two ports open. The forepeak stowage for sails and anchors is reached from the deck.

The 40 is a big boat, and has many standard items of equipment. Sails (top, stay, main, and mizzen) are included. There are 10 opening ports and 4 opening hatches. The large skylight just aft of the mainmast also opens. There are 11 winches. Steering is wheel.

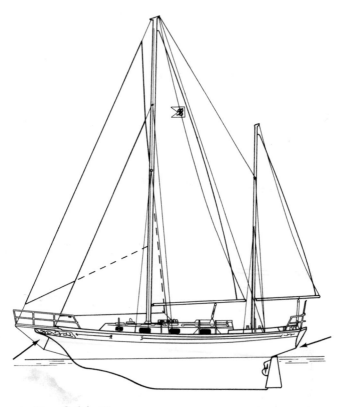

Bayfield 40

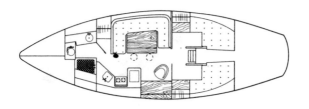

Appendix
Glossary
Index

APPENDIX

One-Design Class Associations

National **A Scow** Class
  Association
Jim Smith, Sec.
P.O. Box 311
Fontana, WI 53125

U.S. **Albacore** Association
Carl Cheney, Pres.
15800 Perkins Lane
Bowie, MD 20716

Apollo Sailing Class Association
AMF Alcort Joanne Girard
Box 1345
Waterbury, CT 06720

Bandit 15 Class Association
Fred Merry, Pres.
1935 King Arthur Cir.
Maitland, FL 32751

Banshee Class
William B. Haile, Sec.
18579 Ravenwood Dr.
Saratoga, CA 95070

International **Blue Jay** Class
  Association
Mrs. James M. Mertz,
  Pres.-Sec.
79 Madison Avenue
New York, NY 10016

U.S. **Boardsailing** Association
Susan Noyes, Dir.
P.O. Box 206
Oyster Bay, NY 11771

Boardsailing U.S.A.
Brian Tulley, Prog. Dir.
P.O. Box 2157
Citrus Heights, CA 95611

Buccaneer Class
George Sculley, Sec.
P.O. Box 66474
Houston, TX 77266

Bullseye Class Association
I. W. Tuttle, Sec.
1 Squam Road
Rockport, MA 01966

National **Butterfly** Association
Dan Darrow, USYRU Liaison
15342 W. Clover Lane
Libertyville, IL 60048

C.&C. 35 Association
James E. Butler, Sec.-Treas.
30712 Champine
St. Clair Shores, MI 48082

National **C Scow** Sailing
  Association
Rodney A. Crawford
P.O. Box 175
Excelsior, MN 55331

National **C Scow** Class
  Association
Jim Smith
P.O. Box 311
Fontana, WI 53125

Cal 20 Class Association
Dick Reinhardt
414 Via Mesa Grande
Redondo Beach, CA 90277

Catalina 22 National Sailing
 Association
Loal Scofield, Sec.-Treas.
P.O. Box 1327
Grapevine, TX 77405

International Celebrity Class
 YRA
Edward Lippman, Sec.
Box 1029
Morrisville, PA 19067

Comet Class YRA
Josh Goldman
60 E. 96th St.
New York, NY 10028

International Contender Class
 Association
Jerome White, Sec.
Box 831
Summerland, CA 93067

Coronado 15 Class Racing
 Association
Joe Theobald, Sec.
1117 N. Formosa Avenue
Los Angeles, CA 90046

Day Sailer Association
Dolores E. Bayer, Sec.
3456 Amberway Court
Cincinnati, OH 45239

American International Dragon
 Association
Mr. Jean Fraley, Sec.-Treas.
302 Lakeside Avenue S.
Seattle, WA 98144

Duster Class YRA
David N. Sikora
2143 Maplewood Avenue
Abington, PA 19001

National Class E Scow
 Association
Shirley Klauser, Sec.
349 Lakewood Boulevard
Madison, WI 53704

International E-22 Class
 Association
Gay S. Lynn, Sec.
64 Halls Lane
Rye, NY 10580

18 Square Meter Sailing
 Association
John Brink, Sec.-Treas.
508 Miller Avenue
Pacifica, CA 94044

El Toro International YRA
Edna Robinson, Sec.
P.O. Box 487
San Leandro, CA 94577

Ensign Class Association
J. Rutledge Delgado, Sec.
410 Oakdale St.
La Porte, TX 77571

International FJ Class
 Association
Mike Wyatt
475 Manhattan Pkwy
Painesville, OH 44077

U.S.A. Finn Association
John M. McIntosh Jr., Sec.
P.O. Box 22669
Savannah, GA 31403

U.S. International Fireball
 Association
Loretta McHenry, Sec.
179 E. Main Street
Cortland, OH 44410

International 505 Class YRA
Lillian Gsegner, Sec.
16918 Hereford Road
Monkton, MD 21111

International Flying Dutchman
 Class
Peter Wells, Sec.
P.O. Box 152
Rindge, NH 03461

Flying Scot Sailing Association
Ed Eubanks, Sec.
P.O. Box 11187
Columbia, SC 29211

Force 5 Racing Class
Association
AMF Alcort Joanne Girard
P.O. Box 1345
Waterbury, CT 06720

International 470 Association
Gregg K. Dietrich, Pres.
60 First St.
Cambridge, MA 02141

U.S. 420 Association
Sally Cantey, Sec.
132 Nortontown Road
Guilford, CT 06437

Gp-14 Class Association
Edward Blumstein, Sec.
1012 Two Girard Plaza
Philadelphia, PA 19102

Geary 18 International YRA
Joan Busch, Sec.
P.O. Box 99783
San Diego, CA 92109

H Class Association
William G. Harding, Sec.
Box 1
Cataumet, MA 02534

Hampton One Design
Association
Charles Zimmerman, Jr., Sec.
116 Hampton Roads Avenue
Hampton, VA 23661

Hawkfarm One Design Class
Association
Paul C. Altman, Sec.
4 Anchor Dr. Apt. 242
Emeryville, CA 94601

Highlander Class International
Association
Gorden Stafford, Sec.
4920 Marybrook Dr.
Dayton, OH 45429

Hobie Class Association
Michele Krcelic, U.S. Dir.
P.O. Box 1008
Oceanside, CA 92054

Interlake Sailing Class
Association
Larry & Barb King, Sec.-Treas.
2405 St. James Woods
Toledo, OH 43617

U.S. Isotope Class Association
Howard Estes
3412 Forest Dr.
Raleigh, NC 27604

International J/24 Class
Association
Dick Tillman, Dir.
645 Caribbean Road
Satellite Beach, FL 32937

J/30 Class Association
Ann Stuursma, Sec.
2228 Elmwood Dr. SE
Grand Rapids, MI 49506

Javelin Class Association
Gay Reiber
6214 Norman Lane
Mayfield Village, OH 44143

Jet 14 Class Association
Mary Ungemach, Sec.
26 Pontiac Dr.
Wayne, NJ 07470

International Laser Class
Association
Sue Holt, Sec.
550 Delmar Road
Pte Claire, PQ H9R 4A6
Canada

Laser II Class Association
Sue Holt, Sec.
550 Delmar Road
Pte Claire, PQ H9R 4A6
Canada

Lido 14 International Class
Association
P.O. Box 1252
Newport Beach, CA 92663

International Lightning Class
Association
Beatrice Parrish, Dir.
808 High St.
Wortington, OH 43085

National **M Scow** Class
  Association
Jim Smith
P.O. Box 311
Fontana, WI 53125

M-20 Sailing Association
John Sharpless, Sec.
2114 Regent St.
Madison, WI 53705

U.S. **Mariner** Class Association
Sue B. Jurechko, Sec.-Treas.
806 Hudson Dr.
Yardley, PA 19067

International **MC** Class Racing
  Association
Ruth F. Smith, Sec.
P.O. Box 88
Flowery Branch, GA 30542

Mercury Class YRA
Ray Johnson, Sec.
P.O. Box 216
Carmel Valley, CA 93924

U.S. **Mirror** Class Association
Edward Willoughby, Sec.
6455 Anslow Lane
Troy, MI 48084

Mistral Class
Mistral J. T. Skemp
7222 Parkway Dr.
Dorsey, MD 21076

International **Mobjack**
  Association
Mary Anne Seymour-Schultz
3366 Edgemont St.
Philadelphia, PA 19134

International **Moth** Class
  Association
Ben Krothe, Sec.
317 Ocean Avenue
Ocean City, NJ 08226

National One Design Class
  Association
Jolly Booth, Sec.
1225 E. Bronson St.
South Bend, IN 46615

N. A. Offshore **One-Design**
  Association
Thomas K. Fisher, Pres.
840 W. Milwaukee Avenue
Detroit, MI 48202

Olson 30 Class Association
Pete Harris, Sec.
130 Driftwood Court
Aptos, CA 95002

U.S. **Optimist** Dinghy
  Association
Robert Meagher, Sec.
P.O. Box 330971
Miami, FL 33133

International **Penguin** Class
  Dinghy Association
Laurence G. Cole
36 Ocean Avenue
Northport, NY 11768

Phantom Class Racing
  Association
D. Bruce Connolly, Sec.
250 Cornwell Avenue
Cheshire, CT 06410

National **Pintail** Class
  Association
Gordon Townsend, Sec.-Treas.
2560 W. Wallings Road
Broadview Hts, OH 44147

Prindle Class Association
Leslie Lindeman, Sec.
1810 E. Borchard Avenue
Santa Ana, CA 92705

Ranger 20 Class Association
Evelyn Aplin, Sec.
Box 814
Bellingham, WA 98227

National **Rebel** Class
  Association
Yvonne Flanigan, Sec.
2100 Hondo Dr.
Plano, TX 75074

Rhodes 19 Class Association
Fred Brehob
17 Corinthian Lane
Marblehead, MA 01945

Rhodes Bantam Class
  Association
Robert M. Schultz, Sec.-Treas.
5679 Meryton Place
Cincinnati, OH 45224

San Juan 21 Class Association
Fred G. W. Rehm, Sec.
1900 North Lane
Camden, SC 29020

San Juan 24 Class Association
Guy Essmeier, Sec.
5609 2nd Ave, NW #25
Seattle, WA 98107

Santana 20 Class Association
Jane Schock, Sec.
P.O. Box 1844
Newport Beach, CA 92663

American **Shark** Association
Tom Fowler, Sec.-Treas.
2 Meadowlark Road
Ithaca, NY 14850

Shields Class Association
Nicholas J. Baker, Sec.
285 Winter St.
Weston, MA 02193

Snipe Class International
  Racing Association
Lowry Lamb, Sec.
Privateer Road
Hixson, TN 37343

U.S. Soling Association
Larry Booth, Treas.
470 W. Willow
Fox Point, WI 53217

Sonar International
Jean Ross
44 Pasture Lane
Darien, CT 06820

International **Star** Class YRA
Doris Jirka, Sec.
1545 Waukegan Road
Glenview, IL 60025

Sunfish Racing Class
  Association
AMF Alcort Joanne Girard
P.O. Box 1345
Waterbury, CT 06720

Super Sunfish Racing Class
  Association
AMF Alcort Joanne Girard
P.O. Box 1345
Waterbury, CT 06720

Supercat Race Association
Stephen A. Edmonds, Sec.
P.O. Box 10184
Riviera Beach, FL 33404

Surfsprint Association
Sue Holt, Sec.
550 Delmar Road
Pointe Claire, PQ H9R 4A6
  Canada

Sweet 16 Sailing Association
Sheri Berger, Sec.-Treas.
2913 S. 46 St.
Kansas City, KS 66106

U.S. **Tanzer 16** Class
  Association
David Permar, Sec.
P.O. Box 26003
Raleigh, NC 27611

Tartan 10 Class Association
David K. Hamister, Sec.
24212 Lake Road
Bay Village, OH 44140

The **Ten** Class Association
Jim Melton
124 S. Main St.
Andover, OH 44003

Thistle Class Association
Honey Abramson, Sec.
1811 Cavell Avenue
Highland Park, IL 60035

U.S. **Tornado** Association
Jim Young
2189 Abraham Lane
Oshkosh, WI 54901

Trac 14 Catamaran Class
  Association
Joanne Girard
P.O. Box 1345
Waterbury, CT 06720

National Triton Association
Thomas D. Stevens, Sec.
300 Spencer Avenue
East Greenwich, RI 02818

AMF 2100 Class Association
Joanne Girard, Sec.
P.O. Box 1345
Waterbury, CT 06720

International 210 Class
  Association
Richard L. Schulz, Sec.-Treas.
1831 Manitoba Avenue
S. Milwaukee, WI 53172

U.S. 1 Class Association
John Slauter, Sec.
17753 Burrows Road
Thompson, OH 44086

U.S. Wayfarer Association
Gerald Lieberman, Sec.
15956 Lauderdale Dr.
Birmingham, MI 48009

Windflite Sailboard Class
  Association
AMF Alcort Joanne Girard
Box 1345
Waterbury, CT 06720

Windglider Class U.S.A.
Marshall Souder, Sec.
P.O. Box 848
Evanston, IL 60204

Windmill Class Association
Walter Bailey, Sec.
3620 Spring Valley Road
Birmingham, AL 35223

International Windsurfer Class
  Association
Diane Schweitzer, Sec.
P.O. Box 2950
Torrance, CA 90509

National X Scow Class
  Association
Jim Smith
P.O. Box 311
Fontana, WI 53125

American Y-FLYER YRA
Gregory W. Kleffner, Sec.
12241 Rain Hollow Dr.
Maryland Hgts, MO 63043

N. American Yngling
  Association
Noel Field, Jr., Sec.
2200 Industrial Bank Bldg.
Providence, RI 02903

Glossary

Basic definitions of terms are given according to their use in the text. No attempt is made to give a complete definition.

Backstay A wire support for the mast, usually running from the stern to the head of the mast.

Ballast Weight, usually metal, placed low in a boat to provide stability.

Barber hauler A line, attached to the jib or jib sheet, used to adjust the angle of sheeting by pulling the sheet toward the centerline of the boat.

Battens Flexible strips of wood or plastic, most commonly used in the mainsail to support the aft portion, or roach, so that it will not curl.

Bilgeboards Similar to centerboards, and used to prevent leeway. Bilgeboards are located on either side of the centerline at the bilges.

Binnacle A support for the compass, raising it to a convenient position.

Board boat A small boat, usually mono rig. May have a shallow cockpit well.

Bobstay Wire stay underneath the bowsprit; helps to counteract the upward pull exerted by the forestay.

Boom crutch Support for the boom, holding it up and out of the way when the boat is anchored or moored. Unlike a gallows frame, a crutch is stowed when boat is sailing.

Boomkin (bumpkin) Short spar extending aft from the transom. Used to anchor the backstay or the sheets from the mizzen.

Boom vang A system used to hold the boom down, particularly when boat is sailing downwind, so that the mainsail area facing the wind is kept to a maximum. Frequently extends from the boom to a location near the base of the mast. Usually tackle- or lever-operated.

Boot top A stripe near the waterline.

Bowsprit A short spar extending forward from the bow. Normally used to anchor the forestay.

Bridge deck The transverse partition between the cockpit and the cabin.

Bridle A short length of wire with a line attached at the midpoint. A bridle is used to distribute the load of the attached line. Often used for boom travelers and for spinnaker downhauls.

Bulkhead An interior partition, commonly used to stiffen the hull. May be watertight.

Bulwark A vertical extension above the deck designed to keep water out and to assist in keeping people in.

Centerboard A board lowered through a slot in the centerline of the hull to reduce sideways skidding or leeway. Unlike a daggerboard, which lifts vertically, a centerboard pivots around a pin, usually located in the forward top corner, and swings up and aft.

Chain plate The fitting used to attach stays to the hull.

Chine A line, running along the side of the boat, where the bottom forms an angle to the side. Not found on round-bottom boats.

Clew For a triangular sail, the aftmost corner.

Coach roof Also trunk. The cabin roof, raised above the deck to provide headroom in the cabin.

Coaming A vertical extension above the deck to prevent water from entering the cockpit. May be broadened to provide a base for winches.

Companionway The main entrance to the cabin, usually including the steps down into the cabin.

Cunningham A mainsail control device, using a line to pull down the mainsail a short distance from the luff to the tack. Flattens the sail.

Daggerboard A board dropped vertically through the hull to prevent leeway. May be completely removed for beaching or for sailing downwind.

Dodger A screen, usually fabric, erected to protect the cockpit from spray and wind.

Downhaul A line used to pull a spar, such as the spinnaker pole, or a sail, particularly the mainsail, down.

Dry-sailing When boats, especially smaller racers, are kept on shore instead of being left anchored or moored, they are dry-sailed. The practice prevents marine growth on the hull or the absorption of moisture into it.

Fairlead A fitting used to alter the direction of a working line, such as a bullseye, turning block, or anchor chock.

Foot For a triangular sail, the bottom edge.

Forestay Wire, sometimes rod, support for the mast, running from the bowsprit or foredeck to a point at or near the top of the mast.

Forepeak The compartment farthest forward in the bow of the boat. Often used for anchor or sail stowage.

Foretriangle The triangle formed by the forestay, mast, and foredeck.

Fractional rig A design in which the forestay does not go to the very top of the mast, but instead to a point $3/4$, $7/8$, etc., of the way up the mast.

Gooseneck The fitting that connects the boom to the mast.

Gunter rig Similar to a gaff rig, except that the spar forming the "gaff" is hoisted to an almost vertical position, extending well above the mast.

Halyard Line, usually of wire, which is used to pull up or hoist a sail.

Head For a triangular sail, the top corner. Also a marine toilet.

Hiking stick An extension of the tiller which allows the helmsman to sit at a distance from the tiller.

Inspection port A watertight covering, usually small, which may be removed so the interior of the hull can be inspected or water removed.

Jiffy reefing A fast method of reefing. Lines pull down the luff and the leech of the sail, reducing its area.

Jumper stay A short stay supporting the top forward portion of the mast. The stay runs from the top of the mast forward over a short jumper strut, then down to the mast, usually at the level of the spreaders.

Keelson A structural member above and parallel to the keel.

Kick-up Describes a rudder or centerboard that rotates back and up when an obstacle is encountered. Useful when a boat is to be beached.

Lazarette A stowage compartment at the stern.

Lazy jack Light lines from the topping lift of the mast, forming a cradle into which the mainsail may be lowered.

Lead Refers to the direction in which a line goes. A boom vang, for example, may "lead to the cockpit."

Leech The aft edge of a triangular sail.

Leech line A line running through the leech of the sail, used to tighten it.

Loose-footed Describes a mainsail attached to the boom at the tack and clew, but not along the foot.

Luff The forward edge of a triangular sail. In a mainsail the luff is that portion that runs up the mast.

Masthead rig A design where the forestay runs to the peak of the mast.

Mast step Fitting or construction into which the base of the mast is placed.

Mechanical advantage (or purchase). A mechanical method of increasing an applied force. Disregarding the effects of friction, if a force of 100 lbs. applied to a tackle is magnified to a force of 400 lbs., the purchase or mechanical advantage is said to be four to one, or 4:1.

150 percent genoa For rating purposes, the length of a line drawn perpendicular to the luff and intersecting the clew is divided by the length of the base of the foretriangle. For instance, if the former is 30 ft. and the latter 20 ft., the genoa is rated at 30/20 = 1.5, or 150 percent.

Outhaul Usually a line or tackle, an outhaul is used to pull the clew of the mainsail towards the end of the boom, thus tightening the foot of the sail.

Pedestal A vertical post in the cockpit used to elevate the steering wheel into a convenient position.

Pulpit A metal framework on deck at the bow or stern. Provides a safety railing and serves as an attachment for the lifelines.

Rake The fore or aft angle of the mast. Can be deliberately induced (by adjustment of the standing rigging) to flatten sails, balance steering, etc. Normally slightly aft.

Roach The curved portion of a sail extending past a straight line drawn between two corners. In a mainsail, the roach extends past the line of the leech between the head and the clew and is often supported by battens.

Rocker The upward curvature of the keel towards the bow and stern.

Roller reefing Reduces the area of a sail by rolling it around a stay, the mast, or the boom. Most common on headsails.

Rub-rail Also rubbing strake or rub strake. An applied or thickened member at the rail, running the length of the boat; serves to protect the hull when alongside a pier or another boat.

Running backstay Also runner, or preventive backstay. A stay that supports the mast from aft, usually from the quarter rather than the stern. When the boat is sailing downwind, the runner on the leeward side of the mainsail must be released so as not to interfere with the sail.

Running rigging That portion of the rigging used to control sails and equipment.

Sandwich construction Layered materials such as FRP-foam-FRP. Usually adhesively bonded. Typically strong and light. Often used in hulls; very widely used in decks.

Scupper. Drain in cockpit, coaming, or toe-rail allowing water to drain out and overboard.

Seat locker A storage locker located under a cockpit seat.

Self-bailing cockpit A watertight cockpit with scuppers, drains, or bailers which remove water.

Self-tacking Normally applied to a sail which requires no adjustment other than sheeting when the boat is tacked.

Sheer strake The topmost planking in the sides, often thicker than other planking.

Sheets Lines used to control the position of a sail.

Shrouds Lateral supports for the mast, usually of wire or metal rod.

Slab reefing Also points reefing, and sometimes jiffy reefing. Reduction of the area of the mainsail by partially lowering the sail and resecuring the new foot by tying it to the boom with points, or light lines attached to the sail.

Splashboard A raised portion of the hull forward of the cockpit intended to prevent water entering.

Spreaders Also crosstrees. Short horizontal struts extending from the mast to the sides of the boat, changing the upward angle of the shrouds.

Standing rigging Permanent rigging used to support the spars. May be adjusted during racing, in some classes.

Stem The most forward structural member in the bow.

Tabernacle A hinged mast step located on deck. Since it is hinged, the mast may be lowered easily.

Tack On a triangular sail, the bottom forward corner.

Taffrail The rail at the stern of the boat.

Tang A fitting, often of sheet metal, used to attach standing rigging to a spar, or to the hull.

Toe-rail A low rail, often slotted, along the side of the boat. Slots allow drainage and the attachment of blocks.

Thwart A transverse structural member in the cockpit. In small boats, often used as a seat.

Topping lift A line or wire rope used to support the boom when boat is anchored or moored.

Trampoline The fabric support that serves for seating between the hulls of a catamaran.

Trapeze Wire gear enabling a crew member to place all of his weight outboard of the hull, thus helping to keep the boat level.

Traveler A fitting across the boat to which sheets are led. In many boats the traveler may be adjusted from side to side so that angle of the sheets can be changed to suit conditions.

Twing Similar to a Barber hauler, a twing adjusts the angle of sheeting.

Ventilator Construction designed to lead air below decks. May have a cowl, which can be angled into or away from the wind; and may be constructed with baffles, so that water is not allowed below.

Whisker pole A short spar, normally kept stowed, which may be used to push the clew of a jib away from the boat when the boat is running downwind.

Window A transparent portion of a jib or mainsail.

Wishbone A boom composed of two separate curved pieces, one on either side of the sail. With this rig, sails are usually self-tending and loose-footed.

Index

Notes

Notes

Notes

Notes

Notes

Notes

Notes

Notes

Notes

Notes

Notes

SAIL LOGOS

One Designs Small Boats *Continued*

Snipe	Soling	Sonar	Spindrift
Star	Sundancer	Sunfish	Tanzer
Tempest	Thistle	Thunderbird	Tornado
US 1	Vagabond	Victoria	Wayfarer
Widgeon	Windmill	Windrose 5.5	Y Flyer

Tech Dinghy

Typhoon

West Wight Potter

Cruisers Auxiliaries

Achilles 24	Alajuela	Annapolis	Bahama
Bayfield	Beachcomber	Bristol	Cal
Capri	Catalina	Catalina	Clark

Cape Dory

Columbia